PREVENTION'S
Quick and Healthy
LOW-FAT COOKING

FEATURING
WEEKNIGHT MEALS
IN MINUTES

EDITED BY DAVID JOACHIM, *PREVENTION* MAGAZINE HEALTH BOOKS

RODALE PRESS, INC.
EMMAUS, PENNSYLVANIA

This book is simultaneously being published by Rodale Press as *Prevention's Healthy Weeknight Meals in Minutes.*

Copyright © 1997 by Rodale Press, Inc.
Illustrations copyright © 1997 by Sara Swan
Photographs copyright © 1997 by Rodale Press, Inc.

Printed in the United States of America on acid-free ⊗, recycled paper ♻

Front Cover: Pinto Bean Chili (page 32) and
Jalapeño Buttermilk Cornbread (page 31)

Cover Photography: Tad Ware & Company, Inc.

Library of Congress Cataloging-in-Publication Data

Prevention's quick and healthy low-fat cooking : featuring weeknight
  meals in minutes / edited by David Joachim, food editor ; Prevention
Magazine Health Books.
     p.   cm.
    The trade paper ed. is published simultaneously as: Prevention's
healthy weeknight meals in minutes.
    Includes index.
    ISBN 0–87596–369–2 hardcover
    1. Low-fat diet—Recipes.   I. Joachim, David.   II. Prevention
Magazine Health Books.   III. Prevention's healthy weeknight meals in
minutes.
RM237.7.P742   1996
641.5′638—dc20   96–35996

2 4 6 8 10 9 7 5 3 1 hardcover

OUR PURPOSE

> "*We inspire and enable people to improve
> their lives and the world around them.*"

RODALE 🍃 BOOKS

Prevention's Healthy Weeknight Meals in Minutes
Editorial Staff

Editor: David Joachim
Managing Editor: Jean Rogers
Contributing Writer: Mary Carroll
Researchers and Fact-Checkers: Sandra Salera Lloyd,
Michelle Szulborski Zenie
Book and Cover Designer: Debra Sfetsios
Design Coordinator: Darlene Schneck
Studio Manager: Joe Golden
Book Layout: Tad Ware & Company, Inc.
Illustrator: Sara Swan
Photographer: Tad Ware Photography
Food Stylist: Robin Krause
Recipe Development: Mary Carroll
Nutritional Consultants: Linda Yoakam, M.S., R.D.; Anita Hirsch, R.D.
Director, Book Manufacturing: Helen Clogston
Manufacturing Coordinator: Melinda B. Rizzo

Prevention *Magazine Health Books*
Vice-President and Editorial Director: Debora T. Yost
Art Director: Jane Colby Knutila
Research Manager: Ann Gossy Yermish
Copy Manager: Lisa D. Andruscavage

Contents

Introduction

*Y*ou can't beat home-cooked meals. They're less expensive and healthier than going out, and they bring the family together. More than any other time in the past ten years, people are reaping the benefits of cooking at home. A Better Homes and Gardens study showed that most Americans eat home-cooked meals five to six nights a week.

But we're also busier than ever. According to the U.S. Department of Agriculture, most of us decide what's for dinner only four hours before it's time to eat. And half of all working adults eat lunch at their desks. Let's face it: At the end of a long day, the last thing you want to do is worry about dinner.

We've designed this book to put healthy dinners on your table night after night—without a minute's thought. We show you how to cut shopping time and what to keep on hand for quick weeknight meals that you can feel good about. When you get home from work, just pick a dinner and follow the simple game plan. Dinner will be on the table in 45 minutes or less.

You'll even find tips for eating smart away from home. Want to know the healthiest fast-food chains? How to get a nutritious airplane meal? How to pack low-fat lunches for you and your kids? The top 20 healthy snacks? It's all here.

Today's busy families need good food without a lot of fuss. With this book you can have healthy burgers, chili, turkey pot pie, macaroni and cheese, chocolate snack cake—all your everyday favorites—in minutes. The best part is, you'll have more time to enjoy your meals. And that's what good food is all about.

David Joachim
Prevention Magazine Health Books

CHAPTER 1

FAST, NO-FUSS
WAYS TO
UPGRADE YOUR
EATING

STAYING HEALTHY IN A BUSY WORLD

Eating has evolved from a simple life-sustaining activity into our national preoccupation. And also our national worry. Because we think we don't have time to eat well.

In this accelerated society, the days of browsing the supermarket and endless time to cook have been replaced by browsing the Internet and endless deadlines. We skip fresh in pursuit of fast and see less of our kitchens than our computers. We manage to slap together a peanut butter sandwich or dial out for pizza between faxes, and we consider ourselves fed.

Anyone with the least amount of health awareness can get very discouraged scanning daily newspaper stories. One scientific study after another reveals something new to avoid: red meat, cheese, butter, alcohol, salt, too many refined foods. Our icons, like olive oil or oat bran, come under attack and sometimes fall.

We look for a way to get back to home-cooked meals—something that will sustain us and satisfy both body and soul. But the boss calls a late meeting and it's one more night of fast food or microwave popcorn.

What if we were to tell you that you *can* have dinner on the table— a weeknight meal that's delicious, a hit with the family and healthy to boot—before the pizza guy rings your doorbell? We're not talking five-page gourmet recipes with long lists of specialized ingredients. We're talking simple, good-tasting food. And the techniques to prepare it fast and healthy.

Cooking at home is the only sure way to control what we eat. Home-cooked meals are usually healthier and lower in fat than take-out or restaurant meals. We can monitor the freshness of ingredients and the nutritional variety—components of well-being and good health. And if you know the ropes, cooking healthy takes no more time than waiting for that pizza or heating up a frozen TV dinner. The secret is shopping smart, buying quick-cooking ingredients and planning ahead. These are the keys to healthy weeknight meals that won't put a cramp in your busy lifestyle.

TAKE CONTROL OF YOUR EATING

Cooking quick, energy-rich meals for yourself and your family is a health priority; just like getting enough sleep or exercise. In these busy times, you need to keep your body at peak condition just to fight fatigue and illness.

Fear of fat has led many of us astray, say nutritionists. We stock up on low-nutrient fat-free convenience foods and ignore fresh, well-balanced meals. Just using a lot of no-fat and low-fat ingredients doesn't equal instant nutrition. That's oversimplifying the facts, and it could be dangerous to your health, according to Michele Tuttle, M.P.H., R.D., director of consumer affairs at the Food Marketing Institute in Washington, D.C. If you focus too much on cutting out fat by eating fat-free packaged foods, you'll probably miss or unbalance other important nutrients, like iron, zinc, beta-carotene, folic acid and vitamins A, C, D and E. And many fat-free convenience foods have extra calories and salt to make up for lack of taste.

"This is why as a nation we're getting fatter even though we're eating fat-free products," says Susan G. Purdy, author of *Have Your Cake and Eat It, Too* and *Let Them Eat Cake*. If you cook a variety of foods and cut back on fat—not eliminate it—you won't be making the severe taste trade-offs that lead to failure with healthy eating. You'll love your food, and you'll love the way you feel.

We all know that taste is tops. Despite our good intentions, we won't stick with healthy eating long-term unless it also tastes great. "So my rule in making healthy meals is: appetizing first, healthy second," says Martha Rose Shulman, award-winning author of *Provençal Light*, *Mediterranean Light* and *Mexican Light*. Shulman keeps her kitchen stocked with foods that inspire her to cook this way: quality fresh foods that cook fast. "What you have on hand, you'll use," she says. "Beautiful, quick-cooking ingredients make you gravitate toward beautiful, quick-cooking meals."

Stocking up on the right ingredients is just one of the kitchen shortcuts cooking experts employ to create healthy meals in a matter of minutes. But the big timesaver is planning, says Brenda Ponichtera, R.D., author of *Quick & Healthy Recipes and Ideas* and *Quick & Healthy Volume II*. "Gathering recipes that don't take long to prepare and that your family enjoys is the first step. Then plan menus around these recipes. When my patients take time to plan, their week is so much easier." We know you're pressed for time. So we've taken that first step for you. All you need to do is pick a dinner from the more than 100 menus provided here.

START HEALTHY, STAY HEALTHY

Plan on starting your morning with energy-rich foods. A healthy breakfast means good self-esteem and energy all day long, says Elizabeth Somer, R.D., author of *Food and Mood*. Skipping breakfast can lead to fatigue and mood swings later in the day. "This is especially important for women, who are always dieting. They often skip breakfast, then they have uncontrollable cravings later in the day," says Somer. Take five minutes to eat something quick and healthy for breakfast.

What you eat in the morning creates a foundation of health you build on the rest of the day. Even a glass of fruit juice and a glass of skim milk will sustain you longer than a sweet roll or a low-cal breakfast bar, says Evelyn Tribole, M.S., R.D., a nutritionist in private practice in Beverly Hills, California, and author of *Healthy Homestyle Cooking*.

Many of us skip breakfast because we've fallen into an eating rut and need to expand our culinary horizons, says Susan Asanovic, M.S., R.D., owner of the food and nutrition consulting firm La Table Dans Le Bon Sens in Wilton, Connecticut. Vary your diet. Try a quick new fruit, like papaya ("a nutritional superstar," says Asanovic), or a new cereal for breakfast. You can even pack along your own take-out breakfast—a low-fat burrito or leftover pasta from dinner—to eat later at the office. That'll begin satisfying your body's morning nutritional needs and build resources for all-day energy.

What about those super-rushed days when breakfast is small and lunch preempted by nonstop work? Count on afternoon snacks and dinner to fill in the nutritious foods you missed, says Anita Hirsch, M.S., R.D., nutritionist at Rodale Press, Inc. and staff nutritionist for *Quick and Healthy Cooking* magazine. When you're eating in a hurry, up the value of everything you eat with nutrient-dense foods. Cruciferous vegetables, soyfoods like tofu and complex carbohydrates like brown rice can do wonders for your health, according to Nan Kathryn Fuchs, Ph.D., a nutritionist in private practice in Sebastopol, California, nutrition editor of *Women's Health Letter*, and author of *Overcoming the Legacy of Overeating*. Dr. Fuchs's basic marinara sauce counteracts the stress of a hectic day with extra nutrition from carrots, chard and broccoli, which give it a rich flavor her family loves.

As you venture into this new approach to eating, you might need to reset your food attitudes. Slow and steady is the key to lasting changes that build a good foundation of health, says Ponichtera. "Ask yourself, 'Can I switch from whole milk to 2 percent? Regular mayonnaise to reduced-fat?' If good-tasting lower-fat versions of your favorites are available, try them with an open mind. Try to make changes you can stick with. You may prefer the taste of low-fat products instead of fat-free products. And that's fine if it can be a permanent change."

GUIDELINES FOR GOOD HEALTH

Experts say that if you can change only two things about your diet, concentrate on lowering fat and adding fiber. This simple strategy will focus all your menu planning on the base of the USDA Food Guide Pyramid and gradually adjust your thinking of the typical dinner plate.

The Food Guide Pyramid illustrates for Americans the current scientific suggestions for healthy eating. At the top of the pyramid are the least-recommended foods—those to be eaten in smallest quantity, like fats, oils and sweets. At the base of the pyramid are the basic building blocks of nutrition needed to prevent chronic diseases like cancer, heart disease and diabetes. The pyramid redefines our priorities: eat mostly whole grains and cereals, plus fresh fruits and vegetables. Use less whole milk and meat to avoid saturated fats. Instead of the 8-ounce T-bone steak, you might serve 2 or 3 ounces of lean chicken or fish, with ½ cup cooked rice or couscous and steamed broccoli, plus 1 cup tossed salad with a low-fat dressing.

The USDA's *Healthy Eating Index*, which monitors how we eat, found that fewer than one out of five people eat the recommended five servings of fruits and vegetables per day. We're also missing out on the recommended amount of grains. Less than one-third of Americans have enough variety in their diets. Experts recommend eating 16 different food items over a three-day period. Less than 20 percent of us manage to cut saturated fats to 10 percent of total calories or to cut total fat intake to 30 percent or less—the recommended limits. And only 35 percent reduce their daily salt intake to 2,400 milligrams or less.

What does this say about our eating habits? Caught in the time trap, we rush past the best nutrient-rich foods, like fresh fruits and vegetables, grains and legumes, says Tuttle. "It just shows that we have a way to go in eating healthy. We're not eating according to the Food Guide Pyramid, and we need to move in that direction."

Five servings of fresh fruits and vegetables a day is surprisingly easy to get, says Asanovic. Just frequent salad bars and buy precut, prewashed lettuce, carrots, celery sticks and other produce. Stock up on fruit salad for lunch and greens and other vegetables to take home for dinner stir-fries or vegetable salads. The best supermarkets prep twice daily, so the items are fresh. To get the best possible ingredients, Asanovic recommends asking the manager of your favorite store which are the freshly prepared selections. Or buy bagged mesclun or other high-flavor lettuces and serve salad at each meal, suggests Faye Levy, author of *30 Low-Fat Meals in 30 Minutes*; everyone will eat more of the healthy vegetables and less of the higher-fat entrée.

Jeanne Jones, "Cook It Light" nationally syndicated columnist, starts getting her five-a-day with fruit for breakfast: favorites are grilled banana on toast ("which tastes like banana jam," says Jones) and frozen banana blended with skim milk over shredded wheat cereal.

For lunch and dinner get inspiration from other cultures—see how they incorporate vegetables into fast meals, says Dr. Fuchs. For example, Chinese vegetable lo mein is essentially pasta and fast-cooked fresh vegetables. Instead of having one large piece of meat as your main dish, try incorporating vegetables and meats in one dish like a pot pie, stir-fry or pasta with meat or seafood. Even a meal as simple as sautéed Swiss chard, dressed with lemon juice, capers and chopped sun-dried tomatoes over pasta, will get you closer to your five-a-day goal.

Great Cooks' 15-Minute Dinners

- **Pasta with Lean and Luscious Alfredo Sauce:** Puree cottage cheese with yogurt, garlic and Parmesan. Toss with steamed broccoli and pasta. To save time, cook the broccoli in the same water as the pasta, adding it a few minutes before the pasta is done. —From Martha Rose Shulman

- **Mexican Snack Night:** Top baked tortilla chips with warmed low-fat refried beans, shredded low-fat cheese and fat-free sour cream; serve with bowls of chopped avocado, broccoli, jicama and baby carrots. Set it up as a picnic on the living room floor—kids love this one. —From Elizabeth Somer

- **Adobo Chicken with Quinoa:** Marinate boneless skinless chicken breasts in chilies, lime juice and cumin, then grill and serve them over a quinoa pilaf made with onions, celery and garlic. —From Steven Raichlen

- **Tri-Pepper Pasta:** Sauté red, yellow and green bell peppers with plenty of garlic and a hint of olive oil and Parmesan. Serve over pasta. —From Evelyn Tribole

- **Catfish with Red Pepper Sauce:** Puree drained, jarred roasted red peppers with chicken broth. Serve over oven-fried catfish on a bed of steamed spinach. —From Coleen Miner

- **Chinese Feast Night:** Make chicken chop suey with frozen chicken breasts, celery, onions and canned bean sprouts. Serve over rice. —From Brenda Ponichtera

- **French Bread Pizza Dinner:** Top French bread with low-fat spaghetti sauce and shredded low-fat mozzarella cheese. Bake until the cheese melts. Serve with tossed salad, baby carrots and a low-fat dip made from cottage cheese or low-fat yogurt blended with an envelope of soup mix. —From Anne Fletcher

- **Moroccan Nights:** Toss cooked couscous with steamed vegetables and a low-fat vinaigrette dressing. —From Paulette Mitchell

STAYING HEALTHY AWAY FROM HOME

When you travel, all bets are off. Or are they? Can you eat healthy on the road, as well as on the run?

"People say to me, 'When I travel, I give up eating healthy; it just can't be done.' But I find it's not hard at all," says Tuttle. "Hotels offer skim milk, bagels, fresh fruit and cereals for breakfast. If you're having a full day of meetings with preset meals, take advantage of breakfast where you have control. Even at preset dinners you can ask for more salad, skim milk or healthy choices."

Consulting with nutritional clients all over the world keeps cookbook author and syndicated columnist Jeanne Jones's travel schedule pretty hectic. How does she manage to eat light in every port of call? It becomes a simple matter of learning what to look for on a variety of restaurant menus, Jones explains. Educate yourself to recognize lighter dishes. These include fresh green salads with low-fat dressing on the side; lean cuts of meat, poultry and fish that are baked or broiled without sauce; side dishes of steamed or stir-fried vegetables; baked potatoes; and simple fruit desserts. When scanning the menu at a restaurant, steer clear of dishes that sport *fried, deep-fried, cream sauce* and other high-fat indicators in the title. Instead, look for terms like *grilled, broiled, light, lean* and *low-fat*. You can even call ahead to see which healthy selections the restaurant offers. When we tested this theory, most chefs were quite willing to accommodate special requests—and show off their skill with fresh foods.

Some savvy travelers carry their own low-fat salad dressings, salt substitutes or sweetener in their bag or briefcase. Any restaurant can fix green salad without dressing, and you can request extra lemon wedges and vinegar and a tiny bit of oil on the side. Or as Jones does, you can dilute a half teaspoonful of dressing with lemon juice to get the flavor without much fat.

Another option experts use when traveling: book hotel rooms with a kitchenette or refrigerator to save on restaurant meals. Stock it with low-fat breakfast foods, fruit and whole-grain breads. Asanovic packs boxed tofu, whole-grain crackers and low-sodium cups of soup. She sometimes brings a cooler with yogurt, fruit, cut-up carrots and low-fat cheese to put in the hotel mini-bar refrigerator for snacking. As a last resort, especially if there are no accommodating restaurants in town, you can buy healthy sandwich fixings, a salad or fruit at the local market—and pack a picnic for the park or to eat in your hotel room.

Paulette Mitchell, a cooking instructor and consultant in Minneapolis, Minnesota, and author of *The Fifteen-Minute Vegetarian Gourmet*, *The Fifteen-Minute Single Gourmet* and *Complete Book of Dressings*, survives on the road by changing the order of importance of her meals: "Breakfast becomes number one, because you can usually get healthy breakfast foods at most restaurants: oatmeal, fresh fruit, juice, whole-wheat bread." For lunch Mitchell grabs a low-fat muffin and juice or a sandwich—something light. Dinner is usually broiled fish or chicken with a big salad.

What about vacations—the time when fun takes precedence over following the rules, and diets go out the window?

Nutrition experts recommend indulging—to a point. Treat time can be important on vacations, says Anne Fletcher, M.S., R.D., a nutrition consultant in Minnesota and author of *Thin for Life: Ten Keys to Success from People Who Have Lost Weight and Kept It Off*. As long as you know you're going to go back to your regular diet when you're at home, indulge yourself a bit. This doesn't mean having treats all day long, Fletcher warns, but allowing yourself one to two treats a day when you travel. "In a restaurant, I might enjoy treats like really fine seafood, sorbet, shrimp cocktail, a cappuccino or fresh fruits out of season—foods that are low-fat, that maybe I can't get at home because they're too expensive or my family doesn't like them." Healthy doesn't get put on hold, but you still have the feeling of indulgence.

FLYING HIGH

Everyone has a war story of airline travel: sitting four hours on the tarmac, being stranded in airports far from home, finding nothing remotely edible on the menu. Like a good scout, be prepared when you fly. Bring your own healthy snacks for the plane and enough to tide you over during unexpected layovers: a bagel, boxes of serving-size cereal, bottled water, self-sealing bags of rice cakes, precut fresh vegetables and fruits. "I like to carry dried prunes in individual packets and a low-cal power bar," says Tribole. "It's saved me more than once from those high-fat peanut packs."

It helps to order a special meal before you fly. Get familiar with the airline first, Tribole recommends, since each has different dietary strengths. Some have great seafood meals, others good vegetarian. Call at least 24 hours before flight time and cross your fingers; and, like Jones, plan for emergencies. "I always order a special meal ahead of time," says Jones, "but I have solutions if the meal doesn't show up." Even with standard coach fare, Jones is innovative. On one flight, she scraped the sauce off a chicken breast, chopped the chicken up and put it on the undressed salad. "There was just enough of the sauce that I couldn't completely get off the chicken to dress the salad. I spooned the cooked vegetables from the entrée over the chicken and enjoyed a terrific chicken salad."

Steven Raichlen, a chef and award-winning author of the *High-Flavor, Low-Fat Cooking* series, recommends looking for healthy newcomers in airports before you board. Many airports now have sushi bars, stands that sell nonfat frozen yogurt, fresh fruit stalls or cafés

BEST BETS IN ETHNIC EATING OUT

- **Cajun:** shrimp Creole, seafood jambalaya, boiled shrimp

- **Chinese:** wonton soup, hot-and-sour soup, chicken chow mein, chicken chop suey, vegetable lo mein, Szechwan shrimp, steamed rice, vegetable stir-fries (ask for a "dry stir-fry" made without oil or share a plateful and get double portions of steamed rice), lychee nuts

- **French:** consommé, bouillabaisse (avoid the rouille sauce), salade Niçoise, roast chicken, grilled seafood or chicken, tomato coulis, sorbets, fresh berries

- **Greek:** shish kebab, baked fish, simple rice dishes, yogurt-cucumber sauce, souvlaki, pita bread, plain yogurt with honey

- **Indian:** lentil soups, dal, tandoori chicken, or fish, bean- or grain-based curries, rice pilaf, basmati rice, raita, chapati or naan breads, chutney

- **Italian:** minestrone soup, Italian breads and breadsticks, pasta with marinara sauce, pasta with meatballs, most seafood dishes, chicken cacciatore, Italian sorbets or ices

- **Japanese:** miso soup, grilled fish and lean meats, vegetarian sushi rolls, sukiyaki, teriyaki chicken or vegetables, udon noodles, rice noodles, steamed rice

- **Mexican:** gazpacho soup, salsa, steamed corn tortillas, soft tacos, chicken or beef fajitas (hold the guacamole and sour cream), baked fish, vegetarian chili, mesquite-grilled chicken or fish

- **Middle Eastern:** hummus, tabbouleh, lentil soup, rice

where you can grab a cup of decaf café latte made with skim milk to fill you up between flights.

"If all goes wrong, you can always ask the flight attendant for pretzels," says Melanie Barnard, *Bon Appétit* columnist and author of *Low-Fat Grilling.* Or, as Barnard does, count on room service at your hotel.

ENERGY-BOOSTING FOODS

Dragging through your day? Overscheduled and overworked? How about a quick energy boost? Step right up to an array of healthy foods that will help you breeze through even the most sluggish afternoon. And they're all in your own kitchen—or can be.

A little nutrition know-how goes a long way toward choosing the best energy-boosting foods. Carbohydrates, fat and protein are the three main sources of dietary energy, with carbohydrates being the most important, according to Peter Miller, Ph.D., executive director of the Hilton Head Health Institute in Hilton Head, South Carolina. "Carbohydrates provide an efficient, long-lasting energy source," Dr. Miller says, especially the complex carbs like whole grains, beans, pasta and breads. All give you a more immediate supply of energy to burn. Fats and protein take longer to digest and can slow you down. The trick for consistent energy is "to combine a little protein with a lot of carbohydrate-rich foods," says Somer.

It's also vital to drink lots of water to keep your energy level up, says Somer. Water is essential in the fight against fatigue. A symptom of mild dehydration is fatigue, and often your thirst is not a good indication of your water needs. If you're thirsting for a glass of water, you probably need two.

Avoid dependence on coffee and sugar. They provide quick fixes but little lasting energy. More than three cups of coffee can fuel your fatigue rather than your energy level, says Somer. Sugar-loaded foods cause you to drop even lower when the buzz wears off. Instead of sugar, plan your snacks around nutrient-dense foods that won't deplete essential energy reserves (see page 13).

We're beginning to see more and more how a diet centered on fresh fruits, vegetables, grains and legumes can build these energy reserves. A healthy diet is like a healthy bank account we can draw on in times of stress because it provides important nutrients.

ANTIOXIDANTS

Fresh fruits and vegetables are loaded with antioxidants like vitamin C, vitamin E and beta-carotene. Studies show that antioxidants may help protect our bodies from age-related diseases. Antioxidants are our front-line defense against free radicals, those molecules that damage cells through oxidation, altering the cell's genetic structure and promoting the growth of cancer. Since these nutrients need to be replenished each day, the easiest way to get enough of them is by planning a few servings of fruits and vegetables into every meal.

Fruits or juices can start the day, and you can regularly add vegetable salads to lunch and dinner. An easy way to build vegetables into in-between meals is to always carry carrot and celery sticks in your purse or briefcase.

For a healthy boost of beta-carotene, choose dark-green and sunny-colored vegetables: spinach, leaf lettuce, broccoli, kale, collards, beet greens, winter squash, pumpkin, carrots, sweet potatoes and red, orange and green sweet peppers. Get into the habit of adding half a cupful of one or more beta-rich vegetables to soups, stews and salads, says Dr. Fuchs. Or just serve them steamed or microwaved with a little lemon juice. Another great source of beta-carotene is tropical papaya or mango, delicious as a snack or pureed as an easy dessert topping for low-fat angel food cake or frozen yogurt.

For your daily dose of vitamin C, start your day with a citrus fruit or juice (oranges are tops for nutrient value, says Dr. Fuchs), or add sliced strawberries to morning oatmeal. When you slide up to the salad bar at lunch, scoop up some high-vitamin-C broccoli florets.

As for vitamin E, the richest sources include fortified cereals, sunflower seeds, oils, sweet potatoes and wheat germ. "I put small amounts of wheat germ in everything," says Somer, including the pancake batter for weekend breakfasts.

POWER SNACKING

Snacking has gotten a bad rap, but actually it can be a powerful source of sustained energy. Here's the way it works: If you're eating healthy snacks, snacking is healthy. See the box on page 13 for quick ideas.

Plan a few of these healthy snacks into each day, suggests Fletcher. Don't leave snacking to chance or wait until you're hungry to decide —because you'll usually grab the doughnuts sitting out in the coffee room, a bag of salty chips from the vending machine or the box of cookies you have stashed in the cupboard. When Fletcher surveyed people who'd lost weight and kept it off, she found that most of them planned snacks into their daily eating. "My rule is: If I'm hungry after several hours and it's not time for lunch, it's time for a snack. So I try to have something on hand," says Fletcher. "It's long periods without eating that lead to bingeing and overeating." Think healthy, and it becomes a habit, says Asanovic. It takes no longer to pack fruit at home than to walk to a vending machine at work.

But for those last-minute stops at vending machines and convenience stores, here's a quick list of the best low-fat snacks we found:

- Barbara's Bakery Fat-Free Organic Sourdough Pretzels
- Barbara's Bakery Organic Whole Wheat Pretzels
- Guiltless Gourmet Baked Not Fried Tortilla Chips
- Frito-Lay Low Fat Baked Tostitos
- Baked Lay's Low Fat Original Potato Chips
- Fit Foods Original Flavor Low Fat Baked Potato Chips
- Mr. Phipps Tater Crisps
- Bugles Light
- Health Valley 100% Natural Fruit Bar
- Health Valley Fat-Free Granola Bar
- Fat-Free Snackwells Cereal Bars
- Keebler Reduced-Fat Pecan Sandies
- R.W. Frookie Oatmeal Raisin Fat-Free Cookie
- Entenmann's Fat-Free Oatmeal Raisin Cookies
- Häagen-Dazs Fat-Free Sorbet 'N Yogurt Bars

BROWN BAG BONUSES

Packing your own lunch has its advantages: You can be sure just how many calories and fat grams go into your midday meal, and you can have something tasty to look forward to all morning—as long as you avoid brown bag boredom.

To get beyond the peanut-butter-and-jelly syndrome, experts say, use leftovers. Well-planned leftovers lead to luscious lunches. So when you prepare dinner or cook ahead on the weekend, think quantity. Cook double, then pack away portions in serving-size microwaveable containers. You'll have a superstar selection of homemade lunches, ready to grab and go. Just reheat them in your office microwave.

Our experts all had their favorites: leftover meat loaf or baked chicken served cold or sliced into sandwiches; extra stir-fried vegetables tossed with low-fat dressing (by lunch they'll have marinated into an Italian antipasto, great with a crusty whole-grain roll); leftover cooked pasta topped with steamed broccoli, kidney beans and a bit of Parmesan cheese; baked potato halves smothered with steamed

20 FAVORITE QUICK AND HEALTHY SNACKS

1. Low-fat trail mix: low-fat miniature pretzels, oyster crackers, low-fat wheat thins, low-fat cheese crackers

2. Frozen unsweetened raspberries, cherries, bananas

3. Fresh whole fruit like apples, oranges, bananas, peaches and plums

4. Precut carrots, celery, jicama and other salad bar vegetables

5. Low-fat, low-sugar cereals in individual cartons

6. Dried prunes or raisins in individual packets

7. Fruit sorbets or ices (higher vitamin C and often less fat than frozen yogurt)

8. Low-fat, low-sodium instant soups

9. Baked sweet potatoes drizzled with low-sodium soy sauce

10. Baked potatoes with melted low-fat cheese

11. Rice cakes or caramel-flavored popcorn cakes

12. Raita (an Indian spread of nonfat plain yogurt, fresh mint and chopped cucumber) on whole-grain crackers or bread

13. Baked tortilla chips and salsa

14. Pita pizzas with low-fat cheese

15. Nonfat vanilla frozen yogurt in half a cantaloupe

16. Sugar-free root beer with low-fat or fat-free ice cream or frozen yogurt

17. Whole cherry tomatoes

18. Whole-wheat pretzels

19. Fat-free crackers topped with low-fat cheese

20. Air-popped popcorn

TOP CHAIN CHOICES

Food	Fat (g.)	Calories
Arby's		
Light Roast Chicken Deluxe	6	276
Light Roast Turkey Deluxe	7	260
Junior Roast Beef	14	324
Burger King		
BK Broiler Chicken Sandwich	6	550
Plain hamburger	15	330
Broiled chicken salad without dressing	4	200
Garden Salad with 2 tablespoons reduced-calorie Italian dressing	3.5	115
Hardee's		
Grilled Chicken Sandwich	9	290
Regular Roast Beef	11	270
Grilled Chicken Salad	3	150
Pancakes, plain (3)	2	280
Kentucky Fried Chicken		
Tender Roast Chicken breast without skin	4.3	169
Tender Roast Chicken thigh without skin	5.5	106

vegetables and melted low-fat cheese. On chilly days, expand your repertoire to bean or grain soups or stews.

Add minitreats—a couple of low-fat fig newtons, cut-up fresh fruit or a container of low-fat yogurt. You may not need the additional food at lunch, but you'll welcome it at three o'clock.

FAST FOODS

Fast food is a way of life; even the nutritional experts we interviewed went to Burger King or McDonald's when life got especially hectic. Luckily, today's fast food is not always fat food and healthy meals are available at most drive-throughs—you just have to know what to ask for.

Food	Fat (g.)	Calories
McDonald's		
McLean Deluxe	12	350
McGrilled Chicken Classic	4	260
Fajita Chicken Salad	6	160
Side Salad with 1 package Lite Vinaigrette dressing	4	95
Subway		
Turkey Breast Sub	4	276
Ham Sub	4	273
Roast Beef Sub	6	299
Veggie Delite Sub	3	223
(all subs with onions, lettuce, tomatoes, pickles, green peppers and olives only)		
Taco Bell		
Light Chicken Soft Taco	5	180
Light Chicken Burrito	6	290
Light Chicken Burrito Supreme	10	410
Wendy's		
Grilled Chicken Fillet Sandwich	7	290
Junior hamburger	10	270
Plain baked potato	0	310
Large chili	10	310

Elizabeth Somer might decide to swing by a fast-food chain on the way home at night, but she always asks for all the meals to be prepared without sauce and orders orange juice instead of soda. When she gets the meals home, she supplements them with fresh fruit and vegetable slices. "Then the total fat content of the fast food meal has been diluted with all kinds of healthy choices," says Somer, so it fits into a healthy dinner.

Pat Baird, R.D., a nutrition consultant and author of *The Pyramid Cookbook*, pops in to McDonald's for grilled chicken and low-fat milk, or a fajita chicken salad and low-fat frozen yogurt. If you choose carefully, the occasional fast-food meal can be part of a healthy lifestyle.

Just don't make fast foods a daily habit. "Even with lower-fat choices, you get fewer fruits and vegetables and less variety than with at-home meals," says Baird. Most fast food items are high in fat and calories, and most people in the drive-through lane opt for the highest-calorie choices: burger, fries and milkshake. A meal of these three could contain your entire daily quota of calories and fat, and half the sodium.

If fast food is part of your weekly meal plan, become familiar with the lower-fat items on your favorite chain's menu. You can even ask at the counter for nutritional information. Read through it and note which of your favorite items are lowest in fat and calories.

Mainly, when ordering in the fast lane, forget the fried foods. Anything breaded or crispy is probably laden with fat. And avoid meals with the words *cheese*, *triple* or *supreme* in the title, Somer says. These automatically add extra calories and fat. Best bet? Grilled chicken sandwich without sauce. Grilled is leaner, and you'll get more flavor for your fat grams.

It helps to decide what you want before you arrive. Our chart of top choices for fast-food dining can get you started.

LETTUCE DANCE

Bypass the burgers and waltz up to the salad bar for a great way to eat fast and low-fat on rushed lunch hours. To get less fat than that burger would give you, experts recommend:

- A baked potato topped with salad-bar veggies and lemon juice, plus a tablespoon of grated Parmesan cheese

- An antipasto salad of sliced lean turkey breast over green peppers, cauliflower, mushrooms, onions and tomatoes, topped with beans and low-fat Italian dressing

- A lean Cobb salad of chopped romaine, shredded cabbage, broccoli, shredded carrots, shredded beets and three-bean salad with a drizzle of low-fat blue cheese dressing

- Tuna salad mixed with lots of shredded carrots and packed into a whole-wheat roll

- Spinach leaves with chopped egg, shredded carrots, alfalfa sprouts, mushrooms, broccoli and lean sliced turkey breast, with lemon juice and a little grated Parmesan cheese

CHAPTER 2

TIMESAVING
TIPS AND
LOW-FAT
TECHNIQUES

IN AND OUT OF THE KITCHEN

What's the easiest way to save time in the kitchen? Plan ahead. Cooking quick and healthy on the home front isn't an accident. Most experts recommend that you set aside weekly planning time—as little as 10 minutes on Saturday morning will do—to think about what you'll need for that week. Otherwise, kitchen time equals frustration, pure and simple.

Avoid trying to solve the problem of how to fix a healthy meal 30 minutes before you have to set it on the table. That makes it too easy to run out for takeout chicken (again). Instead, if you've planned for the rush, you can open your refrigerator to an amazing array of healthy ingredients and the makings of a great dinner.

Part of your plan is learning to shop smarter and stocking up on healthy ingredients that take only 5 to 15 minutes to fix. Experts say your weekly shopping trip can be trimmed to 20 minutes once a week with practice and this kind of planning. You'll need a little time up front to educate yourself on favorite choices from the varieties of healthy convenience foods that line the supermarket shelves these days. But shopping for and stocking a good selection of these in your kitchen is the first key to making actual meal preparation a snap.

In addition, learn how to make cooking more fun by enlisting help from kids and other family members. If meals are simple, kids love to help, and traditionally time-consuming jobs go faster.

What we eat—and how we approach eating—clearly has an impact on our health and energy. By approaching weeknight meals with planning, smart shopping and the quick-cooking recipes in this book, you'll make cooking dinner a relaxing and enjoyable part of your day.

Making a Plan

It may seem daunting to think of sitting down on Sunday and planning what you'll be eating for the rest of the week. But here are the advantages: only one trip to the supermarket instead of three or four, buying fewer impulse items, and eating more balanced meals with more variety. If you're new to this, try planning three meals the first week, says author Evelyn Tribole, M.S., R.D., a nutritionist in private practice in Beverly Hills, California, and author of *Healthy Homestyle Cooking*. Choose three favorite dinner menus you can double to provide great lunch leftovers. And if you can, cook certain staples like rice ahead of time.

To make it even easier, build your shopping list throughout the week, says Paulette Mitchell, a cooking instructor and consultant in Minneapolis, Minnesota, and author of *The Fifteen-Minute Vegetarian Gourmet, The Fifteen-Minute Single Gourmet* and *Complete Book of Dressings*. She tapes a blank sheet of paper inside her pantry cabinet door and writes down staples she needs as she runs out. This makes it easy to plan on the weekend what her family will be eating for the week. "I revolve our dinners around a few favorite meals, then I try to serve leftovers in slightly different forms the rest of the week," says Mitchell. Plus she builds in a reserve of one-dish meals, such as a big pot of soup, for really rushed evenings.

Keep your meal plans super simple to start. Don't try to orchestrate a symphony when preparing dinner after a busy day; choose two or three dishes that are fast and filling and that leave you with great leftovers. Follow the easy menu plans in this book. Each focuses on one main dish, like Pinto Bean Chili (page 32), then offers accompaniments that can be made while the main dish cooks, like Jalapeño-Buttermilk Cornbread (page 31). The game plan for each menu lets you know what to cook first to streamline dinner preparation. "The meals that succeed in our house are meals that are fast and simple," says author Elizabeth Somer, R.D., author of *Food and Mood*. "Forget the gourmet, focus on healthy." That's what you'll be doing. And that doesn't mean sacrificing flavor, as you'll see when you try the delicious recipes in this book.

As you plan, be sure to include variety—but also repeat family favorites like meat loaf or stew. Familiar good-tasting foods on the menu each night make healthy eating easier for most people, says Tribole.

"You have to view healthy cooking and shopping as a project, and for any project, a plan is essential," says Michele Tuttle, M.P.H., R.D., director of consumer affairs at the Food Marketing Institute in Washington D.C. Lots of people are very resistant to planning meals, but it saves time, food and energy—and makes shopping much easier. "Even if you just plan the big meals like dinner," says Tuttle, "it allows you to think about your week and take into account scheduling constraints, guests and nights out."

SUPERMARKET SAVVY

You're standing in the supermarket line, watching the woman ahead of you pile her groceries onto the checkout counter. Silently you evaluate your choices and compare. Once again, you've picked up that bag of chocolate chip cookies and a few cartons of ice cream—they looked good, you forgot your list and you were hungry (real hungry, judging by the opened cookie bag). Shopping isn't your favorite thing, anyway.

A good shopping strategy would have gotten you home with better choices. Being smart in the supermarket is crucial—next in importance after good planning—for healthy weeknight meals. Read the hints from leading nutritionists and chefs that follow—and see how they learned to make wise choices that don't foil good eating intentions.

1. Use Your List. The experts agree: Without a list, shopping takes longer. You'll be less focused, says Tribole, and more likely to be seduced by impulse buys.

With practice, you can create your week's menus and shopping list in less than ten minutes. You can still be flexible and watch for sales: If lean ground beef is half price, you can switch from chicken to meat loaf and buy extra to freeze for next week's spaghetti and meatballs.

Several kitchen experts had a neat device that makes shopping fast and fun: a diagram of their grocery store. Most stores have these, or you can make your own. Run off multiple copies and use them as shopping lists, says Steven Raichlen, a chef and award-winning author of the *High-Flavor, Low-Fat Cooking* series. Raichlen groups items by where they are located in the store: dairy is first, then paper products, dry goods, produce. When we tested this theory, we got in and out of the store in no time flat.

2. Shop the Same Store. In unfamiliar markets, you waste valuable time going down aisle after aisle, hunting for your favorite foods, says Somer. "I've gotten to the point where I know exactly what I want in my store and I can pick it up without even looking at it." If you use a list to cluster your items in certain aisles, says Tuttle, you can go through each aisle only once and get your groceries fast.

"Even if another store is having a sale, I stick with my favorite store," says Colleen Miner, author of *Together in the Kitchen* and a chef on a weekly Minneapolis television show. "If I want to shop quickly, I go where I know where everything is."

Every once in a while, Miner suggests, spend a few minutes looking at new products you might like to try. New convenience products come out every month that can make it easy for you to maintain a healthy lifestyle. If you don't see what you want, be sure to ask the store manager to stock it.

3. Shop the Slow Times. When you shop is as important as how you shop. Choosing the right time can save you the extra ten minutes of waiting in long checkout lines. If you go right after work, you'll join hundreds of other hungry, frazzled shoppers during the typical supermarket's rush hour. Also avoid Saturdays, the worst day to shop. Best time? Later in the evening around seven or eight o'clock, says Tuttle, when most people are eating dinner.

If you're an early riser with jam-packed evenings, stop in before work. This worked for several of our experts, who even had time to unpack and store groceries at home before starting off to work.

4. Increase Your Label IQ. Part of educating yourself to make quick and nutritious meals is understanding and reading food nutrient labels. First pay attention to serving size, says Tribole. If you don't, the rest of the information on the label is meaningless. "Ask yourself what your realistic serving size for this food is. If the label on the can of soup says two servings but you usually heat up the whole can for lunch, you have to multiply all the nutrients by two," she says.

Then look at what that amount gives you as a percentage of your recommended daily allowance of fat, sodium and calories.

If the product you're buying has 60 percent of a day's worth of sodium, you know that when you add it to the rest of your meals that day it will shoot you way past your limit. "So ask yourself if it's worth it to you taste-wise and flavor-wise," says Tribole. There are no forbidden foods, she stresses, just the need to be aware of what you're eating and try to achieve a balanced diet in the long run. "As a general rule, I advise people to aim for no more than 5 grams of fat and no more than 300 milligrams of sodium per serving," says Anita Hirsch, M.S., R.D., nutritionist at Rodale Press and staff nutritionist for *Quick and Healthy Cooking* magazine.

Here are basic steps to increase your label reading IQ without enrolling in a nutrition course:

- Look at the first few ingredients—they are ranked in order of quantity.
- Check the portion or serving size.
- Check the amount of calories, fat and sodium for each portion. Is it within your daily amount?
- Watch for excess sugar in disguise ("Words ending in *-ose* mean sugar," warns Nan Kathryn Fuchs, Ph.D., a nutritionist in private practice in Sebastopol, California, nutrition editor of *Women's Health Letter* and author of *Overcoming the Legacy of Overeating.*).
- Check "percentage of daily value" of important nutrients like calcium, vitamins A and C and iron. Reread labels occasionally, even with your favorite foods, advises Tribole. You'd be surprised how often they change.

5. Bulk Up. Shop in bulk, suggests author Anne Fletcher, M.S., R.D., a nutrition consultant in Minnesota and author of *Thin for Life: Ten Keys to Success from People Who Have Lost Weight and Kept It Off.* Most experts we interviewed buy big bags of frozen vegetables and frozen boneless, skinless chicken breasts to have on hand for speedy meals.

Stock up on staples you use regularly. Say you eat pasta three times a week. Buy a lot at once—even a one- or two-month supply, says Tuttle. "Get in the habit of thinking a week in advance or even longer," she says. "Why not have a few extra loaves of bread in the freezer, a few extra boxes of cereal if you have room in your pantry?" Stocking up means fewer trips to the store—you only shop when you need to replenish perishable items.

For extra convenience, supplement your shopping trips with delivery service. Chef Raichlen makes use of free local delivery services from markets he shops regularly. Call fish markets, bakeries, smaller grocery stores and dairy delivery companies—you may find home delivery a real bargain and a way to cut your shopping time in half.

6. Mind Your P's: Perimeter and Produce. Two important guidelines once you're in the store: Stick to the outer perimeter where the basics are, and focus most of your shopping time in the produce section.

"Most fresh foods are located along the perimeter walls where plumbing and electrical fixtures are housed," says Tribole. Packaged nonperishables usually line the center aisles. Fill up your cart with perimeter shopping first and you'll be less likely to browse in the tempting center of the store.

Secondly, try to spend most of your time in the produce aisle, since fresh fruits and vegetables form the foundation of most of the healthy recipes in this book. It's also a major resource for great snack foods, says Somer. "Look for precut vegetables and fresh snacking fruit—bananas, oranges, kiwis." And don't forget those cruciferous vegetables. Hirsch recommends buying a different cruciferous vegetable each time you shop—broccoli one week, cauliflower the next—so they're always part of your meals.

7. Eat First. Don't shop when you're hungry, warns Tuttle—a growling tummy can tempt you to grab less nutritious snacks like doughnuts or an extra bag of trail mix from the bulk bins. Plan to have a piece of fruit or a glass of juice before you leave for the store.

8. Collect Convenience. Look for foods that are healthy but also cook fast: instant brown rice, precut produce. "I buy foods that don't require a lot of preparation," says Marie Simmons, *Bon Appétit* columnist and author of *Fresh & Fast: Inspired Cooking for Every Season & Every Day*. Simmons loads her shopping cart with cored and peeled pineapple, red potatoes that don't have to be peeled and spinach in bags. "Fresh is the key, good taste is the key." Make it easy on yourself.

COOK IN QUANTITY

Every expert we talked with follows another important rule: Cook favorite dishes in quantity. Why waste time making rice twice, when you can cook up a big pot that'll last all week?

Dr. Fuchs recommends having containers of cooked whole grains—brown rice, millet, pasta—frozen in one-, two- or four-serving portions. They're great for five-minute dinners; you can reheat these smaller portions in two to four minutes in the microwave. "It's also useful if you're cooking for different taste buds in one family—you

QUICKEST-COOKING MEATS, SEAFOOD AND POULTRY

Beef
- Extra-lean ground beef
- Flank steak
- Stew meat

Poultry
- Boneless skinless chicken breasts
- Boneless skinless turkey breasts
- Turkey tenderloin
- Ground chicken or turkey

Pork
- Boneless loin chops
- Lean ham

Lamb
- Loin chops
- Stew meat

Seafood
- Fish fillets
- Scallops
- Shrimp
- Crabmeat
- Clams
- Mussels

like brown rice, your husband likes white," says Dr. Fuchs. "You can have a supply of both in the freezer, and it takes no time to reheat them."

"I routinely cook up batches of favorite soups to freeze," says nutrition consultant and author Patricia Baird, R.D. With homemade stock, experts recommend using a fat separator or chilling the soup to allow fat to rise to the top where it can be skimmed off. Soups are best frozen flat on a tray in resealable plastic freezer bags, then stacked. A big pot of vegetable-laden soup starts the week's nutrition off right. "Use vegetables like carrots and winter squash," says Dr. Fuchs. "For extra nutrition put in white beans, rice, barley or millet. For energy, potatoes or yams. When you're reheating the soup, throw in nutritious chopped greens such as spinach or chard."

Experts also suggest asking yourself, What can I do today that will make tomorrow's dinner easier? Doubling up on tasks—like chopping onions—cuts kitchen time in half. Do quantity cooking while you're working around the house, reading, or catching up on chores. "Whenever I am home," says Susan G. Purdy, author of *Have Your Cake and Eat It, Too* and *Let Them Eat Cake*, "something is simmering on the stove or baking in the oven." A soup, casserole or thick hearty stew for the week's meals can cook without too much supervision while you do other things. Just set a kitchen timer to remind you.

Save money by cooking large batches of your own convenience

foods. Susan Asanovic, M.S., R.D., owner of the food and nutrition consulting firm Table Dans Le Bon Sens in Wilton, Connecticut, cooks a huge pot of beans regularly and freezes them. Fletcher's family loves baked potatoes, so she always cooks extra for lunches during the week; topped with vegetables and melted low-fat cheese, they're a favorite 5-minute meal.

Stocking your fridge and freezer with this kind of planned quantity cooking will make you feel rich in time. You'll always have the makings of a wealth of nutritious meals.

PLAN ON THE WEEKEND

Planned-overs, says Tribole, are intentional leftovers, a most important strategy for healthy weeknight meals. A 30-minute cooking session on the weekend gives you a two- or three-meal head start for the week. Look over your menus for the week. If you're having rice twice and macaroni in three meals, cook up a big pot of each on Sunday. Drain well, rinse in cold water to remove excess starch (and keep the stickiness down) and let the rice or pasta cool. Then package in flattened resealable plastic storage bags or small containers.

Spanish rice or macaroni and cheese is super-easy when the grain is already cooked—all you have to do is assemble and bake. A pot of cooked rice can also become the base for an impromptu stir-fry, a quick tomato-rice soup or a salad with low-fat vinaigrette and leftover steamed vegetables. Chef Raichlen uses up leftover cooked beans by adding sautéed onions, garlic and cumin. It's a natural way of thinking for food experts: What can I make ahead to make cooking a breeze?

Include certain perishable staples in your cook-ahead session each week to save actual prep time on busy nights. If you're chopping an onion in the food processor, why not chop two? Busy cooks often have bags of chopped onions in the freezer—they don't freeze solid, so you can scoop out a cup or tablespoon when you need it. Treat other repeat ingredients the same way: a week's worth of minced fresh garlic, chopped fresh parsley and homemade low-fat pesto in the refrigerator are worth their weight in gold on weeknights.

Marinating firm cuts of fish or chicken in self-sealing plastic bags is another popular prep-ahead tactic chefs use to reduce kitchen time. Simply place the cleaned meat in a freezer-weight bag and add lime or lemon juice, a little olive oil, tomato juice, citrus peel, low-fat plain yogurt, curry—whatever appeals to your taste buds. The tanginess of the yogurt or citrus helps reduce the need for salt, and your meat will tenderize as it marinates. Refrigerate the bag for up to two days, turning it occasionally to distribute the marinade evenly. Raichlen depends on low-fat marinades like these to transform lean ingredients into memorable dishes. He keeps a variety of quick marinades on hand during the week (favorites are a Cuban combination of lime juice, minced garlic and ground cumin and an Indian mixture of nonfat plain yogurt, lemon juice, minced onion and saffron).

Once you try this trick for boosting flavor, your summer menus will revolve around the grill, as Raichlen's do. "You can also reduce the marinade as a low-fat sauce," he suggests. Just boil at high heat for 3 to 5 minutes, then drizzle over the cooked meat.

Raichlen also makes yogurt cheese each week. It's a simple overnight procedure: Spoon a container of nonfat plain yogurt into a strainer lined with cheesecloth, place over a bowl and refrigerate overnight. In the morning you have a thick, creamy fat-free base for favorite desserts, dips and sauces. Raichlen uses yogurt cheese for his signature whipped pudding of yogurt cheese, vanilla, lemon peel and a little sugar, and for his winning tart filling that he tops with fresh fruit.

Here are some favorite prep-ahead items we found in our experts' refrigerators and freezers:

- Lemon juice (juice 10 lemons and freeze in ice-cube trays)
- Minced onions (mince 3 to 5 onions in your food processor and freeze in ½-cup portions)
- Minced garlic (mince 2 to 3 whole heads of garlic and store covered with olive oil or lemon juice in the fridge)
- Bread crumbs (place stale bread in a food processor, grind and freeze for breading foods and topping casseroles)
- Cooked beans (soak and cook triple batches, then freeze in resealable plastic bags)
- Cooked brown, white and basmati rice (freeze in 1-cup portions)
- Chopped ginger (chop in the food processor—don't bother to peel it—and freeze in 1-tablespoon portions in ice-cube trays)

ENLIST YOUR FAMILY'S HELP

Even with careful planning and a stockpile of leftovers, you still have to assemble the meal. How do the experts get weeknight dinners from stove to table—and have fun doing it?

"Delegate," says Asanovic. "Enlist family members to help shop, prep and clean up. We all have just 24 hours in a day. Healthy, delicious food is a huge priority, but I don't like drudgery. So I organize, prioritize and stay focused."

Children should be engaged in helping in the kitchen, agrees Simmons. "It's an act of love; you're nurturing and sustaining them as you cook together. Part of health is family time. Give each child a task: setting the table, slicing the bread." And watch dinner appear like magic!

TOP TOOLS FOR THE SPEEDY KITCHEN

When we asked our experts for their favorite timesaving tools, here's what they recommended.

Food Processor. Nothing beats a food processor for cutting vegetables, pureeing, or grating cheese in literally seconds. Raichlen uses it to make instant sauces or sorbets out of frozen berries. You can mince your fresh herbs, onions and garlic in minutes or puree part of a soup to thicken the whole pot.

Keep your food processor plugged in and on the counter, say the experts, so you'll use it often. With lower-fat cooking, there's less cleanup too. Just rinse the work bowl and blade between different uses in the same meal.

Wok. Asian chefs can put a fast delicious dinner on the table because they wok it. Stir-fries cooked quickly at high heat in a wok also retain maximum nutrients, color and flavor for minimum fat. The best woks are carbon steel—the favorite of many chefs because it distributes heat evenly. Follow the manufacturer's directions for seasoning your wok before you use it—only once is needed.

To save time when wokking, keep the heat high. Have ingredients cut and sauces ready, since cooking time can be less than five minutes for a vegetable stir-fry for four people.

Pressure Cooker. Pressure cookers have evolved big time since the days of Grandma's spaghetti sauce on the ceiling. If you want to add the superior nutrition of whole grains to your meals on a regular basis, invest in a pressure cooker. The new models are shiny and efficient, with complex safety backup systems—foolproof and fast.

Most whole grains, longer-cooking vegetables, soups and pasta sauces can be pressure-cooked in half the time. You simply put the food inside, lock on the lid, set the pressure cooker over high heat and let the steam pressure build. The boiling point rises from 212°—the highest you can get in a regular pot—to 250°. It is the best way to maximize nutrients: The food is done sooner and the nutrient-filled steam goes back into the pot.

Experts advise filling the pressure cooker only half to three-quarters full, to allow the steam pressure enough room to build. When high pressure is reached, begin timing. Newer pressure cookers have an indicator on the lid that tells you when they reach high pressure.

Best buys are stainless steel, a solid bottom of copper or aluminum (for best heat conduction) and a six-quart capacity.

Sizzle Plate. A terrific restaurant tool rarely used in home kitchens is making news: the sizzle plate. It's a concave metal dish with a wide rim. You arrange meat, fish, poultry and vegetables in the center, add a drizzle of liquid such as defatted stock or juice, cover it with foil and pop it into the oven. Minutes later, you have a meal. Because it works on the principle of moist-heat cooking, many of the nutrients are retained. Sizzle plates are available in most kitchenware stores. Look for 10″ × 7″ plates in stainless steel for the most versatility.

Microwave. When was the last time you actually *cooked* in your microwave (not just reheated something)? This timesaving device can speed meal preparation dramatically. You can make breakfast in 2 minutes, lunch in 5, dinner in 15 if you depend on microwave magic.

You don't have to gussy up food with oil or butter to keep it moist when you microwave. Just cover it with plastic wrap and vent. The moist heat cooking can produce incredibly low-fat meals. And nutritionists love the microwave because fewer vitamins are lost than in most other cooking methods. "Microwaving retains nutrients best," says Asanovic. Cornell University food scientists found that microwaving lost the least vitamin C in broccoli, compared to boiling and steaming. And you lose more fat, according to a study at Texas A&M University, which looked at the amount of fat from ground beef zapped by microwaves as opposed to other cooking methods.

And there's a bonus for especially busy nights: If you use the microwave for quickly cooked fresh vegetables, there are no pots to clean, dry and put away.

Speedy Stovetop and Oven Tips

Use these four cooking methods for the quickest, healthiest meals.

Grilling. Both outdoor gas and indoor stovetop grilling are speedy ways of retaining flavor and moistness as you cook leaner cuts of meats and fish. Try marinating vegetables and meat overnight in self-sealing plastic bags in the refrigerator. Brush foods with a basting liquid while grilling (try balsamic vinegar or low-fat chicken stock) to further prevent drying out. Cut cleanup by grilling on heavy-duty foil. (Avoid charcoal grills, which take 30 minutes to heat up.)

Broiling. Broiling takes 5 to 10 minutes for most meats and fish and is best for those thinner cuts that tend to dry out or stick on the grill. Coat broiler pans or racks with no-stick cooking spray or line them with foil. Baste leaner meats and chicken fillets with balsamic vinegar, pineapple juice, lemon juice or chicken broth during broiling to enhance their flavor.

Stir-Frying. Usually done in a wok or large skillet where there's room to toss the food, stir-frying is the fastest way to cook most vegetables, as well as boneless chicken and shrimp. This method is preferred by Asian chefs because the high-heat, quick cooking retains much of the original color and texture of vegetables.

Steam-Sautéing (Quick Braising). Braising, or slow cooking in flavored liquids, tenderizes leaner cuts of meat. You can speed up the process with a quick, high-heat sauté to sear meat in a tiny amount of oil or chicken broth. Then add more broth or other flavorful liquid, cover and steam until tender.

KITCHEN SHORTCUTS

- Have all the ingredients and equipment out before you begin to cook.
- Use no-stick cookware to avoid oiling the pan.
- Keep your food processor and blender on the counter for quick access.
- Chop and shred vegetables in your food processor.
- Prepare two or more recipes at the same time.
- Keep your work area clear by cleaning up as you go: replace jar lids, package leftover vegetables, put used bowls and spoons in the dishwasher.

FRESHNESS IN THE FRIDGE

- Store foods in the fridge by types: produce in crisper drawers, beverages in the side door where they can't ice up, fresh foods toward the front where you'll see and use them quickly.
- Store uncooked meats, fish and poultry in the coldest part of your fridge.
- Store leftovers in see-through containers.
- Store washed, torn lettuce in your salad spinner. The small amount of water left in the bottom under the spinner basket will humidify greens and keep them crisp for 5 to 7 days.
- Store fresh herbs standing in a glass of water loosely covered with a plastic bag. Or wrap a moist paper towel around the stems and store them in perforated resealable plastic vegetable bags.
- Store mushrooms and strawberries unwashed in a paper bag or cardboard carton (not the crisper drawer), loosely covered with paper towels to absorb excess water.

MEALS IN MINUTES
WITH YOUR MICROWAVE

BEST BREAKFASTS

• **Egg and Cheese Sandwich:** Make your own egg-and-cheese sandwich. Break an egg into a microwaveable custard cup, beat with a small amount of water and microwave at half power (50%) for 1 minute, or until the egg is cooked. Layer it on a toasted English muffin with a slice of low-fat cheese.

• **Breakfast Pizza:** If you love leftover pizza for breakfast, make your own in a flash. Top a halved English muffin with leftover spaghetti sauce and shredded low-fat cheese and place on a paper towel. Microwave on high power for 1 to 2 minutes, or until the cheese melts.

LIGHTNING LUNCHES

• **Baked Stuffed Potato:** Bake a scrubbed potato by pricking it with a fork and microwaving on high power for 4 to 5 minutes; slit open. Top with frozen or precooked vegetables and shredded low-fat cheese. Microwave for 1 minute longer.

• **Pasta Presto:** Add 1 cup mixed frozen vegetables to 1 cup cooked leftover pasta. Top with 1 tablespoon each lemon juice and grated Parmesan cheese and cover with plastic wrap. Microwave on high power for 2 minutes.

DESPERATION DINNERS

• **Quick Tomato Sauce:** Create a fast tomato sauce by combining 4 cups chopped tomatoes, 2 tablespoons minced garlic and 3 tablespoons minced fresh basil; cover and microwave on high power for 5 minutes, then puree. Toss with pasta.

• **Fast Fish:** Wrap a fish fillet and salad bar vegetables in parchment. Microwave on high power for 4 to 5 minutes, or until the fish flakes when pressed lightly with a fork. Sprinkle the fish with lemon juice.

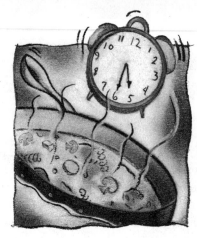

SIMPLE
COMFORT
IN ONE POT

$\mathcal{S}$PEEDY SOUP AND STEW DINNERS

$\mathcal{A}$ big pot of soul-warming soup always tastes as if it's been simmering on low for hours, lovingly tended by a culinary wizard (like Grandma). But most of these savory one-pot dinners are ready in 30 minutes. And leftovers taste even better the next day, when seasonings mellow. Our collection of rush-hour soups and hearty stews will make old-fashioned flavor and good nutrition an easy part of your weeknight menus.

SPEEDY SOUTHWESTERN DINNER

Pinto Bean Chili
Jalapeño Buttermilk Cornbread
Tossed Green Salad

Chili and cornbread can fit into busy weeknights if you cook smart. Use canned pinto beans and precut vegetables from the salad bar, and bake the cornbread while the chili simmers. Then thicken the chili with a quick puree instead of lengthy cooking time.

GAME PLAN

1. Prepare the cornbread and put it in the oven to bake.
2. Start the chili.
3. Make a tossed salad from mixed baby lettuces, shredded carrots and diced tomatoes. Add your favorite low-fat dressing.

JALAPEÑO BUTTERMILK CORNBREAD

SERVES 6

1½	cups yellow or white cornmeal
½	cup all-purpose flour
2	teaspoons baking powder
½	teaspoon baking soda
½	teaspoon salt
1	tablespoon oil
1	tablespoon honey
2	eggs, slightly beaten
1½	cups low-fat buttermilk
⅓	cup frozen whole-kernel corn, thawed and drained
3–4	tablespoons chopped jalapeño peppers (wear plastic gloves when handling)

Coat an 8″ × 8″ baking pan or a 9″ ovenproof skillet with no-stick cooking spray and place it in the oven. Turn the oven to 450° and heat the pan for 3 to 5 minutes, or until it is very hot.

While the pan is heating, in a medium bowl combine the cornmeal, flour, baking powder, baking soda, salt, oil, honey, eggs, buttermilk, corn and jalapeño peppers. Beat vigorously for 30 seconds. Pour into the hot pan.

Reduce the oven to 375° and bake for 20 minutes, or until the cornbread is golden brown and a toothpick inserted in the center comes out clean. Let the cornbread cool slightly, then cut it into 6 pieces.

Preparation time: 6 minutes
Cooking time: 20 minutes

Chef's note: Leftover cornbread can be stored in the refrigerator for up to 3 days if it's wrapped tightly in plastic wrap. Toast thin slices of cornbread and spread them with jam for a quick breakfast.

Per serving: 239 calories, 5.7 g. fat (21% of calories), 5.2 g. dietary fiber, 73 mg. cholesterol, 551 mg. sodium.

PINTO BEAN CHILI

SERVES 4

- 1 *cup defatted reduced-sodium chicken broth*
- 2 *cups chopped onions*
- ½ *cup chopped celery*
- ½ *cup shredded carrots*
- 2–3 *tablespoons minced garlic*
- 2 *teaspoons ground cumin*
- 4 *teaspoons chili powder*
- 1 *can (16 ounces) reduced-sodium pinto beans, undrained*
- 1 *can (16 ounces) reduced-sodium low-fat barbecue baked beans*
- 2 *teaspoons chopped jalapeño peppers (wear plastic gloves when handling)*
- 1 *can (16 ounces) reduced-sodium chopped Italian plum tomatoes (with juice)*
  Salt and ground black pepper
- ⅓ *cup shredded low-fat Monterey Jack cheese*
- ½ *cup nonfat sour cream*

In a large Dutch oven over medium-high heat, bring ½ cup of the broth to a boil. Add the onions; cook and stir for 2 minutes. Add the celery, carrots, garlic, cumin and chili powder; cook and stir for 3 minutes.

Add the pinto beans, baked beans, jalapeño peppers, tomatoes (with juice) and remaining ½ cup of the broth. Increase the heat to high; cover the pot and bring the chili to a boil. Reduce the heat to medium high; simmer the chili, covered, for 15 minutes, stirring occasionally. (Adjust the heat so that the chili is cooking rapidly but not scorching.)

To thicken the chili, place 4 cups in a blender or food processor and carefully puree it on low speed. Return the pureed chili to the pot; add salt and pepper to taste. If desired, add more chili powder and chopped jalapeño peppers to taste.

Spoon the chili into 4 bowls; stir in the Monterey Jack. Top each bowl with a dollop of sour cream.

Preparation time: 10 minutes
Cooking time: 25 minutes

Per serving: 325 calories, 4.1 g. fat (10% of calories), 11.1 g. dietary fiber, 7 mg. cholesterol, 717 mg. sodium.

BEEF IT UP!

*P*ressure cooking gives this speedy stew slow-cooked flavor. And the drop biscuits cook in minutes. To keep the biscuits lean yet tender, we replaced some of the butter with yogurt and low-fat buttermilk. If you don't have a pressure cooker, follow the directions for using a Dutch oven.

GAME PLAN

1. Start the stew.
2. Make the biscuits.
3. Make a simple carrot salad with shredded carrots and raisins. Add your favorite low-fat coleslaw dressing.

SAVORY BEEF STEW

SERVES 4

¼ cup all-purpose flour
½ teaspoon salt
¼ teaspoon dry mustard
1 pound lean sirloin, trimmed of fat and cubed
1½ teaspoons olive oil
½ cup defatted beef broth
½ cups diced onions
2 tablespoons minced garlic
1 cup diced red potatoes
1 medium carrot, chopped

1 can (14 ounces) peeled whole tomatoes (with juice), chopped

2 tablespoons tomato paste

2 tablespoons balsamic vinegar

1 tablespoon brown sugar

1½ teaspoons dried thyme

2 bay leaves

Salt and ground black pepper

Place the flour, salt, dry mustard and sirloin in a resealable plastic storage bag. Shake to combine. Heat the oil in a pressure cooker or heavy Dutch oven over medium-high heat. Transfer the beef to the pan, and brown on all sides.

Add the broth; bring to a boil, scraping the bottom of the pan to loosen any browned bits. Add the onions, garlic, potatoes, carrots, tomatoes (with juice), tomato paste, vinegar, brown sugar, thyme and bay leaves.

Lock the pressure cooker lid in place and bring to high pressure over high heat. Cook for 12 minutes. Release the pressure, and add salt and pepper to taste. Remove the bay leaves before serving.

Preparation time: 10 minutes
Cooking time: 15 minutes

Chef's note: If you don't have a pressure cooker, use a Dutch oven. Increase the amount of beef broth or water to 3 cups and cook for 1½ to 2 hours over medium heat, stirring occasionally.

Per serving: 333 calories, 7.4 g. fat (20% of calories), 4 g. dietary fiber, 65 mg. cholesterol, 599 mg. sodium.

CHIVE BISCUITS

1¾ cups all-purpose flour
 1 tablespoon baking powder
 ½ teaspoon baking soda
 ¼ teaspoon salt
 1 tablespoon snipped fresh chives
 2 tablespoons chilled margarine or butter
 ½ cup nonfat plain yogurt
 ⅓ cup low-fat buttermilk

Preheat the oven to 450°. In a food processor or large mixing bowl, combine the flour, baking powder, baking soda, salt and chives. Add the margarine or butter in small pieces; mix until the pastry is crumbly. Add the yogurt and buttermilk; mix just until the liquid is incorporated.

Drop the dough by large spoonfuls onto a 9″ × 13″ no-stick baking sheet. Bake for 12 minutes, or until lightly browned.

Preparation time: 8 minutes
Cooking time: 12 minutes

Per serving: 277 calories, 6.4 g. fat (21% of calories), 1.5 g. dietary fiber, 1 mg. cholesterol, 647 mg. sodium.

TURKEY TIME

Corn and Turkey Chowder
Green and White Bean Salad
French Bread

*W*ho needs cream and butter? Potatoes bring plenty of creamy richness to this thick soup. It's paired with a colorful bean salad that uses both fresh and canned beans, so it's a snap to make.

GAME PLAN

1. Make the chowder.
2. Make the salad and let it marinate.
3. Heat the French bread.

CORN AND TURKEY CHOWDER

SERVES 4

2¼   cups defatted chicken broth
1½   cups chopped onions
  2   teaspoons chopped garlic
  3   cups cubed cooked red potatoes
3½   cups frozen whole-kernel corn, thawed and drained
  ⅔   cup skim milk
  ½   cup diced cooked skinless turkey breast
       Salt and ground black pepper
  ¼   cup chopped fresh parsley

In a large soup pot over medium-high heat, heat ¼ cup of the broth; when it's simmering, add the onions. Cook and stir for 3 minutes, or until the onions are soft. Add the garlic, potatoes and remaining 2 cups of broth. Bring the soup to a boil. Simmer, covered, for 15 minutes, or until the potatoes are soft.

Puree half the corn in a blender. Add the pureed and whole corn, milk and turkey to the soup. Simmer for 15 minutes. Add salt and pepper to taste and stir in the parsley.

Preparation time: 10 minutes
Cooking time: 35 minutes

Per serving: 351 calories, 0.6 g. fat (1% of calories), 7.2 g. dietary fiber, 12 mg. cholesterol, 238 mg. sodium.

GREEN AND WHITE BEAN SALAD

SERVES 4

3   *cups diagonally sliced green beans*
1   *cup canned Great Northern beans, rinsed and drained*
2   *teaspoons olive oil*
¼   *cup minced fresh parsley*
¼   *cup minced fresh basil*
⅓   *cup balsamic vinegar*
2   *teaspoons honey mustard*
¼   *cup minced sweet or red onions*
½   *teaspoon salt*
    Ground black pepper

Bring a pot of water to a boil; add the green beans. Cook for 30 seconds, or until they turn bright green. Rinse under cold water and transfer to a medium bowl.

Add the Great Northern beans, oil, parsley, basil, vinegar, mustard and onions. Stir well. Let the salad marinate at room temperature for 30 minutes. Add the salt and pepper to taste.

Preparation time: 10 minutes
Cooking time: 30 seconds
Marinating time: 30 minutes

Per serving: 160 calories, 2.9 g. fat (16% of calories), 1.9 g. dietary fiber, no cholesterol, 295 mg. sodium.

FAST FIESTA

Mexican Chicken Tortilla Soup
Spicy Grilled Corn
Salsa
Sliced Avocados, Tomatoes and
Bell Peppers

his slightly spicy soup is perfect for an elegant summer dinner. The tortillas are cut into strips, then baked instead of fried. Add them to the soup just before serving. Grilled corn is cooked southwestern style, without the husks, for a chewy and flavorful side dish.

GAME PLAN

1. Start the soup.
2. Preheat the grill and prepare the corn for grilling.
3. Arrange a plate with tomatoes, sweet red or yellow bell peppers and a small amount of thinly sliced avocados.
4. Spoon the salsa into a bowl.
5. Bake the tortillas for the soup.
6. Grill the corn and finish the soup.

SPICY GRILLED CORN

SERVES 4

4	*large ears white or yellow corn on the cob, shucked*
1½	*teaspoons olive oil, warmed*
¼	*teaspoon ground cumin*
½	*teaspoon salt*
	Pinch of ground red pepper

Preheat the grill.

Place the corn, oil, cumin, salt and red pepper in a resealable plastic storage bag. Shake to combine.

Transfer the corn to the grill. Grill for 5 to 8 minutes, turning frequently, or until the corn is lightly browned, brushing the ears occasionally with any remaining oil.

Preparation time: 1 minute
Cooking time: 8 minutes

Per serving: 99 calories, 2.7 g. fat (22% of calories), 2.9 g. dietary fiber, no cholesterol, 280 mg. sodium.

MEXICAN CHICKEN TORTILLA SOUP

SERVES 4

3   *cups defatted chicken broth*

½   *cup sliced onions*

1   *cup diced red potatoes*

½   *large green pepper, diced*

2   *teaspoons minced garlic*

2   *boneless skinless chicken breast halves, cut into thin strips*

1   *can (14 ounces) Mexican-style stewed tomatoes*

1   *teaspoon chopped jalapeño peppers (wear plastic gloves when handling)*

½   *teaspoon ground cumin*

4   *(6") corn tortillas*

1   *tablespoon lime juice*

¼   *cup chopped fresh cilantro*

In a large soup pot over medium-high heat, bring ½ cup of the broth to a boil. Add the onions, potatoes, green peppers and garlic. Cook and stir for 5 minutes. Add the chicken; cook and stir for 1 minute.

Add the stewed tomatoes, jalapeño peppers, cumin and remaining 2½ cups of broth. Bring to a boil. Simmer the soup, uncovered, over medium heat for 15 minutes, or until the potatoes are soft.

Meanwhile, preheat the oven to 350°. Coat both sides of the tortillas with olive oil no-stick cooking spray; cut them into thin strips and place on a baking sheet. Bake for 15 minutes, or until crisp.

Add the lime juice and cilantro to the soup; top each bowl with the tortilla strips.

Preparation time: 10 minutes
Cooking time: 15 minutes

Per serving: 240 calories, 2.3 g. fat (8% of calories), 2.3 g. dietary fiber, 34 mg. cholesterol, 497 mg. sodium.

INDIAN SUMMER SUPPER

Butternut Squash Bisque
Red Pepper–Ricotta Bruschetta
Tossed Green Salad

This simple soup is a fast and delicious way to incorporate high-beta-carotene butternut squash into your meals. The "little toasts," or bruschetta, invented by thrifty Italian cooks, are a crunchy accompaniment.

GAME PLAN

1. Start the soup.
2. Make the bruschetta.
3. Make a simple tossed green salad from leaf lettuce, shredded red cabbage and sliced cucumbers. Add your favorite low-fat Italian dressing.
4. Puree the soup.

BUTTERNUT SQUASH BISQUE

SERVES 4

1	large butternut squash
1	teaspoon olive oil
2¼	cups defatted chicken broth
2	teaspoons minced garlic
2	cups chopped onions
1	cup chopped sweet red peppers
¼–½	teaspoon ground red pepper
½	teaspoon ground cumin
	Salt and ground black pepper
¼	cup nonfat plain yogurt

Pierce the squash several times with a sharp knife; place it on a paper towel in the microwave. Microwave on high for 5 minutes. Halve the squash lengthwise and remove the seeds; microwave on high for 5 more minutes.

In a large soup pot over medium-high heat, combine the olive oil and ¼ cup of the broth; bring to a boil. Add the garlic, onions and peppers; cook and stir for 5 minutes.

Scoop the squash from its shell and cut into chunks; add the squash, ground red pepper, cumin and remaining 2 cups of broth to the soup. Reduce the heat to medium. Bring to a boil; simmer, covered, for 15 minutes.

Transfer the soup to a blender or food processor; puree until smooth. Return the soup to the pot; heat through. Add salt and pepper to taste; garnish each serving with yogurt.

Preparation time: 10 minutes
Cooking time: 30 minutes

Per serving: 168 calories, 1.7 g. fat (8% total calories), 6 g. dietary fiber, 0.3 mg. cholesterol, 211 mg. sodium.

RED PEPPER–RICOTTA BRUSCHETTA

SERVES 4

8 *(¾") slices crusty French bread*
½ *cup light ricotta cheese*
2 *tablespoons nonfat mayonnaise*
2 *tablespoons nonfat plain yogurt*
2 *tablespoons grated Parmesan cheese*
½ *cup roasted sweet red peppers (from a jar), drained*

Toast the bread.

In a blender or bowl, combine the ricotta, mayonnaise, yogurt and Parmesan until smooth. Spread on the toasted bread.

Top each bruschetta with red peppers.

Preparation time: 10 minutes

Per serving: 191 calories, 3.4 g. fat (16% of calories), 0.5 g. dietary fiber, 7 mg. cholesterol, 486 mg. sodium.

POWWOW PARTY

Corn and Sweet Potato Stew
Toast with Low-Fat Pimento Cheese
Coleslaw

Inherited from Native American cooking, this delicious combination of fresh corn, tomatoes, chilies and sweet potatoes is a winner for winter months. The toast is topped with an old-fashioned favorite—pimento cheese—made lean with low-fat cheeses.

GAME PLAN

1. Make the stew.
2. Make the spread and refrigerate it.
3. Make a simple coleslaw from shredded red cabbage, shredded carrots and drained canned pineapple chunks. Add your favorite low-fat coleslaw dressing or nonfat plain yogurt.
4. Make the toast.

CORN AND SWEET POTATO STEW

SERVES 4

2½ cups defatted chicken broth
½ cup chopped onions
1 tablespoon minced garlic
1 cup peeled and diced sweet potatoes
1 cup chopped sweet red peppers
½ cup diced zucchini or summer squash
1 cup whole-kernel corn

1   can (14½ ounces) diced tomatoes with green chilies, or
    whole peeled tomatoes (with juice), chopped
1   cup cooked navy beans or brown rice
½   teaspoon dried thyme
1   teaspoon cornstarch
1   tablespoon dry sherry or apple juice
    Salt and ground black pepper
¼   cup low-fat sour cream

In a large soup pot over medium-high heat, bring ½ cup of the broth to a boil; add the onions. Cook and stir for 3 minutes. Add the garlic, sweet potatoes, peppers, zucchini or summer squash, corn, tomatoes (with juice), beans or rice and thyme. Cook and stir for 1 minute.

Add the remaining 2 cups of broth; bring to a boil. Reduce the heat to medium; simmer, covered, for 20 to 25 minutes, or until the sweet potatoes are tender.

In a small bowl, combine the cornstarch and sherry or apple juice; add to the stew. Cook and stir for 3 to 5 minutes, or until slightly thickened. Add salt and pepper to taste; garnish each bowl with sour cream.

Preparation time: 10 minutes
Cooking time: 30 minutes

Per serving: 281 calories, 1.9 g. fat (6% of calories), 7.5 g. dietary fiber, 5 mg. cholesterol, 574 mg. sodium.

TOAST WITH LOW-FAT PIMENTO CHEESE

SERVES 8

4 ounces nonfat cream cheese
1 cup shredded low-fat sharp Cheddar cheese
⅓ cup light ricotta cheese
⅓ cup chopped, drained pimentos (from a jar)
¼ cup nonfat mayonnaise
⅓ cup plain nonfat yogurt
2 tablespoons minced red onions
8 slices reduced-sodium dark rye or whole-wheat bread

In a blender or food processor, combine the cream cheese, Cheddar and ricotta until smooth. Add the pimentos, mayonnaise and yogurt; process until the pimentos are finely chopped. Stir in the red onions. Transfer to a container and refrigerate for 15 minutes.

Toast the bread and cut it into triangles. Serve with the chilled spread.

Preparation time: 5 minutes
Chilling time: 15 minutes

Chef's note: Cube leftover toast as croutons for soup; leftover pimento cheese is great as a sandwich spread for lunch later in the week.

Per serving: 149 calories, 3.4 g. fat (18% of calories), no dietary fiber, 9 mg. cholesterol, 524 mg. sodium.

SIMPLY SCANDINAVIAN

Blender Potato Buttermilk Soup
Marinated Vegetable Salad
Rye Croutons

*Y*our blender and pressure cooker make this Scandinavian soup dinner almost instant. Low-fat buttermilk and potatoes thicken the creamy soup, and a crisp marinated salad adds plenty of vitamin-rich fresh vegetables.

GAME PLAN

1. Make the salad.
2. Make the soup.
3. Slice rye bread into strips, coat with olive oil no-stick cooking spray and bake for 15 minutes at 350°.

BLENDER POTATO BUTTERMILK SOUP

SERVES 4

1   teaspoon olive oil
1   cup chopped onions
3   stalks celery, diced
3   medium baking potatoes, diced
3   cups defatted chicken broth
2   cups low-fat buttermilk
¼   cup sliced green onions
    Salt and ground black pepper

Heat the oil in a pressure cooker over medium-high heat. Add the onions and celery; cook and stir for 2 minutes. Add the potatoes and broth. Lock the pressure cooker lid in place and bring to high pressure. Cook for 5 minutes. Remove the pressure cooker from the heat and release the pressure.

Transfer the soup to a blender or food processor; add the buttermilk and puree. Return the soup to the pot; heat through. Add the green onions and salt and pepper to taste.

Preparation time: 5 minutes
Cooking time: 7 minutes

Per serving: 263 calories, 2.5 g. fat (8% of calories), 5.1 g. dietary fiber, 5 mg. cholesterol, 420 mg. sodium.

MARINATED VEGETABLE SALAD

SERVES 4

½ cup thinly sliced red onions
1 cup diced cucumbers
½ cup sliced mushrooms
½ cup diced sweet red peppers
½ cup diced green peppers
2 tablespoons chopped fresh parsley
2 tablespoons lemon juice
2–3 tablespoons rice vinegar
2 teaspoons olive oil
1 teaspoon minced garlic
Salt and ground black pepper
4 lettuce leaves

In a large bowl, combine the onions, cucumbers, mushrooms, red and green peppers, parsley, lemon juice, vinegar, oil and garlic. Add salt and pepper to taste. Let the salad marinate for 20 minutes at room temperature.

Line 4 salad plates with the lettuce leaves; arrange the salad on top of the lettuce.

Preparation time: 15 minutes
Marinating time: 20 minutes

Per serving: 59 calories, 2.6 g. fat (35% of calories), 1.7 g. dietary fiber, no cholesterol, 5 mg. sodium.

NEW MEXICO NIGHTS

Black Bean Stew with Smoked Turkey
Grilled Cheese Tortilla Wedges
Tossed Salad

This hearty menu of corn-and-black-bean stew and crisp tortillas can take the chill off any winter day. Smoked turkey and lean cheeses add high flavor without high fat.

GAME PLAN

1. Make the stew.
2. Make a simple tossed salad of canned artichoke hearts, romaine lettuce and sliced radishes. Add your favorite low-fat ranch dressing.
3. Make the tortilla wedges.

GRILLED CHEESE TORTILLA WEDGES

SERVES 4

- ¾ cup shredded low-fat Monterey Jack cheese
- 2 tablespoons thinly sliced green onions
- ¼ cup finely diced tomatoes
- ¼ cup nonfat sour cream
- 8 (8") flour tortillas

In a medium bowl, combine the Monterey Jack, green onions, tomatoes and sour cream. Divide between 4 tortillas, spreading evenly. Top with the remaining 4 tortillas.

Coat a 10" no-stick skillet with no-stick cooking spray; set it over medium-high heat. When the skillet is hot, cook the tortilla sandwiches for 3 to 4 minutes, or until the cheese has melted, turning once during cooking. Cut into wedges.

Preparation time: 5 minutes
Cooking time: 15 minutes

Per serving: 301 calories, 8.8 g. fat (27% of calories), 0.2 g. dietary fiber, 15 mg. cholesterol, 512 mg. sodium.

BLACK BEAN STEW WITH SMOKED TURKEY

SERVES 4

¼	cup dry sherry or apple juice
1	tablespoon olive oil
2	cups chopped onions
½	cup chopped celery
½	cup chopped carrots
½	cup chopped sweet red peppers
4	cups cooked black beans
2	ounces diced smoked lean turkey
2	cups whole-kernel corn
2	cups defatted chicken broth
2	tablespoons minced garlic
1	cup chopped tomatoes
2	teaspoons ground cumin
3–4	teaspoons chili powder
½	teaspoon dried oregano
¼	cup chopped fresh cilantro
2	tablespoons honey
2	tablespoons tomato paste

In a large soup pot over medium-high heat, combine the sherry or apple juice and oil; bring to a boil. Add the onions; cook and stir for 3 minutes, or until soft but not browned. Add the celery, carrots and peppers. Cook and stir for 5 minutes.

Add the beans, turkey, corn, broth, garlic, tomatoes, cumin, chili powder, oregano, cilantro, honey and tomato paste. Bring to a boil. Lower the heat to medium; simmer for 15 minutes.

Puree 1 cup of the stew in a blender, then return it to the pot.

Preparation time: 15 minutes
Cooking time: 25 minutes

Per serving: 495 calories, 5.6 g. fat (10% of calories), 13.4 g. dietary fiber, 6 mg. cholesterol, 432 mg. sodium.

NEW DOWN-HOME DINNER

Pesto Chili
Cheesy Whole-Wheat Breadsticks
Fresh Fruit Plate

This rich-tasting pesto chili combines Texas heartiness with French flair. The crusty breadsticks are surprisingly quick—use a good-quality store-bought whole-wheat bread dough.

GAME PLAN

1. Make the chili.
2. Make the breadsticks.
3. Slice fresh fruit such as kiwifruit, pears, apples, melon and bananas. Arrange it on a platter.

CHEESY WHOLE-WHEAT BREADSTICKS

SERVES 4

2 teaspoons cornmeal
2 tablespoons grated Parmesan cheese
1 tablespoon minced garlic
¼ teaspoon ground red pepper
4 ounces frozen whole-wheat bread dough, thawed
1 egg white, slightly beaten

Preheat the oven to 450°. Line a baking sheet with parchment paper and sprinkle it with the cornmeal. Set aside.

In a large bowl, knead the cheese, garlic and red pepper into the dough. Form 8 balls. Roll each ball into a long breadstick; arrange on the baking sheet. Brush with beaten egg white.

Bake for 12 to 15 minutes, or until the breadsticks are crisp and golden brown.

Preparation time: 10 minutes
Cooking time: 15 minutes

Per serving: 106 calories, 2.4 g. fat (21% of calories), 0.3 g. dietary fiber, 4 mg. cholesterol, 210 mg. sodium.

PESTO CHILI

SERVES 4

¼   *cup water*
1   *teaspoon olive oil*
1   *cup chopped onions*
2   *teaspoons minced garlic*
1   *cup diced red potatoes*
1   *cup diced carrots or peeled winter squash*
½   *cup chopped celery leaves*
2   *cups canned chopped tomatoes (with juice)*
2   *cups canned reduced-sodium kidney beans, drained*
2   *cups defatted reduced-sodium chicken broth*
2   *teaspoons reduced-sodium tomato paste*
2   *tablespoons minced fresh parsley*
2   *teaspoons dried basil*
1   *cup chopped fresh spinach leaves*
2   *teaspoons toasted pine nuts*
¼   *cup grated Parmesan cheese*

In a large soup pot over medium-high heat, bring the water and oil to a boil. Add the onions and 1 teaspoon of the garlic. Cook and stir for 5 to 6 minutes, or until the onions are soft but not browned.

Add the potatoes, carrots or squash, celery leaves, tomatoes (with juice) and beans. Cook and stir for 2 minutes. Add the broth and tomato paste; bring to a boil. Cover and simmer over medium heat for 15 minutes, or until the potatoes are soft.

In a blender or food processor, combine the parsley, basil, spinach, pine nuts and Parmesan; puree. Stir into the soup.

Preparation time: 10 minutes
Cooking time: 25 minutes

Per serving: 299 calories, 6 g. fat (17% of calories), 10.8 g. dietary fiber, 6 mg. cholesterol, 161 mg. sodium.

SUPER STEW SUPPER

Chick-Pea and Pasta Stew
Cheddar Corn Muffins
Cucumber Salad

*S*alad bar vegetables make this stew quick to prepare. The muffins are rich-tasting without the fat; applesauce and low-fat buttermilk lighten the batter.

GAME PLAN

1. Make the muffins.
2. Make the stew.
3. Make a simple salad of sliced cucumbers, chopped green onions, minced red onions, rice vinegar and a drizzle of honey. Arrange it on lettuce leaves.

CHEDDAR CORN MUFFINS

MAKES 12

1	cup unbleached all-purpose flour
¼	cup cornmeal
1	teaspoon baking powder
½	teaspoon baking soda
½	teaspoon salt
½	cup shredded low-fat sharp Cheddar cheese
½	cup shredded bran cereal
¾	cup low-fat buttermilk
2	tablespoons canola oil or softened butter
2	tablespoons unsweetened applesauce
1	large egg
⅓	cup maple syrup
½	cup whole-kernel corn

Preheat the oven to 400°. Lightly oil and flour a 12-cup muffin tin. Set aside.

In a large mixing bowl, combine the flour, cornmeal, baking powder, baking soda and salt. Add the Cheddar and cereal; toss to coat. In another bowl, whisk together the buttermilk, oil or butter, applesauce, egg, maple syrup and corn. Combine the contents of both bowls, folding just until the dry ingredients are moistened. Spoon the batter into the muffin tin.

Bake for 15 to 20 minutes, or until the muffins are golden brown and springy to the touch, and a toothpick inserted in the center of one muffin comes out clean.

Preparation time: 10 minutes
Cooking time: 20 minutes

Per muffin: 123 calories, 3.8 g. fat (26% of calories), 1.7 g. dietary fiber, 21 mg. cholesterol, 276 mg. sodium.

FAST FROM THE FREEZER: INSTANT SOUP IDEAS

On really busy nights, there's always soup for dinner. Each of these tasty concoctions can be put together in less than 10 minutes—with ingredients from your freezer and pantry shelves.

• **Spicy Mexican Soup:** In a 10″ no-stick skillet over medium-high heat, combine 2 cups frozen mixed vegetables, ½ cup medium salsa, 1 teaspoon olive oil and 1 teaspoon chopped mild green chili peppers (wear plastic gloves when handling); cook and stir for 5 minutes. Add 3 cups defatted chicken broth and 1 cup chopped cooked boneless, skinless chicken; bring to a boil. Cook for 5 minutes, stirring occasionally. Add salt and ground black pepper to taste. Serve with nonfat sour cream and chopped fresh cilantro. Serves 4.

• **Boffo Beef and Vegetable Soup:** Trim excess fat from 3 ounces frozen sirloin steak; cut it into small pieces. Dredge the beef in flour. In a medium saucepan over medium-high heat, combine 1 cup frozen mixed vegetables, 1 teaspoon olive oil, ¼ teaspoon ground cumin and the beef; cook and stir for 5 minutes, or until the beef is no longer pink in the center. Add 2 cups defatted beef stock, 1 cup reduced-sodium tomato sauce and salt and ground black pepper to taste; bring to a boil. Cook and stir for 5 minutes. Serves 4.

CHICK-PEA AND PASTA STEW

SERVES 4

1 teaspoon olive oil

¼ cup dry red wine or red grape juice

1 cup chopped onions

2 cloves garlic, minced

1 cup chopped tomatoes

⅓ cup chopped fresh parsley

⅓ cup frozen sliced carrots

⅓ cup chopped celery

½ cup cooked and diced red potatoes

1 cup cooked macaroni

1 cup canned chick-peas, drained

4 cups defatted chicken broth

2 teaspoons dried basil

¼ teaspoon dried oregano

½ teaspoon dried chives

Salt and ground black pepper

In a large soup pot over medium-high heat, combine the oil and red wine or grape juice; bring to a boil. Add the onions; cook for 5 minutes, or until soft but not browned. Add the garlic, tomatoes, parsley, carrots and celery. Cook and stir for 5 minutes.

Add the potatoes, macaroni, chick-peas, broth, basil, oregano and chives; bring to a boil. Lower the heat to medium and cook, uncovered, for 15 minutes, or until the vegetables are soft.

Puree 1 cup of the stew in a blender or food processor, then return it to the pot. Add salt and pepper to taste.

Preparation time: 15 minutes
Cooking time: 25 minutes

Per serving: 211 calories, 2.8 g. fat (11% of calories), 5.8 g. dietary fiber, no cholesterol, 598 mg. sodium.

BETTER BREAD SPREADS

• **Bagels with Sweet Ricotta Spread:** Toast 2 halved bagels. In a small bowl, mash together 1/3 cup low-fat ricotta cheese, 2 tablespoons finely chopped dates and 1 tablespoon honey. Spread over the toasted bagels. Serves 4.

• **Pita Wedges with Chick-Pea Spread:** Toast 4 pita rounds in a toaster oven for 2 minutes, then cut them with scissors into 6 to 8 wedges each. In a small bowl, mash 1 cup cooked chick-peas with 1/4 cup low-fat mayonnaise or nonfat plain yogurt and 2 tablespoons honey mustard. Season to taste with salt, pepper and celery seed. Use as a dip for the pita wedges. Serves 4.

• **Whole-Wheat Hamburger Buns with Japanese Tofu Spread:** Split and toast 2 whole-wheat hamburger buns. In a small bowl or food processor, cream 4 ounces drained soft tofu, 1 teaspoon tahini or peanut butter, 1 tablespoon reduced-fat mayonnaise, 1 tablespoon miso and 1 teaspoon minced black olives. Add lemon juice, salt and pepper to taste. Spread on the toasted buns. Serves 4.

• **Tortilla Wraps with Spicy Bean Spread:** Wrap 4 whole-wheat tortillas in plastic wrap and microwave for 1 minute on high power to warm. In a small bowl, mash 1 1/2 cups canned black beans, drained, with 1 tablespoon lemon juice, 1 teaspoon chili powder, 2 tablespoons spicy salsa, a pinch of ground cumin and 1 teaspoon minced garlic. Add salt and pepper to taste. Spoon onto the tortillas and roll up. Serves 4.

• **Creamy Banana Spread on Toast:** Toast 2 to 4 slices of rye or whole-wheat bread. In a small bowl, mash together 1/2 ripe banana, 4 ounces reduced-fat cream cheese, 1 teaspoon lemon juice and 1 teaspoon honey. Stir in 1/4 cup raisins and spread on the toast. Serves 4.

Savory Beef Stew (page 34)

Butternut Squash Bisque (page 42) and Red Pepper–Ricotta Bruschetta (page 43)

Curried Chick-Peas (page 68)

Black Bean and Corn Salad (page 79)

Whole-Grain Corn Waffles (page 81) and Three-Berry Compote (page 82)

Cold Sesame Noodles (page 93) and Cucumber Salad (page 94)

Orzo with Grilled Shrimp (page 98)

Mediterranean Pasta with Feta and Olives (page 103)

WINTER FIRESIDE DINNER

> *Lentil Vegetable Stew*
> *Herbed Egg-White Popovers*
> *Broccoli or Cabbage Slaw*

*P*aired with airy popovers, this nutritious and fast-cooking lentil stew makes a perfect quick meal for winter weather. To lower the popovers' traditionally high fat content, we've replaced most of the eggs and all of the butter with egg whites and skim milk.

GAME PLAN

1. Make the stew.
2. Make the popovers.
3. Make a simple salad from packaged broccoli or cabbage slaw and low-fat coleslaw dressing.

HERBED EGG-WHITE POPOVERS

MAKES 6

- 2 *eggs*
- 2 *egg whites*
- 2 *tablespoons snipped fresh herbs (thyme, oregano, chives, parsley)*
- 1 *tablespoon grated Parmesan cheese*
- 1 *cup all-purpose flour*
- 1 *cup skim milk*
- ½ *teaspoon salt*

Preheat the oven to 450°. Generously coat six 6-ounce custard cups or a popover pan with no-stick cooking spray.

In a medium bowl, beat the eggs and egg whites. Add the herbs, Parmesan, flour, milk and salt; beat just until incorporated. Pour into the custard cups or popover pan.

Bake for 20 minutes; reduce the heat to 350° and bake for 10 minutes longer, or until the popovers are puffed and lightly browned.

Preparation time: 5 minutes
Cooking time: 30 minutes

Per popover: 127 calories, 2.3 g. fat (17% of calories), 0.6 g. dietary fiber, 72 mg. cholesterol, 258 mg. sodium.

LENTIL VEGETABLE STEW

SERVES 4

¼ *cup dry sherry or apple juice*
1 *cup chopped onions*
1 *cup shredded carrots*
½ *cup diced unpeeled sweet potatoes*
½ *cup diced sweet red peppers*
4 *large cloves garlic, chopped*
1 *cup dry lentils, sorted and rinsed*
4 *cups defatted chicken broth*
¼ *teaspoon ground cumin*
1 *teaspoon curry powder*
¼ *teaspoon ground cinnamon*
  Salt and ground black pepper

In a 10″ skillet over medium-high heat, bring the sherry or apple juice to a boil; add the onions. Cook and stir for 2 minutes, or until soft but not browned. Add the carrots, sweet potatoes, peppers and garlic. Cook and stir for 1 minute, or until the liquid has evaporated.

Add the lentils, broth, cumin, curry powder and cinnamon; bring to a boil. Cover and cook for 25 to 30 minutes, or until the lentils are very soft and the stew is thick. Add salt and pepper to taste.

Preparation time: 10 minutes
Cooking time: 30 minutes

Per serving: 274 calories, 0.9 g. fat (3% of calories), 3.5 g. dietary fiber, no cholesterol, 356 mg. sodium.

CHAPTER 4

ON-THE-GO BEAN AND GRAIN DINNERS

High on the list of top foods for good health, whole grains and beans can now fit into a fast-paced lifestyle. Quick-cooking rices, canned beans, premade polenta and risotto are practically ready to eat when you buy them. These low-fat, cholesterol-free protein sources make a solid foundation for your weeknight meals. Try these tempting recipes and discover why two-thirds of the world's cultures rely on the hearty taste and nutrition of grains and beans.

FAST INDIAN FARE

> *Curried Chick-Peas*
> *Saffron Rice*
> *Warm Chapatis*
> *Mango Chutney, Yogurt and Chopped*
> *Dried Fruits*

*C*hick-peas, or garbanzo beans, take on a lovely golden color and deep flavor when mixed with curry powder, ginger and garlic. This curry in a hurry is ready in 25 minutes, served with hot rice, chapatis and bowls of condiments. Chapatis are Indian flatbreads similar to tortillas. They are available in Indian groceries and large supermarkets.

GAME PLAN

1. Make the curry.
2. Make the rice.
3. Warm 4 chapatis in the microwave by wrapping them in plastic wrap and heating them on high power for 1 minute.
4. Arrange the chutney, yogurt and chopped dried fruit in separate bowls.

CURRIED CHICK-PEAS

SERVES 4

1½ *cups defatted chicken broth*
 2 *cups chopped onions*
 3 *tablespoons grated fresh ginger*
 1 *tablespoon minced garlic*
 1 *sweet red pepper, diced*

2 cups cauliflower florets
1 can (16 ounces) cooked reduced-sodium chick-peas, undrained
1–2 tablespoons curry powder
1 teaspoon cornstarch
¼ cup cold water
Salt and ground black pepper

Coat a large Dutch oven with no-stick cooking spray; set it over medium-high heat and add ½ cup of the broth. When the broth is simmering, add the onions; cook and stir for 3 minutes. Add the ginger, garlic, peppers, cauliflower and chick-peas; cook and stir for 2 minutes.

Add the remaining 1 cup of broth; cook and stir for 5 minutes. Add the curry powder and stir well. Cook, uncovered, for 15 minutes, stirring occasionally, or until the vegetables are soft.

In a small bowl, mix the cornstarch with the cold water; add it to the pot. Cook and stir until the curry is slightly thickened. Add salt and pepper to taste; if desired, add more curry powder to taste.

Preparation time: 5 minutes
Cooking time: 25 minutes

Per serving: 199 calories, 2.7 g. fat (12% of calories), 8.6 g. dietary fiber, no cholesterol, 597 mg. sodium.

SAFFRON RICE

SERVES 4

1½ cups uncooked white basmati rice
¼ teaspoon saffron
¼ cup hot water
1 teaspoon safflower or olive oil
1½ cups chopped onions
1 (2") cinnamon stick, broken into thirds
2 whole cloves
1 tablespoon honey or sugar
½ teaspoon ground cardamom
4 cups defatted chicken broth
Salt

Rinse the rice under cold water until the water runs clear; drain well. Place the saffron in a small bowl with the hot water; let it stand for 10 minutes.

Heat the oil in a heavy no-stick skillet or Dutch oven over medium-high heat; add the onions. Cook and stir for 3 minutes, or until the onions are soft. Add the saffron mixture, cinnamon, cloves, honey or sugar, cardamom and rice. Cook and stir for 1 minute.

Add the broth. Bring to a boil; lower the heat to medium, cover and cook for 12 minutes, or until all the liquid has been absorbed. Fluff the rice with a fork; add salt to taste. Remove the whole cloves and cinnamon stick.

Preparation time: 5 minutes
Cooking time: 15 minutes

Per serving: 299 calories, 2.8 g. fat (8% of calories), 1 g. dietary fiber, no cholesterol, 383 mg. sodium.

ARABIAN NIGHTS

Couscous and Lentil Skillet Dinner
Salad of Bitter Greens and Mint
Pita Bread

Cooked lentils, vegetables and couscous create a speedy main dish in this Middle Eastern meal. If you don't have lentils, you can use any other leftover cooked or canned beans. The light yogurt sauce on the minty salad is traditionally served as a dip with couscous and pita bread dinners.

GAME PLAN

1. Make the couscous and lentil dish.
2. Warm 4 pita rounds in a 350° oven for 10 minutes, or until crisp.
3. Make the salad.

SALAD OF BITTER GREENS AND MINT

SERVES 4

½ cup plain nonfat yogurt
½ teaspoon dried mint leaves, crushed
1 clove garlic, pressed
⅛ teaspoon salt
½ teaspoon olive oil
4 cups washed and torn bitter lettuces (endive, arugula, radicchio)

In a salad bowl, combine the yogurt, mint, garlic and salt. Add the oil and the greens. Toss well.

Preparation time: 5 minutes

Per serving: 31 calories, 0.7 g. fat (20% of calories), 1.2 g. dietary fiber, no cholesterol, 100 mg. sodium.

COUSCOUS AND LENTIL SKILLET DINNER

SERVES 4

    2   teaspoons olive oil
    1   onion, thinly sliced
    1   cup shredded carrots
    1   cup diced tomatoes
    ¼   teaspoon ground turmeric
    ¼   teaspoon ground cumin
    ¼   teaspoon ground cinnamon
    1   cup cooked lentils
    2   green onions, sliced
 ¼–½   teaspoon chopped jalapeño peppers (wear plastic
        gloves when handling)
    2   cups uncooked couscous
    3   cups defatted chicken broth
    ¼   cup chopped fresh parsley
        Salt and ground black pepper

Heat the oil in a 10″ no-stick skillet over medium heat; add the onions, carrots and tomatoes. Cook and stir for 5 minutes, or until the vegetables soften, adding up to ¼ cup water if needed to prevent sticking.

Add the turmeric, cumin, cinnamon and lentils; cook and stir for 1 minute. Add the green onions, jalapeño peppers, couscous and broth; bring to a boil. Cover and remove the skillet from the heat. Let it sit for 5 minutes, or until all the liquid has been absorbed.

Add the parsley and salt and pepper to taste. Fluff the couscous with a fork.

Preparation time: 5 minutes
Cooking time: 15 minutes

Per serving: 483 calories, 3.4 g. fat (6% of calories), 18.9 g. dietary fiber, no cholesterol, 283 mg. sodium.

FANCY PIZZA PARTY

> *Savory Black Bean Pizza*
> *Cumin Carrots*
> *Tossed Salad*

*B*lack beans make a striking and deliciously fiber-rich pizza. Here the pizza is paired with cumin-scented steamed carrots—good hot or cold.

GAME PLAN

1. Make the pizza.
2. Make the carrots.
3. Make a simple tossed salad from baby lettuces. Add your favorite low-fat Italian dressing or lemon juice.

SAVORY BLACK BEAN PIZZA

SERVES 4

1 *(12″) uncooked low-fat pizza crust*
1 *cup low-fat reduced-sodium pizza sauce*
1 *can (16 ounces) black beans, drained and rinsed*
2 *teaspoons minced garlic*
   Pinch of ground cumin
½ *sweet red pepper, sliced into rings*
½ *cup thinly sliced red onions*
¾ *cup shredded low-fat mozzarella cheese*
½ *cup shredded fat-free Monterey Jack cheese*
¼ *cup nonfat sour cream*
2 *tablespoons chopped fresh cilantro*

Preheat the oven to 500°. Place the crust on an ungreased baking sheet and top with the pizza sauce; spread over the crust, leaving a ½″ border.

In a small bowl, mix the beans with the garlic and cumin; spread over the sauce. Top with the peppers, onions, mozzarella and Monterey Jack.

Place the pizza on the lowest rack of the oven. Bake for 12 to 15 minutes, or until bubbly. Let cool for 5 minutes, then top with the sour cream and cilantro. Cut into wedges.

Preparation time: 5 minutes
Cooking time: 15 minutes

Per serving: 522 calories, 9.1 g. fat (15% of calories), 8 g. dietary fiber, 22 mg. cholesterol, 1,303 mg. sodium.

CUMIN CARROTS

SERVES 4

1   *pound peeled baby carrots*
½   *cup apple juice*
2   *teaspoons olive oil or butter*
½–1   *teaspoon honey*
½–1   *teaspoon ground cumin*
2   *tablespoons minced fresh parsley*

In a covered saucepan over medium heat, steam the carrots in the apple juice for 5 minutes, or until crisp-tender; drain and toss with the oil or butter, honey, cumin and parsley.

Preparation time: 5 minutes
Cooking time: 5 minutes

Per serving: 63 calories, 2.4 g. fat (29% of calories), 2.7 g. dietary fiber, no cholesterol, 103 mg. sodium.

SPANISH INTERLUDE

Paella Primavera
Tossed Romaine and Radish Salad
French Bread

anned chick-peas and quick-cooking rice make this traditional springtime dinner a snap to make. Pick up precut vegetables and bagged washed lettuce for the simple salad.

GAME PLAN

1. Make the paella.
2. Make the salad.
3. Heat the French bread.

TOSSED ROMAINE AND RADISH SALAD

SERVES 4

1 *cup torn romaine lettuce*
1 *cup shredded red cabbage*
½ *cup sliced radishes*
2 *tablespoons honey*
4½ *teaspoons olive oil*
¼ *cup lemon juice*
½ *cup honey mustard*

In a salad bowl, combine the lettuce, cabbage and radishes. In a covered jar, shake together the honey, oil, lemon juice and mustard. Pour over the salad; toss well.

Preparation time: 5 minutes

Per serving: 170 calories, 6.1 g. fat (31% of calories), 0.9 g. dietary fiber, no cholesterol, 211 mg. sodium.

PAELLA PRIMAVERA

SERVES 4

2 teaspoons olive oil

2 cups thinly sliced onions

2 tablespoons minced garlic

¼ cup hot water

1 teaspoon saffron

1 can (8 ounces) artichoke hearts, drained and quartered

1 cup cooked chick-peas

½ sweet red pepper, cut into strips

1 tablespoon minced fresh basil

2 cups chopped escarole or chard

1 cup uncooked basmati rice, rinsed

1½ cups defatted chicken broth, warmed

½ cup frozen or fresh peas, thawed

Salt and ground black pepper

Heat the oil in a 10″ no-stick skillet or stovetop casserole over medium-high heat. Add the onions and garlic; cook and stir for 3 minutes, or until the onions are soft but not browned.

In a small bowl, combine the hot water and saffron. Let stand for 5 minutes, then add to the onions. Add the artichokes, chick-peas, peppers, basil, escarole or chard and rice. Cook and stir for 3 minutes. Add the broth; bring to a boil.

Cover, reduce the heat to medium, and simmer for 10 minutes, or until the rice is tender. Stir in the peas; add salt and pepper to taste.

Preparation time: 10 minutes
Cooking time: 20 minutes

Per serving: 353 calories, 8.5 g. fat (20% of calories), 5.5 g. dietary fiber, no cholesterol, 349 mg. sodium.

FAST RICE AND BEAN BAKE

Spanish Rice Bake
Marinated Pinto Bean Salad
Sautéed Zucchini

A combination of stovetop cooking and oven baking makes this Spanish dinner super-easy. Balsamic vinegar in the salad dressing brings out the fuller flavor of the beans without adding oil.

GAME PLAN

1. Make the salad.
2. Cook the rice.
3. Sauté sliced zucchini in defatted chicken broth; sprinkle it with chopped fresh parsley.

SPANISH RICE BAKE

SERVES 4

¾ cup defatted chicken broth
2 cups thinly sliced onions
2 teaspoons minced garlic
2 cups sliced mushrooms
2 cups cooked rice
1 can (16 ounces) whole peeled tomatoes (with juice), chopped
½ cup chopped green onions
¼ cup shredded carrots
¼–½ cup shredded low-fat Monterey Jack cheese

Preheat the oven to 400°. In a large Dutch oven over medium-high heat, bring the broth to a boil. Add the onions, garlic and mushrooms; cook and stir for 5 minutes. Add the rice, tomatoes (with juice), green onions and carrots; cook and stir for 2 minutes.

Sprinkle the Monterey Jack over the rice mixture. Transfer the pot to the oven; bake uncovered for 10 minutes, or until the cheese melts.

Preparation time: 5 minutes
Cooking time: 20 minutes

Per serving: 199 calories, 2.1 g. fat (9% of calories), 3.1 g. dietary fiber, 5 mg. cholesterol, 311 mg. sodium.

MARINATED PINTO BEAN SALAD

SERVES 4

1	can (16 ounces) pinto beans, drained and rinsed
½	cup balsamic vinegar
1–2	tablespoons minced garlic
2	tablespoons lemon juice
2–3	tablespoons honey
½	cup diced sweet red peppers
½	cup diced sweet yellow or green peppers
½	cup whole-kernel corn
½	cup diced celery
½	cup minced fresh parsley
	Salt and ground black pepper

In a large bowl, combine the beans, vinegar, garlic, lemon juice, honey, red peppers, yellow or green peppers, corn, celery and parsley; toss well. Let stand at room temperature for 30 minutes. Add salt and pepper to taste; add more garlic and/or honey, if desired.

Preparation time: 10 minutes
Marinating time: 30 minutes

Per serving: 220 calories, 1.1 g. fat (4% of calories), 1.3 g. dietary fiber, no cholesterol, 438 mg. sodium.

SOUTHWEST SENSATION

Black Bean and Corn Salad
Garden Stir-Fry with Wild Rice
Rye Croutons

Corn, black beans and wild rice make this Southwestern summer meal colorful and high in lean protein. The stir-fry's tangy wild rice and vegetable combination complements the savory salad.

GAME PLAN

1. Make the salad.
2. Slice rye bread into thick rounds and place on a baking sheet. Spray with olive oil no-stick cooking spray. Bake at 350° for 15 minutes, or until crisp.
3. Make the stir-fry.

BLACK BEAN AND CORN SALAD

SERVES 4

 1 *cup whole-kernel corn*
 2 *cans (16 ounces each) black beans, rinsed and drained*
 ¼ *cup chopped fresh parsley*
 2 *tablespoons minced red onions*
 ¼ *cup balsamic vinegar*
1–2 *tablespoons olive oil*
 1 *teaspoon lemon juice*
 1 *teaspoon minced garlic*
 1 *teaspoon honey or brown sugar*
    Salt and ground black pepper
    Lettuce leaves

In a large bowl, combine the corn, beans, parsley, onions, vinegar, oil, lemon juice, garlic, and honey or brown sugar. Let the salad marinate for 30 minutes at room temperature. Add salt and pepper to taste.

Arrange the lettuce leaves on 4 salad plates; spoon the salad over the lettuce.

Preparation time: 5 minutes
Marinating time: 30 minutes

Per serving: 260 calories, 5.3 g. fat (15% of calories), 13.3 g. dietary fiber, no cholesterol, 672 mg. sodium.

GARDEN STIR-FRY WITH WILD RICE

SERVES 4

¾ cup defatted chicken broth
½ cup chopped green onions
2 cloves garlic, finely minced
1 cup sliced sweet red peppers
1 cup sliced sweet yellow peppers
3 cups cooked wild rice
1 tablespoon reduced-sodium soy sauce

In a 10″ no-stick skillet over medium-high heat, bring the broth to a boil. Add the green onions, garlic, and red and yellow peppers; stir-fry for 5 to 8 minutes, or until the vegetables are crisp-tender. Add the rice and soy sauce; cook and stir for 2 minutes.

Preparation time: 10 minutes
Cooking time: 10 minutes

Per serving: 168 calories, 0.7 g. fat (4% of calories), 3.3 g. dietary fiber, no cholesterol, 201 mg. sodium.

BREAKFAST FOR DINNER

Whole-Grain Corn Waffles
Three-Berry Compote
Sliced Fresh Fruit

*L*ighter textured whole-wheat pastry flour makes these waffles airy and delicious. If you mix the batter in a blender, you can pour the batter directly from the blender onto the hot waffle iron. The berry compote adds elegance to a simple meal.

GAME PLAN

1. Make the compote.
2. Slice an assortment of fresh fruit such as melon, bananas, peaches and plums; arrange on a plate.
3. Make the waffles.

WHOLE-GRAIN CORN WAFFLES

SERVES 8

1½	cups whole-wheat pastry flour
½	cup cornmeal
¼	teaspoon salt
2	cups low-fat buttermilk
2	eggs
1	egg white
1	tablespoon honey or brown sugar
2	tablespoons oil
½	cup whole-kernel corn

Coat the waffle iron with no-stick cooking spray, if necessary, then preheat it.

In a blender, combine the flour, cornmeal, salt, buttermilk, eggs, egg white, honey or brown sugar, and oil; puree until smooth. Stir in the corn.

Pour about a fourth of the batter into the waffle iron; bake for 5 minutes, or until the waffle is golden brown and cooked through. Repeat with the remaining batter. Keep the cooked waffles warm in the oven on a covered ovenproof plate.

Preparation time: 5 minutes
Cooking time: 20 minutes

Chef's note: Leftover waffles can be frozen for up to 2 weeks—just reheat them in the toaster oven.

Per serving: 196 calories, 5.9 g. fat (26% of calories), 4.2 g. dietary fiber, 56 mg. cholesterol, 158 mg. sodium.

THREE-BERRY COMPOTE

SERVES 4

1 *cup blueberries*
1 *cup raspberries*
1 *cup boysenberries or blackberries*
¼ *cup maple syrup*
¼ *teaspoon ground nutmeg*
½ *teaspoon grated orange rind*

In a medium bowl, combine the blueberries, raspberries, maple syrup, nutmeg and orange rind. Let marinate at room temperature for 30 minutes.

Preparation time: 5 minutes
Marinating time: 30 minutes

Chef's note: If fresh berries are unavailable, use thawed frozen ones.

Per serving: 101 calories, 0.4 g. fat (4% of calories), 3.7 g. dietary fiber, no cholesterol, 5 mg. sodium.

A BETTER BURGER

Bean-and-Grain Burgers
Potato Wedges with Sour Cream Dip
Lettuce, Red Onions, Tomatoes and
Cucumbers

These vegetarian burgers taste like a Southwestern barbecue when topped with salsa and mayonnaise. Serve them with our low-fat version of french fries: oven-baked potato wedges with a lively sour cream dip.

GAME PLAN

1. Make the potato wedges.
2. Make the burgers.
3. Mix the sour cream dip for the potatoes.
4. Arrange a platter with lettuce leaves and sliced red onions, tomatoes and cucumbers.

POTATO WEDGES WITH SOUR CREAM DIP

SERVES 4

 2 *large baking potatoes, each cut into 8 wedges*
 ½ *teaspoon salt*
 1 *teaspoon ground paprika*
 ½ *cup low-fat sour cream*
 1 *teaspoon honey mustard*

Preheat the oven to 400°. Line a baking sheet with foil; set aside.

Place the potatoes, salt and paprika in a large bowl or a resealable plastic storage bag. Toss to combine. Transfer the potatoes to the baking sheet; lightly coat the surface of the potatoes with no-stick cooking spray. Bake for 20 minutes, or until the potatoes are tender and crisp.

In a small bowl, combine the sour cream and mustard. Serve with the hot potatoes.

Preparation time: 5 minutes
Cooking time: 20 minutes

Per serving: 148 calories, 2.1 g. fat (13% of calories), 2.5 g. dietary fiber, 9 mg. cholesterol, 302 mg. sodium.

INSTANT INTERNATIONAL TOPPINGS FOR COOKED GRAINS

- **Indonesian:** Stir together equal amounts of peanut butter, reduced-sodium soy sauce and defatted chicken broth. Add chopped green onions, minced fresh ginger and minced garlic to taste. Use to top barley, quinoa, rice, couscous or whole-grain pastas.

- **Italian:** Mix chopped fresh basil, parsley and oregano with pizza sauce or Italian-style stewed tomatoes. Add grated Parmesan and part-skim mozzarella cheese. Use to top polenta or pasta.

- **Russian:** Stir together equal amounts of low-fat sour cream, part-skim ricotta cheese and nonfat plain yogurt. Add diced tomatoes, sweet red peppers, green onions and cucumbers. Top with toasted caraway seeds. Use to top rice, buckwheat or couscous.

- **Mediterranean:** Stir-fry medium peeled deveined shrimp or slivered skinless boneless chicken breast in defatted chicken broth and fresh lemon juice. Add minced fresh garlic, chopped green onions and salt and ground black pepper to taste. Use to top couscous, quinoa, rice, polenta or pasta.

BEAN-AND-GRAIN BURGERS

SERVES 4

  1 *can (16 ounces) black beans, rinsed and drained*

  2 *eggs*

  ⅓ *cup shredded reduced-sodium low-fat Cheddar cheese*

  ¼ *cup cooked rice*

  ¾ *cup dry bread crumbs or dry cornbread stuffing*

  2 *tablespoons chopped fresh parsley*

  3 *cloves garlic, minced*

  2 *large green onions, chopped*

1–2 *teaspoons reduced-sodium barbecue sauce*

  1 *teaspoon chopped jalapeño peppers (wear plastic gloves when handling), optional*

  4 *whole-wheat hamburger buns, split*

     Salsa

     Nonfat mayonnaise

In a medium bowl, mash the beans; add the eggs, Cheddar, rice, bread crumbs or cornbread stuffing, parsley, garlic, green onions, barbecue sauce and jalapeño peppers (if using). Mix well.

Coat a 10″ no-stick skillet with no-stick cooking spray. Using a large spoon, mound the burger mix into 4 patties (mixture will be wet); transfer to the skillet. Cook over medium-high heat for 5 minutes, then turn and flatten with a spatula. Cook for 3 to 5 minutes, or until firm and lightly browned.

Toast the hamburger buns. Place the burgers in the buns and top with salsa and mayonnaise.

Preparation time: 5 minutes
Cooking time: 10 minutes

Per serving: 388 calories, 9.4 g. fat (20% of calories), 6.7 g. dietary fiber, 114 mg. cholesterol, 798 mg. sodium.

ASIAN GET-AWAY

> *Vegetable Tofu Stir-Fry*
> *Rice-Noodle Nests with Green Onions*
> *Sliced Fresh Peaches*

*N*ests of lightly seasoned rice noodles hold a colorful stir-fry of vegetables and tofu in this fast Asian menu.

GAME PLAN

1. Make the stir-fry.
2. Make the rice-noodle nests and top them with the stir-fry.
3. Slice the peaches; arrange them on a platter and drizzle them with lemon juice.

VEGETABLE TOFU STIR-FRY

SERVES 4

8	ounces firm tofu, drained and cubed
1	teaspoon plus 1 tablespoon reduced-sodium soy sauce
2	tablespoons dry sherry or apple juice
½	teaspoon dark sesame oil
1	teaspoon cornstarch
¼	teaspoon ground black pepper
½	cup defatted chicken broth
1	cup roasted sweet red peppers (from a jar)
1	cup broccoli florets
1	cup whole snow peas

Place the tofu in a large shallow pan. In a measuring cup, combine 1 teaspoon of the soy sauce, the sherry or apple juice and the oil; drizzle over the tofu. Let the tofu marinate for 15 minutes at room temperature.

In a small bowl, stir together the cornstarch, pepper and remaining 1 tablespoon soy sauce. Set aside.

In a wok over medium-high heat, bring the broth to a boil. Add the red peppers and broccoli; stir-fry for 3 to 4 minutes, or until the vegetables are crisp-tender. Add the snow peas, tofu and any remaining marinade. Cover the wok; cook for 2 minutes, or until the snow peas are bright green.

Quickly stir the cornstarch mixture, then add to the wok. Cook and stir until the sauce thickens slightly.

Preparation time: 5 minutes
Cooking time: 8 minutes
Marinating time: 15 minutes

Per serving: 137 calories, 5.8 g. fat (35% of calories), 3.4 g. dietary fiber, no cholesterol, 235 mg. sodium.

RICE-NOODLE NESTS WITH GREEN ONIONS

SERVES 4

> 1   package (1 pound) rice sticks (vermicelli rice noodles)
> 2–3   teaspoons reduced-sodium soy sauce
> ¼   cup minced green onions

Place the rice sticks in a large bowl. Cover with cold water and soak for 20 minutes.

Heat water to boiling in a large pot; drain the rice sticks and add to the pot. Cook for 3 minutes, or until they are heated through and soft but not mushy. Drain well. Toss with the soy sauce and green onions. Arrange in nests on 4 dinner plates.

Soaking time: 20 minutes
Cooking time: 3 minutes

Chef's note: Leftover unsauced cooked noodles can be refrigerated for up to 10 days. To reheat, simply drop them in boiling water for 30 seconds, then toss with sauce.

Per serving: 401 calories, 0.1 g. fat (0% of calories), 0.1 g. dietary fiber, no cholesterol, 100 mg. sodium.

Fast Far East Feast

Szechwan Vegetable Stir-Fry
Jasmine Rice and Barley
Lychee Fruit Salad

Quick-cooking jasmine-scented rice originates in Thailand. Its subtle fragrance combines wonderfully with barley in the perfect side dish for a spicy Szechwan stir-fry.

GAME PLAN

1. Make the rice and barley.
2. Make the stir-fry.
3. Make a simple fruit salad of canned lychee nuts and mandarin oranges tossed with chopped fresh mint.

SZECHWAN VEGETABLE STIR-FRY

SERVES 4

½   cup defatted chicken broth
½   cup broccoli florets
½   cup shredded carrots
2   green onions, cut into slivers
2   tablespoons grated fresh ginger
½   teaspoon honey
½–1   teaspoon crushed or ground red pepper
2   tablespoons water
2   tablespoons hoisin sauce

In a wok over medium-high heat, bring the broth to a boil. Add the broccoli and carrots; cook and stir for 1 minute. Add the green onions, ginger, honey and pepper; cover the wok and cook for 2 minutes, or until the vegetables are crisp-tender.

In a small bowl, stir together the water and hoisin sauce; add to the wok. Cook and stir for 1 minute, or until the sauce thickens slightly.

Preparation time: 5 minutes
Cooking time: 8 minutes

Per serving: 27 calories, 0.2 g. fat (5% of calories), 1 g. dietary fiber, no cholesterol, 152 mg. sodium.

JASMINE RICE AND BARLEY

SERVES 4

1	*cup uncooked jasmine rice*
2¼	*cups defatted chicken broth*
½	*cup quick-cooking barley*
1	*teaspoon chopped peanuts (optional)*
¼	*teaspoon salt*

Rinse the rice under cold water until the water runs clear.

In a medium saucepan, bring the broth to a boil. Add the rice, barley, peanuts and salt. Cover and reduce the heat to low. Cook for 15 minutes, or until all the liquid has been absorbed and the grains are tender. Fluff with a fork.

Preparation time: 2 minutes
Cooking time: 18 minutes

Per serving: 270 calories, 0.8 g. fat (3% of calories), 3.6 g. dietary fiber, no cholesterol, 325 mg. sodium.

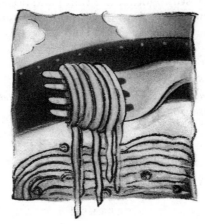

CHAPTER 5

FAST AND HEALTHY WAYS TO USE YOUR NOODLE

PERFECT PASTA DINNERS

How could we live without pasta? It's the backbone of fast, healthy, home-cooked meals—and the favorite dinner of 90 percent of the chefs we interviewed. Ready in 10 to 15 minutes, most pasta entrées are perfect for really rushed evenings. Just set water on to boil when you walk in the door, prepare one of the delicious pasta toppings in this chapter and you're ready to eat. By itself, pasta is very low in fat. With the lean meat, seafood and vegetable sauces in this chapter, you can keep it that way. Plan to pack leftover pasta for quick at-the-desk weekday lunches.

SALAD ON THE GRILL

Grilled Chicken Pasta Caesar Salad
Antipasto Toast
Asparagus

This menu combines all the best elements of pasta salad and Caesar salad—in a hurry. The antipasto toast is almost a meal in itself. Piled with an array of bright vegetables, it brings you the flavors of an Italian table without the fat.

GAME PLAN

1. Make the salad.
2. Make the toast.
3. Steam fresh asparagus; drizzle it with lemon juice.

GRILLED CHICKEN PASTA CAESAR SALAD

SERVES 4

1 *pound boneless skinless chicken breasts*
8 *ounces bow-tie pasta*
1 *tablespoon olive oil*
¼ *cup balsamic vinegar*
3 *tablespoons grated Parmesan cheese*
3 *cloves garlic, minced*
2 *stalks celery, thinly sliced*
4 *green onions, thinly sliced*
1 *sweet red pepper, diced*
1 *can (8 ounces) mandarin orange slices, drained*

Preheat the grill. One at a time, place the chicken breasts between 2 pieces of plastic wrap and flatten them slightly with the flat side of a meat mallet. Coat them with no-stick cooking spray. Grill for 3 to 5 minutes on each side, or until cooked through. Cut into strips and set aside.

Cook the pasta according to package directions; drain well.

Meanwhile, in a large salad bowl, whisk together the oil, vinegar, Parmesan and garlic. Add the chicken, pasta, celery, green onions, peppers and oranges. Toss well.

Preparation time: 10 minutes
Cooking time: 10 minutes

Per serving: 466 calories, 9 g. fat (17% of calories), 1.7 g. dietary fiber, 73 mg. cholesterol, 171 mg. sodium.

Antipasto Toast

SERVES 4

8	*thick slices Italian or French bread*
2	*cups chopped tomatoes*
1	*teaspoon minced garlic*
2	*tablespoons roasted red peppers, drained*
¼	*cup chopped fresh parsley*
2	*teaspoons olive oil*
1	*teaspoon balsamic vinegar*

Preheat the grill. Grill the bread on both sides until lightly toasted.

In a small bowl, combine the tomatoes, garlic, peppers, parsley, oil and vinegar. Spoon on top of the toasted bread.

Preparation time: 5 minutes
Cooking time: 5 minutes

Per serving: 211 calories, 4.9 g. fat (20% of calories), 1.5 g. dietary fiber, no cholesterol, 363 mg. sodium.

FAR EAST SUPPER

Cold Sesame Noodles
Cucumber Salad
Pita Bread

*T*his menu centers on a refreshing chilled pasta dish, made with fast-cooking Japanese udon noodles, and a sweet-and-sour cucumber salad. Both dishes can be made earlier in the day and refrigerated for dinner.

GAME PLAN
1. Make the sesame noodles and chill them.
2. Make the cucumber salad.
3. Warm several rounds of whole-wheat pita bread and cut it into triangles.

COLD SESAME NOODLES

1	pound Japanese udon noodles
1	tablespoon tahini
1	tablespoon peanut butter
½	cup plain nonfat yogurt
2	tablespoons reduced-sodium soy sauce
1½	tablespoons honey
1½	cups chopped cooked boneless skinless chicken breasts
1	cup julienned carrots
3	green onions, sliced diagonally
¼	cup chopped fresh parsley

Cook the noodles according to package directions; drain well.

Meanwhile, in a large bowl, stir together the tahini, peanut butter, yogurt, soy sauce and honey. Add the chicken, carrots, green onions, parsley and pasta; mix well. Cover and refrigerate for 30 minutes.

Preparation time: 10 minutes
Cooking time: 8 minutes
Chilling time: 30 minutes

Per serving: 311 calories, 4.5 g. fat (13% of calories), 3.7 g. dietary fiber, 37 mg. cholesterol, 530 mg. sodium.

CUCUMBER SALAD

SERVES 4

6   *medium cucumbers, peeled, halved lengthwise, seeded and sliced*

2   *tablespoons minced green onions*

2   *tablespoons brown sugar or maple syrup*

½   *cup rice vinegar*

3–4   *tablespoons reduced-sodium soy sauce*

2   *teaspoons finely chopped dry-roasted peanuts*

¼   *teaspoon crushed red pepper flakes*

In a large bowl, combine the cucumbers, green onions, brown sugar or maple syrup, vinegar and soy sauce. Marinate for 15 minutes at room temperature.

Add the peanuts and red pepper flakes. Toss well. Add more soy sauce to taste, if desired.

Preparation time: 10 minutes
Marinating time: 15 minutes

Per serving: 104 calories, 1.4 g. fat (10% of calories), 0.2 g. dietary fiber, no cholesterol, 421 mg. sodium.

SWIFT AND SIMPLE STIR-FRY

*Stir-Fry of Swiss Chard, Red Peppers
and Broad Noodles
Garlic Bread Crostini
Sliced Summer Tomatoes with Basil*

This great pasta dinner is on the table in less than 15 minutes. It features a colorful combination of vitamin-rich chard and sweet red peppers. The crostini side dish is a crunchy accompaniment, but watch out— it's addictive!

GAME PLAN

1. Start the noodles.
2. Make the crostini.
3. Make the stir-fry.
4. Slice tomatoes and arrange them on a plate; sprinkle them with shredded fresh basil and a small amount of olive oil.

STIR-FRY OF SWISS CHARD, RED PEPPERS AND BROAD NOODLES

SERVES 4

8	*ounces broad egg noodles*
¾	*cup defatted chicken broth*
2	*cups sliced onions*
2	*cups chopped cooked skinless chicken breasts*
2	*cloves garlic, minced*
1	*sweet red pepper, julienned*
3	*cups chopped red Swiss chard stems and leaves*
1–2	*teaspoons hot-pepper oil*
1	*tablespoon tahini (see note)*
2	*teaspoons reduced-sodium soy sauce*

Cook the noodles according to package directions; drain well.

Meanwhile, coat a 10″ no-stick skillet with no-stick cooking spray; set it over medium-high heat. When the skillet is hot, add ¼ cup of the broth; bring to a boil. Add the onions, chicken, garlic, peppers and chard; cook and stir for 3 minutes, or until the onions are soft. Add the remaining ½ cup of broth; cover and cook for 4 minutes, or until the liquid has almost evaporated.

In a small bowl, mix the hot-pepper oil, tahini and soy sauce; add to the stir-fry. Toss with the noodles.

Preparation time: 5 minutes
Cooking time: 10 minutes

Chef's note: Tahini is a Middle Eastern paste made from ground sesame seeds. Look for it in the ethnic section of your supermarket or in Middle Eastern groceries.

Per serving: 393 calories, 6.6 g. fat (15% of calories), 2.9 g. dietary fiber, 102 mg. cholesterol, 265 mg. sodium.

GARLIC BREAD CROSTINI

SERVES 4

½ *loaf Italian bread*
2 *cloves garlic, halved*
2 *tablespoons prepared pesto*
2 *tablespoons grated Parmesan cheese*

Preheat the oven to 350°. Cut the bread into 12 thin slices and arrange them on a baking sheet.

Rub garlic on one side of each slice, then spread with the pesto and sprinkle with the Parmesan. Bake for 10 minutes, or until lightly browned.

Preparation time: 5 minutes
Cooking time: 10 minutes

Per serving: 208 calories, 6.8 g. fat (29% of calories), no dietary fiber, 4 mg. cholesterol, 444 mg. sodium.

ASIAN FANTASIA

Orzo with Grilled Shrimp
Onion, Caper and Orange Salad
Steamed Cauliflower

*O*rzo is a tiny rice-shaped pasta that cooks quickly—perfect for rushed weeknights. This lively menu has a Szechwan twist, cooled by a refreshing salad of oranges and capers.

GAME PLAN

1. Make the salad.
2. Make the pasta.
3. Steam cauliflower; drizzle it with lemon juice.

ONION, CAPER AND ORANGE SALAD

SERVES 4

2   tablespoons olive oil
¼   cup balsamic vinegar
2   tablespoons honey or sugar
5   cups torn romaine lettuce
2   cans (8 ounces each) mandarin orange slices, drained
1   tablespoon drained capers
¼   cup minced red onions
     Salt and ground black pepper

In a salad bowl, whisk together the oil, vinegar and honey or sugar. Add the lettuce, oranges, capers and onions. Toss well. Add salt and pepper to taste.

Preparation time: 5 minutes

Per serving: 164 calories, 6.9 g. fat (36% of calories), 1.8 g. dietary fiber, no cholesterol, 93 mg. sodium.

ORZO WITH GRILLED SHRIMP

SERVES 4

2	tablespoons reduced-sodium soy sauce
1	tablespoon rice vinegar
2	tablespoons honey
1	teaspoon cornstarch
2	teaspoons dark sesame oil
12	ounces medium uncooked shrimp, peeled and deveined
1	cup orzo
¼	cup defatted chicken broth
1	tablespoon minced garlic
2	teaspoons chopped fresh ginger
¼	cup sliced green onions
½–1	teaspoon minced jalapeño peppers (wear plastic gloves when handling)
½	cup shredded carrots
½	cup diced sweet red peppers

In a resealable plastic storage bag, combine the soy sauce, vinegar, honey, cornstarch, oil and shrimp. Seal the bag; shake well. Refrigerate for 15 minutes, turning occasionally.

Preheat the grill. Remove the shrimp, reserving the marinade; grill for 3 minutes, or until pink and cooked through.

Cook the orzo according to package directions.

Meanwhile, in a 10″ no-stick skillet over medium-high heat, bring the broth to a boil. Add the garlic, ginger, green onions, jalapeño peppers, carrots and red peppers. Cook and stir for 2 to 3 minutes. Add the orzo, grilled shrimp and reserved marinade. Cook and stir for 1 to 2 minutes, or until the sauce thickens.

Preparation time: 10 minutes
Cooking time: 15 minutes
Marinating time: 15 minutes

Per serving: 351 calories, 3.3 g. fat (9% of calories), 1.2 g. dietary fiber, 131 mg. cholesterol, 456 mg. sodium.

MEDITERRANEAN IN A FLASH

Olive-Tuna Rotelle
Chilled Broccoli Salad with Red Peppers
French Bread

*C*anned tuna packed in water makes a quick, low-fat protein in this pasta dinner. The colorful and slightly spicy broccoli salad pairs well with the meaty tuna sauce.

GAME PLAN

1. Make the broccoli salad and chill it.
2. Make the pasta.
3. Slice the French bread; arrange it in a bread basket.

OLIVE-TUNA ROTELLE

SERVES 4

8	*ounces rotelle*
½	*cup defatted chicken broth*
2	*cups chopped onions*
1	*carrot, chopped*
4	*cloves garlic, chopped*
1	*can (6 ounces) chunk light tuna packed in water, drained*
4	*cups chopped tomatoes*
2	*cups chopped sweet red peppers*
¼	*cup chopped fresh basil*
1	*tablespoon chopped black olives*
2	*teaspoons dried oregano*
¼	*cup tomato paste*

Cook the rotelle according to package directions; drain well.

Meanwhile, in a 10″ no-stick skillet over medium-high heat, bring the broth to a boil. Add the onions, carrots and garlic. Cook and stir for 3 to 5 minutes, or until the onions are soft. Add the tuna, tomatoes, peppers, basil, olives, oregano and tomato paste; bring to a boil. Cook and stir for 10 minutes. Toss with the pasta.

Preparation time: 10 minutes
Cooking time: 15 minutes

Per serving: 422 calories, 3.6 g. fat (8% of calories), 7.3 g. dietary fiber, 12 mg. cholesterol, 414 mg. sodium.

CHILLED BROCCOLI SALAD WITH RED PEPPERS

SERVES 4

1½ pounds broccoli
½   large sweet red pepper, diced
2   tablespoons minced shallots or garlic
3   tablespoons balsamic vinegar
1   tablespoon olive oil
1   teaspoon honey
    Salt and ground black pepper

Separate the broccoli florets from the stems; trim the stems and cut into slices ½″ thick. Steam the broccoli for 3 minutes, or until crisp-tender. Drain well.

In a large salad bowl, combine the peppers, shallots, vinegar, oil and honey. Add the broccoli; toss well. Cover and refrigerate for 30 minutes, stirring occasionally. Add salt and pepper to taste.

Preparation time: 5 minutes
Cooking time: 3 minutes
Chilling time: 30 minutes

Per serving: 101 calories, 4 g. fat (32% of calories), 0.5 g. dietary fiber, no cholesterol, 40 mg. sodium.

SPRINGTIME PASTA PRONTO!

> *Pasta Primavera*
> *Garlic Bread*
> *Cherry Tomatoes, Carrot Sticks and*
> *Jicama Sticks*

Primavera means "springtime" in Italian, and this quick pasta dinner is great for warmer weather. If you're in a hurry, substitute a colorful mix of precut vegetables from the salad bar.

GAME PLAN

1. Heat water for the pasta.
2. Make the garlic bread.
3. Make the pasta sauce and cook the pasta.
4. Arrange carrot and jicama sticks on a platter with whole cherry tomatoes.

GARLIC BREAD

SERVES 4

1 loaf French or Italian bread
4 large cloves garlic, finely minced

Preheat the oven to 350°. Cut the bread into thick slices almost all the way through; place the loaf on a no-stick baking sheet and spread the slices. Coat both sides of each slice with olive oil no-stick cooking spray. Sprinkle with the garlic. Press the slices back together.

Bake for 15 minutes, or until hot and crusty.

Preparation time: 5 minutes
Cooking time: 15 minutes

Per serving: 311 calories, 4.2 g. fat (12% of calories), 0.1 g. dietary fiber, no cholesterol, 662 mg. sodium.

PASTA PRIMAVERA

SERVES 4

½ cup defatted chicken broth or dry white wine
4 cloves garlic, minced
½ cup chopped onions
1 large sweet red pepper, coarsely chopped
1 cup shredded carrots
1 cup thinly sliced zucchini or yellow summer squash
1 cup trimmed and halved snow peas
¼ cup chopped fresh basil
1 package (9 ounces) fresh fettuccine
1½ cups light ricotta cheese
½ cup low-fat sour cream
¼ cup grated Parmesan cheese
   Salt and ground black pepper

In a large skillet over medium-high heat, heat the broth or wine; when it is simmering, add the garlic and onions. Cook and stir for 3 to 5 minutes, or until the onions are soft but not browned. Add the peppers, carrots and squash; cover and cook for 5 minutes, or until the vegetables are soft. Add the snow peas and basil; cover and cook for 30 seconds. Remove the skillet from the heat.

Cook the fettuccine according to package directions; drain.

Meanwhile, in a blender or food processor, puree the ricotta, sour cream and Parmesan; add to the sautéed vegetables. Add the fettuccine and toss to coat; season to taste with salt and pepper.

Preparation time: 10 to 15 minutes
Cooking time: 10 minutes

Chef's note: You can substitute about 8 ounces of dry pasta for the fresh fettuccine.

Per serving: 388 calories, 8.9 g. fat (20% of calories), 3.6 g. dietary fiber, 26 mg. cholesterol, 365 mg. sodium.

DINNER ON A GREEK ISLAND

*Mediterranean Pasta
with Feta and Olives
Greek Salad
Italian Bread*

Tangy feta cheese adds surprising richness and wakes up this simple pasta dinner—without adding a lot of fat. The sauce tastes great the next day, so make extra for an easy work lunch.

GAME PLAN

1. Heat the Italian bread.
2. Boil the water for the pasta.
3. Make the salad.
4. Make the pasta and sauce.

MEDITERRANEAN PASTA WITH FETA AND OLIVES

SERVES 4

 1 *pound penne or rotelle*
 2 *cups low-fat reduced-sodium marinara or other tomato sauce*
 1/4 *teaspoon crushed red pepper flakes*
 1 1/2 *teaspoons chopped pitted kalamata olives*
 6 *ounces feta cheese, crumbled*
 1/4 *cup chopped fresh parsley*

Cook the penne or rotelle according to package directions; drain well.

Meanwhile, heat the sauce in a 3-quart saucepan over medium heat. Add the red pepper flakes, olives and feta. Cook and stir for 3 minutes, or until the cheese begins to melt. Remove from the heat; add the parsley. Toss with the hot pasta.

Preparation time: 5 minutes
Cooking time: 8 minutes

Per serving: 610 calories, 11.5 g. fat (17% of calories), no dietary fiber, 37 mg. cholesterol, 748 mg. sodium.

GREEK SALAD

SERVES 4

3	*cups torn romaine lettuce*
1	*cup torn escarole or curly endive*
¼	*cup thinly sliced red onions*
¼	*cup thinly sliced radishes*
1	*medium tomato, cut into 8 wedges*
2	*tablespoons lemon juice*
2	*teaspoons olive oil*
1	*tablespoon nonfat plain yogurt*
1	*teaspoon honey*
¼	*teaspoon dried oregano*
	Salt and ground black pepper

In a large salad bowl, combine the lettuce, escarole or endive, onions, radishes and tomatoes.

In a jar, combine the lemon juice, oil, yogurt, honey and oregano; shake to combine. Add salt and pepper to taste. Pour over the salad; toss well.

Preparation time: 10 minutes

Per serving: 50 calories, 2.5 g. fat (42% of calories), 1.8 g. dietary fiber, no cholesterol, 15 mg. sodium.

LIGHT DINNER AL FRESCO

Lemon Vegetable Pasta and
Grilled Shrimp
Baked Tomatoes
Tossed Salad

*C*rispy baked tomatoes put a new twist on a simple dinner and complement the lemony shrimp. Let them bake while you prepare the pasta.

GAME PLAN

1. Make the baked tomatoes.
2. Make the pasta and grilled shrimp.
3. Make a simple salad with baby lettuces, lemon juice and grated Parmesan.

LEMON VEGETABLE PASTA AND GRILLED SHRIMP

SERVES 4

8	ounces medium shrimp, peeled and deveined
2	tablespoons lemon juice
2	tablespoons chopped fresh garlic
8	ounces fettuccine
¼	cup chopped green onions
⅓	cup diced sweet red peppers
¼	cup pesto
¼	cup nonfat plain yogurt
1	teaspoon grated lemon rind

Place the shrimp, lemon juice and garlic in a resealable plastic storage bag; refrigerate for 15 minutes, turning occasionally.

Preheat the grill.

Cook the fettuccine according to package directions; drain well.

Meanwhile, drain the shrimp, reserving the marinade. In a 10″ no-stick skillet over medium heat, bring the lemon marinade to a boil. Add the green onions and peppers; cook and stir for 2 to 3 minutes, or until all the liquid has evaporated. Remove from the heat; add the pesto, yogurt and lemon rind.

Grill the shrimp for 2 minutes, or until pink and cooked through. Add to the sauce; toss with the pasta.

Preparation time: 5 minutes
Cooking time: 8 minutes
Marinating time: 15 minutes

Per serving: 322 calories, 10.1 g. fat (28% of calories), 0.7 g. dietary fiber, 90 mg. cholesterol, 317 mg. sodium.

BAKED TOMATOES

SERVES 4

4   *plum tomatoes*
1   *teaspoon olive oil*
2   *tablespoons dry bread crumbs*
½   *teaspoon dried basil*

Preheat the oven to 350°. Trim ¼″ from each tomato top and bottom (so they will sit flat), then slice the tomatoes in half horizontally. Place the tomatoes on a baking sheet. Lightly brush the tops with the oil. In a small bowl, mix the bread crumbs and basil. Sprinkle over the tomatoes; press down slightly.

Bake for 20 minutes, or until the bread crumbs are slightly browned.

Preparation time: 3 minutes
Cooking time: 20 minutes

Per serving: 50 calories, 1.7 g. fat (28% of calories), 1.6 g. dietary fiber, no cholesterol, 40 mg. sodium.

Uptown Italian Evening

Pasta Puttanesca
Apple-Romaine Salad
Green Beans

We've lightened up this classic Italian peasant pasta by using less olive oil. Paired with a sweet apple salad tossed with tangy poppy seed dressing, it makes a weeknight feast. You can save time on salad prep by using packaged greens.

GAME PLAN

1. Make the pasta.
2. Make the salad.
3. Steam green beans; toss them with a tiny amount of olive oil, salt and ground black pepper.

PASTA PUTTANESCA

SERVES 4

8	*ounces penne*
1	*tablespoon olive oil*
1	*cup chopped onions*
4	*cloves garlic, minced*
5	*cups chopped fresh tomatoes or 1 can (28 ounces) chopped Italian plum tomatoes (with juice)*
¼	*cup chopped fresh basil*
¼	*teaspoon crushed red pepper flakes*
2	*teaspoons dried oregano*
1	*teaspoon honey or sugar*
¼–½	*cup grated Parmesan cheese*

Cook the penne according to package directions; drain well.

Meanwhile, heat the oil in a 10″ no-stick skillet over medium heat. Add the onions and garlic; cook and stir for 3 minutes, or until the onions are soft. Add the tomatoes (with juice), basil, red pepper flakes, oregano, and honey or sugar; bring to a boil. Cook and stir for 10 minutes. Add the penne and Parmesan; toss well.

Preparation time: 10 minutes
Cooking time: 15 minutes

Per serving: 363 calories, 7.4 g. fat (18% of calories), 4.1 g. dietary fiber, 5 mg. cholesterol, 144 mg. sodium.

APPLE-ROMAINE SALAD

SERVES 4

2   *cups torn romaine lettuce*
1   *cup chopped sweet red apples*
⅓   *cup shredded carrots*
2   *tablespoons honey*
2   *teaspoons olive oil*
1   *teaspoon poppy seeds*
¼   *cup lemon juice*
1½   *tablespoons nonfat plain yogurt*
    Salt and ground black pepper

In a large salad bowl, toss together the lettuce, apples and carrots. In a covered jar, combine the honey, oil, poppy seeds, lemon juice and yogurt. Add to the greens; toss well. Add salt and pepper to taste.

Preparation time: 10 minutes

Per serving: 126 calories, 7.2 g. fat (49% of calories), 1.5 g. dietary fiber, no cholesterol, 9 mg. sodium.

MANICOTTI IN MINUTES

30-Minute Manicotti
Italian Bean Salad
Carrots and Chives

*T*he microwave makes manicotti a low-fat, no-sweat dish. With a light bean salad and steamed baby carrots, you've got a nourishing dinner in no time.

GAME PLAN
1. Make the manicotti. Then, make the bean salad.
2. Steam whole baby carrots; toss them with snipped chives.

30-MINUTE MANICOTTI

SERVES 4

8	*manicotti shells, uncooked*
2	*cups light ricotta cheese*
1	*cup finely chopped spinach*
1	*egg*
¼–⅓	*cup grated Parmesan cheese*
2	*tablespoons minced fresh basil*
¼	*cup chopped fresh parsley*
¼	*teaspoon ground nutmeg*
2	*cups low-fat reduced-sodium Italian-style tomato sauce*
1½	*cups shredded nonfat mozzarella cheese*

Cook the manicotti shells according to package directions. Transfer to a bowl of cold water and set aside.

Meanwhile, in a large bowl, combine the ricotta, spinach, egg, Parmesan, basil, parsley and nutmeg. Set aside.

Pour 1 cup of the tomato sauce into an 11″ × 7″ microwaveable baking dish. Fill each manicotti shell with about ¼ cup of the cheese mixture. Arrange the filled shells in the pan; spoon the remaining 1 cup of tomato sauce on top. Sprinkle with the mozzarella. Cover tightly with vented plastic wrap.

Microwave on medium-high power (70%) for 15 minutes, or until the noodles are tender when pricked with a knife point and the sauce is bubbly; rotate the dish every 5 minutes during cooking. Let stand covered for 5 minutes before serving.

Preparation time: 10 minutes
Cooking time: 15 minutes
Standing time: 5 minutes

Per serving: 332 calories, 6.8 g. fat (19% of calories), 2.1 g. dietary fiber, 74 mg. cholesterol, 568 mg. sodium.

ITALIAN BEAN SALAD

SERVES 4

2   *cups canned cannellini beans, drained and rinsed*
2   *small shallots, minced*
3   *tablespoons lemon juice*
3   *tablespoons nonfat plain yogurt*
2   *tablespoons minced fresh parsley*
2   *teaspoons Dijon mustard*
1   *teaspoon olive oil*
1   *teaspoon salt*
½   *teaspoon minced fresh tarragon*
4   *cups mixed baby lettuces*
½   *cup balsamic vinegar*
     Ground black pepper

In a large bowl, mix the beans, shallots, lemon juice, yogurt, parsley, mustard, oil, salt and tarragon. Let marinate for 15 minutes at room temperature, stirring occasionally.

In a salad bowl, toss together the lettuces and vinegar. Arrange on 4 salad plates and top with the bean mixture. Sprinkle with black pepper to taste.

Preparation time: 5 minutes
Marinating time: 15 minutes

Per serving: 146 calories, 2.3 g. fat (11% of calories), 7.4 g. dietary fiber, no cholesterol, 809 mg. sodium.

FAST FETTUCCINE DINNER

Fettuccine with Sun-Dried Tomato Sauce
Minted Sugar Snap Peas
Spinach Salad

Sun-dried tomatoes give you big flavor with little fat; look for ones packed without oil near the produce section of your supermarket. If fresh sugar snap peas are out of season, replace them with a package of trimmed snow peas.

GAME PLAN

1. Start the pasta.
2. Make a spinach salad from bagged spinach, sliced red onions and fresh raspberries. Add a low-fat vinaigrette.
3. Make the peas.

FETTUCCINE WITH SUN-DRIED TOMATO SAUCE

SERVES 4

8	ounces fettuccine
½	cup defatted chicken broth
2	cloves garlic, minced
1	cup shredded carrots
1	cup diced sweet red peppers
1	cup broccoli florets
1	package (3 ounces) dry-pack sun-dried tomatoes, chopped
½	cup chopped fresh basil
1	can (15 ounces) whole peeled tomatoes (with juice), chopped
3	tablespoons grated Parmesan cheese

Cook the fettuccine according to package directions; drain well.

Meanwhile, coat a 10″ no-stick skillet with no-stick cooking spray; set it over medium-high heat. When the pan is hot, add the broth; bring it to a boil. Add the garlic, carrots, peppers, broccoli and sun-dried tomatoes. Cook and stir for 2 minutes, or until the vegetables are soft. Add the basil and tomatoes (with juice); bring to a boil.

Reduce the heat to medium; cook and stir for 5 minutes. Remove from the heat; stir in the pasta and cheese.

Preparation time: 10 minutes
Cooking time: 15 minutes

Per serving: 312 calories, 4.1 g. fat (11% of calories), 4.7 g. dietary fiber, 4 mg. cholesterol, 438 mg. sodium.

MINTED SUGAR SNAP PEAS

SERVES 4

 3 *cups sugar snap peas*
 ⅓ *cup apple juice*
 2 *teaspoons chopped fresh mint*
 ¼ *teaspoon grated lemon rind*
 1 *teaspoon butter*

In a 10″ no-stick skillet, combine the peas and apple juice. Bring to a boil over medium-high heat. Cover and cook for 2 minutes, or until the peas are crisp-tender. Using a slotted spoon, transfer the peas to a colander; rinse with cold water to stop the cooking process.

Add the mint and lemon rind to the steaming liquid; bring to a boil. Cook and stir for 1 minute, or until the liquid has reduced by half. Add the butter and peas; toss well.

Preparation time: 5 minutes
Cooking time: 5 minutes

Per serving: 64 calories, 1.2 g. fat (16% of calories), 2.9 g. dietary fiber, 3 mg. cholesterol, 15 mg. sodium.

Grilled Southwestern-Style Drumsticks (page 136) and Spicy Corn on the Cob (page 137)

Turkey Pot Pie with Buttermilk Biscuit Crust (page 154)

*Turkey Tenderloin with Sun-Dried Tomato-Mushroom Sauce (page 158) and
Garlic Mashed Potatoes (page 157)*

Grilled Raspberry Turkey Breasts (page 159)

Grilled Marinated Flank Steak (page 162) and Asian Vegetable Sauté (page 163)

Texas Beef Soft Tacos (page 170) and Sweet Potato Salad (page 171)

Stuffed Pork Loin Chops (page 175) and Glazed Honey Carrots (page 176)

Pork BBQ Sandwiches (page 181) and Oven-Fried
Pepper-Dusted Potato Wedges (page 182)

PENNE PIZZAZZ

Penne with Roasted Red Pepper Sauce
Escarole Salad with Parmesan
Steamed Carrots with Lime Juice

*E*ggplant and roasted red peppers bring healthy Mediterranean flavors to this fresh-tasting sauce. To reduce the amount of oil needed, salt is used to soften the eggplant before cooking it.

GAME PLAN

1. Make the pasta.
2. Make the salad.
3. Steam baby carrots; toss them with fresh lime juice and minced parsley.

PENNE WITH ROASTED RED PEPPER SAUCE

SERVES 4

1	*medium eggplant, peeled and diced*
	Salt
10	*ounces penne*
½	*cup defatted chicken broth*
3	*cloves garlic, minced*
1	*cup chopped tomatoes*
1	*jar (8 ounces) roasted red peppers, drained and diced*
¼	*teaspoon crushed red pepper flakes*
1	*teaspoon honey*

Place the eggplant in a medium bowl; sprinkle generously with salt. Let stand at room temperature for 15 minutes to soften; rinse and drain well.

Cook the penne according to package directions; drain well.

Meanwhile, in a 10″ no-stick skillet over medium-high heat, bring the broth to a boil. Add the garlic; cook and stir for 1 minute. Add the tomatoes, peppers, red pepper flakes and honey; cook for 10 minutes, stirring occasionally. Add the eggplant; cook for 15 minutes, or until the sauce is thick, stirring occasionally. Add the pasta; toss well.

Preparation time: 10 minutes
Cooking time: 30 minutes

Per serving: 335 calories, 1.9 g. fat (5% of calories), 1.7 g. dietary fiber, no cholesterol, 53 mg. sodium.

ESCAROLE SALAD WITH PARMESAN

SERVES 4

 3 *cups torn escarole or curly endive*
 ¼ *cup chopped fresh parsley*
 ¼ *cup chopped green onions*
 ¼ *cup chopped green peppers*
 ¼ *cup chopped sweet red peppers*
 ½ *cup whole-kernel corn*
 ¼ *cup lemon juice*
 2 *teaspoons olive oil*
 1 *tablespoon grated Parmesan cheese*
    Salt and ground black pepper

In a large salad bowl, mix the escarole or endive, parsley, green onions, green peppers, red peppers and corn. Add the lemon juice, olive oil and Parmesan; toss well. Add salt and pepper to taste.

Preparation time: 10 minutes

Per serving: 65 calories, 2.9 g. fat (36% of calories), 2 g. dietary fiber, 1 mg. cholesterol, 41 mg. sodium.

QUICK PASTA SAUCES

• **Creamy Alfredo:** In a blender or food processor, puree ½ cup low-fat ricotta cheese and ½ cup low-fat cottage cheese until smooth. Stir in 2 tablespoons minced green onions, 1 tablespoon minced garlic, and salt and ground black pepper to taste. Toss with 4 cups hot cooked pasta and your favorite sautéed or steamed mixed vegetables. Serves 4.

• **Mama's Vegetable Marinara:** Heat 2 cups low-fat pasta sauce and add ⅓ cup grated carrots, ⅓ cup finely chopped broccoli and 2 teaspoons minced garlic. Toss with 4 cups hot cooked pasta. Serves 4.

• **Smoky Turkey and Tomato:** Simmer 1 ounce diced smoked turkey, 2 cups chopped tomatoes, 2 tablespoons minced garlic and 1 cup finely chopped broccoli florets in a covered no-stick skillet for 10 minutes. Puree half of the sauce to thicken it and return it to the skillet. Add salt and ground black pepper to taste. Toss with 4 cups hot cooked pasta. Serves 4.

• **Lighter Garlic Sauce with Broccoli:** Simmer 3 tablespoons minced garlic in ¼ cup defatted chicken broth for 5 minutes; add 2 cups steamed broccoli florets, 1 tablespoon olive oil and 3 tablespoons grated Parmesan cheese. Heat through. Toss with 4 cups hot cooked pasta. Serves 4.

• **Peas and Ham:** Simmer 2 cups fresh peas, ½ cup diced onions and 2 ounces diced turkey ham in ½ cup defatted chicken broth for 5 minutes. Stir in ½ cup low-fat ricotta cheese and 2 tablespoons minced parsley. Toss with 4 cups hot cooked pasta. Serves 4.

A Taste of the South Seas

Stir-Fry of Asian Noodles and Vegetables
Island Vegetable Salad
Sliced Kiwifruit

*A*sian rice vermicelli (also called rice sticks) is fast and tasty: The noodles need only a quick soak in boiling water to soften. To cut prep time on the salad, use a selection of precut veggies from the salad bar.

Game Plan

1. Make the salad and let it marinate.
2. Make the stir-fry.
3. Peel and slice kiwifruit and arrange it on a plate.

Stir-Fry of Asian Noodles and Vegetables

serves 4

8	*ounces rice sticks (vermicelli rice noodles)*
½	*cup defatted chicken broth*
½	*cup thinly sliced onions*
4½	*teaspoons minced garlic*
4½	*teaspoons grated fresh ginger*
½	*cup diagonally sliced carrots*
2	*cups broccoli florets*
1	*cup thinly sliced sweet red peppers*
1	*can (15 ounces) whole straw mushrooms, rinsed and drained*
1	*teaspoon cornstarch*
2	*tablespoons mirin (rice wine) or apple juice*
1	*tablespoon sugar or honey*

1 teaspoon dark sesame oil

1–2 tablespoons reduced-sodium soy sauce

Place the rice sticks in a large bowl. Cover with boiling water and let soak for 5 to 10 minutes, or until tender; drain well.

Meanwhile, in a wok over medium-high heat, bring the broth to a boil. Add the onions, garlic, ginger and carrots; stir-fry for 3 to 4 minutes, or until the carrots are crisp-tender. Add the drained noodles, broccoli, peppers and mushrooms; stir-fry for 2 minutes.

In a small bowl combine the cornstarch, mirin or apple juice, sugar or honey, oil and soy sauce. Add to the wok; cook and stir for 2 to 3 minutes, or until the sauce thickens.

Preparation time: 10 minutes
Soaking time: 10 minutes
Cooking time: 10 minutes

Per serving: 316 calories, 1.9 g. fat (5% of calories), 6.1 g. dietary fiber, no cholesterol, 651 mg. sodium.

ISLAND VEGETABLE SALAD

SERVES 4

2 *cups sliced vegetables (such as sweet red peppers, carrots, broccoli)*

2 *green onions, julienned*

1 *clove garlic, minced*

2 *tablespoons rice vinegar*

4½ *teaspoons olive oil*

½ *teaspoon honey*

Salt and ground black pepper

Steam the vegetables for 5 minutes; rinse briefly under cold water and drain well.

In a large salad bowl, combine the steamed vegetables, green onions, garlic, vinegar, oil and honey. Let the salad marinate at room temperature for 20 minutes, stirring occasionally. Add salt and pepper to taste.

Preparation time: 10 minutes
Cooking time: 5 minutes
Marinating time: 20 minutes

Per serving: 81 calories, 5.3 g. fat (55% of calories), 2 g. dietary fiber, no cholesterol, 10 mg. sodium.

A FAMILY FAVORITE

Baked Macaroni and Cheese
Roasted Asparagus
Garden Salad

*H*ere's a new twist on a classic dinner—ready in 45 minutes! While the macaroni boils, cook the sauce, then bake the pasta and the asparagus. It's that simple.

GAME PLAN

1. Make the macaroni and cheese.
2. Roast the asparagus.
3. Make a simple salad of leaf lettuce and chopped tomatoes. Add lemon juice and a tiny amount of olive oil.

BAKED MACARONI AND CHEESE

SERVES 4

8	ounces elbow macaroni
1	tablespoon olive oil
1	tablespoon all-purpose flour
½	teaspoon dry mustard
1¼	cups skim milk
1¼	cups shredded low-fat extra-sharp Cheddar cheese
½	cup light ricotta cheese
2	tablespoons chopped green onions
	Salt and ground black pepper
¼	cup toasted bread crumbs

Preheat the oven to 375°. Coat an 8″ × 8″ baking pan with no-stick cooking spray. Set aside.

Cook the macaroni according to package directions. Drain well.

Meanwhile, heat the oil in a 3-quart no-stick saucepan over low heat; stir in the flour and mustard. Cook and stir for 1 minute. Gradually stir in the milk. Bring to a boil; cook and stir for 1 minute. Add the Cheddar. Remove the pan from the heat.

In a blender or food processor, puree the ricotta cheese. Add to the sauce. Stir in the green onions and pasta; add salt and pepper to taste. Spoon into the baking pan. Top with the bread crumbs. Bake for 20 minutes, or until the top is golden brown.

Preparation time: 5 minutes
Cooking time: 25 minutes

Per serving: 415 calories, 10.8 g. fat (24% of calories), 0.2 g. dietary fiber, 24 mg. cholesterol, 606 mg. sodium.

ROASTED ASPARAGUS

SERVES 4

1   *pound asparagus*
1   *teaspoon olive oil*
    Salt and ground black pepper
½   *teaspoon balsamic vinegar*

Preheat the oven to 350°. Wash the asparagus and snap off any tough ends. In a shallow roasting pan, toss the asparagus with the oil; add salt and pepper to taste. Arrange in a single layer in the pan.

Bake at 350° for 10 minutes; increase the heat to 450° and bake for 5 minutes, or until tender and brown, shaking once during roasting.

Sprinkle with the vinegar.

Preparation time: 2 minutes
Cooking time: 15 minutes

Per serving: 36 calories, 1.5 g. fat (31% of calories), no dietary fiber, no cholesterol, 12 mg. sodium.

CHAPTER 6

BEST BETS
FROM THE
BARNYARD

QUICK CHICKEN AND TURKEY DINNERS

Versatile and quick, poultry provides a simple source of lean protein for everyday meals. Boneless cuts of chicken and turkey cook very fast, and you can toss them with a variety of nutritious sauces, grains, vegetables and pastas for dinner in under 45 minutes. No wonder poultry is America's favorite entrée for pressed evenings. Try one of these menus tonight and see why.

FAST FRENCH

Chicken Breasts in Sweet Orange Sauce
Herbed Basmati Rice
Steamed Asparagus
French Bread

A fast-lane approach to duck à l'orange, this easy chicken dinner is truly elegant and—believe it or not—very low in fat. The fragrant basmati rice echoes the chicken's citrus flavor and soaks up extra sauce.

GAME PLAN

1. Start the chicken.
2. While the chicken is cooking, start the rice.
3. Steam asparagus and toss it with lemon juice.
4. Warm the French bread.

CHICKEN BREASTS IN SWEET ORANGE SAUCE

SERVES 4

> 4   *skinless chicken breast halves (bone-in)*
> ¾–1   *cup defatted chicken broth*
> 1   *cup orange juice*
> 2   *tablespoons orange marmalade*
> 2   *teaspoons chopped orange rind (see note)*
> 2   *tablespoons honey*
> 1   *teaspoon cornstarch*
> *Salt and ground black pepper*

Coat a 10″ no-stick skillet with no-stick cooking spray and set it over medium-high heat. When the pan is hot, add the chicken and brown it on both sides. Add ¾ cup of the broth; reduce the heat to medium. Cover and cook for 20 minutes, or until the chicken is no longer pink in the center, adding more broth as needed to prevent sticking. Place the chicken on a serving platter and cover to keep warm.

In a small bowl, combine the orange juice, marmalade, orange rind, honey and cornstarch; stir well. Pour into the skillet and bring to a boil. Cook and stir until the sauce thickens. Add salt and pepper to taste. Pour it over the chicken.

Preparation time: 5 minutes
Cooking time: 30 minutes

Chef's note: Use a potato peeler to strip off the sweet and flavorful colored part of the rind (or zest), paring off as little as possible of the bitter white interior membrane. Then chop the rind with a chef's knife or scissors.

Per serving: 238 calories, 3.2 g. fat (12% of calories), 1.1 g. dietary fiber, 73 mg. cholesterol, 128 mg. sodium.

HERBED BASMATI RICE

SERVES 4

1½ cups uncooked basmati rice
1 teaspoon grated lemon rind
¼ cup lemon juice
3½ cups defatted chicken broth
½ cup chopped fresh parsley
2 green onions, chopped (including greens)
   Salt

Rinse the basmati rice under cold water until the water runs clear; drain well.

Coat a heavy saucepan with olive oil no-stick cooking spray; set it over medium-high heat. When the pan is hot, add the rice; cook and stir for 1 minute. Add the lemon rind, lemon juice and broth; bring to a boil. Reduce the heat to low; cover and cook for 15 to 20 minutes, or until all the broth has been absorbed.

Fluff the rice with a fork. Stir in the parsley and green onions; add salt to taste.

Preparation time: 5 minutes
Cooking time: 20 minutes

Per serving: 259 calories, 1.6 g. fat (5% of calories), 0.1 g. dietary fiber, no cholesterol, 427 mg. sodium.

MEXICAN WRAP UP

Pepper, Onion and Chicken Fajitas
Low-Fat Guacamole
Shredded Lettuce Salad

rap up your weeknight dinner with this fast Mexican favorite: just line up bowls of ingredients for a build-your-own fajita dinner. The guacamole is a surprise—green beans stretch the fat of a single avocado into a delicious low-fat dip.

GAME PLAN

1. Marinate the chicken.
2. Make the guacamole.
3. Make the fajitas.
4. Make a simple salad with leaf lettuce, diced tomatoes and shredded carrots. Add your favorite low-fat dressing.

LOW-FAT GUACAMOLE

SERVES 6

1½ cups frozen green beans, thawed
1 small avocado, cubed
2 large cloves garlic, minced
2–3 tablespoons lemon juice
1 tablespoon chopped jalapeño peppers (*wear plastic gloves when handling*)
2 tablespoons chopped fresh cilantro

In a blender or food processor, puree the green beans, avocado, garlic and lemon juice until very smooth. Stir in the peppers and cilantro.

Preparation time: 5 minutes

Chef's note: Leftover guacamole makes a great sandwich filler; it keeps for 2 days in the fridge.

Per serving: 57 calories, 5.4 g. fat (76% of calories), 4.7 g. dietary fiber, no cholesterol, 63 mg. sodium.

PEPPER, ONION AND CHICKEN FAJITAS

SERVES 4

1   *pound boneless skinless chicken breasts, sliced across the grain into ¼" strips*

¼   *cup lime juice*

1   *teaspoon ground cumin*

1   *tablespoon minced garlic*

1   *teaspoon olive oil*

1   *sweet red pepper, cut into strips*

1   *sweet yellow or green pepper, cut into strips*

2   *medium red onions, sliced*

¼   *cup chopped fresh cilantro*

8   *(10") low-fat flour tortillas*

1   *cup low-fat sour cream*

1   *cup reduced-sodium salsa*

Place the chicken, lime juice, cumin and garlic in a resealable plastic storage bag. Refrigerate for at least 35 minutes or up to 24 hours, turning occasionally.

Heat the oil in a heavy 10" no-stick skillet over medium-high heat until almost smoking; add the red peppers and yellow or green peppers. Cook and stir for 3 minutes, or until the peppers begin to brown slightly. Add the onions; cook and stir for 5 minutes, or until the onions are tender and slightly charred. Transfer the vegetables to a plate; cover to keep warm.

Add the chicken and marinade to the pan; cook and stir for 4 minutes, or until the chicken is no longer pink. Add the vegetables and cilantro; cook and stir for 1 minute.

Wrap the tortillas in plastic wrap; microwave them for 1 minute on high power. Divide the chicken mixture among the 8 tortillas; top with sour cream and salsa before rolling up.

Preparation time: 10 minutes
Cooking time: 10 minutes
Marinating time: 35 minutes

Per serving: 429 calories, 8.4 g. fat (17% of calories), 13.2 g. dietary fiber, 88 mg. cholesterol, 937 mg. sodium.

GREAT SALSAS FOR GRILLED POULTRY

*G*rilled turkey or chicken and one of these 5-minute salsas means dinner in a jiffy.

Latin Jazz: In a medium bowl, combine 2 cups chopped papaya, 1 teaspoon chopped mild green chili peppers (use plastic gloves when handling), 1 tablespoon lime juice, 1 tablespoon minced fresh cilantro and 2 teaspoons minced fresh garlic. Makes 2 cups.

Florida Keys: In a medium bowl, combine 2 cups chopped fresh oranges, ¼ cup minced red onions, ¼ cup white vinegar, 2 tablespoons minced fresh cilantro or parsley, 2 teaspoons sugar or honey, ¼ teaspoon ground cumin and salt and ground black pepper to taste. Makes about 2 cups.

California Coast: In a medium bowl, combine 1 cup minced artichoke hearts, 1 cup chopped tomatoes, 1 cup chopped sweet red peppers, ¼ cup chopped fresh parsley or cilantro, ¼ cup balsamic vinegar and salt and ground black pepper to taste. Makes about 3 cups.

A FRENCH TWIST ON CHICKEN

*Sautéed Chicken
in Rosemary-Mushroom Sauce
Lemon Broccoli
Spinach Salad*

*D*espite the elegant name and upscale appearance, this French-style skillet dinner is simple to make, low in fat, and visually stunning—a great menu for drop-in company.

GAME PLAN

1. Make the chicken.
2. Make a salad of bagged washed spinach and sliced radishes. Add your favorite low-fat ranch dressing.
3. Make the broccoli.

SAUTÉED CHICKEN IN ROSEMARY-MUSHROOM SAUCE

SERVES 4

1	tablespoon olive oil
4	skinless chicken breast halves (bone-in)
½	cup white wine or apple juice
1	cup sliced onions
2	cups sliced mushrooms
2	teaspoons minced garlic
½	cup chopped green peppers
½	teaspoon minced fresh rosemary
1	tablespoon all-purpose flour
2	tablespoons tomato paste

½ *cup defatted chicken broth*

1 *cup chopped tomatoes*

Heat the oil in a 10″ no-stick skillet over medium-high heat; when the oil is hot, add the chicken and brown it on both sides. Transfer the chicken to a plate.

Bring the wine or apple juice to a boil in the same skillet, scraping to loosen any browned bits. Add the onions, mushrooms, garlic, green peppers and rosemary; cook and stir for 5 minutes, or until the onions are soft.

In a small bowl, combine the flour and tomato paste; stir in the broth and tomatoes. Add to the sauce; stir well. Place the chicken, bone side up, on the vegetables; cover and cook for 15 to 20 minutes, or until the chicken is no longer pink in the center.

Preparation time: 10 minutes
Cooking time: 30 minutes

Per serving: 257 calories, 7 g. fat (24% of calories), 2.8 g. dietary fiber, 73 mg. cholesterol, 180 mg. sodium.

LEMON BROCCOLI

SERVES 4

1 *pound broccoli*

¼ *cup lemon juice*

1 *teaspoon butter or olive oil*

1 *teaspoon grated lemon rind*

Trim the broccoli stems and cut them into ½″ slices. Steam the broccoli for 5 minutes, or until crisp-tender. Drain well; toss with the lemon juice, butter or oil and lemon rind.

Preparation time: 10 minutes
Cooking time: 5 minutes

Per serving: 40 calories, 1.3 g. fat (24% of calories), no dietary fiber, 3 mg. cholesterol, 34 mg. sodium.

SOUTHWEST GRILL

Grilled Southwestern-Style Drumsticks
Spicy Corn on the Cob
Steamed Green Beans
Cooked Rice

*A*s fast as the best-tasting food from a restaurant drive-through but surprisingly low in fat, this kid-pleasing entrée will soon become a family favorite. The spicy corn on the cob grills in its own packet of foil while the chicken cooks.

GAME PLAN

1. Marinate the drumsticks.
2. Cook the rice.
3. Grill the corn and drumsticks.
4. Steam fresh green beans; drizzle them with a tiny amount of olive oil.

GRILLED SOUTHWESTERN-STYLE DRUMSTICKS

SERVES 4

8	*chicken drumsticks, skins removed*
1	*tablespoon garlic powder*
1	*tablespoon onion powder*
1	*tablespoon ground paprika*
1	*tablespoon chili powder*
1	*teaspoon ground cumin*
½	*teaspoon salt*
1	*cup dark beer or apple cider*

Place the drumsticks, garlic powder, onion powder, paprika, chili powder, cumin, salt, and beer or apple cider in a resealable plastic storage bag. Shake well. Refrigerate for 20 minutes or up to 24 hours, turning occasionally.

Preheat the grill. Remove the drumsticks from the bag; reserve the marinade. Place the drumsticks on a plate and lightly coat with no-stick cooking spray. Transfer to the grill.

Cook for 20 minutes, or until the chicken is no longer pink in the center, turning occasionally and basting with the reserved marinade.

Preparation time: 3 minutes
Cooking time: 20 minutes
Marinating time: 20 minutes

Per serving: 204 calories, 5.7 g. fat (25% of calories), 1 g. dietary fiber, 82 mg. cholesterol, 376 mg. sodium.

SPICY CORN ON THE COB

SERVES 4

4   *ears corn, shucked*
¼   *teaspoon ground red pepper*
2   *tablespoons balsamic vinegar*
1   *tablespoon olive oil*

Preheat the grill. Place the corn on a sheet of heavy-duty foil.

In a small bowl, stir together the red pepper, vinegar and oil; brush on the corn. Wrap the foil around the corn and place the packet on the grill. Grill for 20 minutes, or until the corn is hot and cooked through, turning once.

Preparation time: 5 minutes
Cooking time: 20 minutes

Per serving: 155 calories, 4.3 g. fat (22% of calories), 2.7 g. dietary fiber, no cholesterol, 6 mg. sodium.

TEXAS BACKYARD BARBECUE

Spicy Chicken Tenders
Buffalo Blue-Cheese Dipping Sauce
with Raw Vegetable Plate
Texas Garlic Toast

*B*uffalo, New York, originated the delicious combination of blue cheese sauce, vegetables and spicy chicken wings. Find the same terrific tastes—without the fat—in this easy menu.

GAME PLAN

1. Make the chicken tenders.
2. Make the dipping sauce and raw vegetables.
3. Toast thick slices of homestyle bread; coat them with olive oil no-stick cooking spray and brush with chopped fresh garlic.

SPICY CHICKEN TENDERS

SERVES 4

2   *pounds boneless skinless chicken breasts or thighs*
⅓   *cup low-fat buttermilk*
½   *cup yellow cornmeal*
½   *cup dry bread crumbs*
½   *teaspoon salt*
1   *tablespoon ground paprika*
1   *tablespoon chili powder*
1   *tablespoon garlic powder*

Cut the chicken into 2″ pieces. Place the chicken and buttermilk in a resealable plastic storage bag. Shake well. Refrigerate for 10 minutes.

Preheat the oven to 400°. Line a large baking sheet with foil.

Place the cornmeal, bread crumbs, salt, paprika, chili powder and garlic powder in a second resealable plastic storage bag. Add the chicken; shake well to coat.

Transfer the chicken to the baking sheet. Coat the chicken with no-stick cooking spray. Bake for 25 minutes, or until the coating is crisp and the chicken is no longer pink in the center.

Preparation time: 5 minutes
Cooking time: 25 minutes
Marinating time: 10 minutes

Per serving: 402 calories, 7.8 g. fat (18% of calories), 3 g. dietary fiber, 139 mg. cholesterol, 549 mg. sodium.

BUFFALO BLUE-CHEESE DIPPING SAUCE WITH RAW VEGETABLE PLATE

SERVES 4

⅓ *cup light ricotta cheese*
¼ *cup nonfat cottage cheese*
¼ *cup nonfat plain yogurt*
 1 *tablespoon crumbled blue cheese*
 1 *tablespoon minced green onions*
    Salt and ground black pepper
    Lettuce leaves
 2 *cups peeled baby carrots*
 1 *cup celery sticks*
 1 *cup whole radishes*

In a blender or food processor, puree the ricotta, cottage cheese, yogurt and half of the blue cheese. Stir in the remaining blue cheese and the green onions. Add salt and pepper to taste. Spoon the sauce into a small serving bowl. Refrigerate for 10 minutes.

Line a platter with lettuce leaves. Place the bowl of sauce in the center; arrange the carrots, celery sticks and radishes around it.

Preparation time: 5 minutes
Chilling time: 10 minutes

Per serving: 75 calories, 1.8 g. fat (20% of calories), 3.1 g. dietary fiber, 6 mg. cholesterol, 224 mg. sodium.

SPEEDY CHINESE

Chinese Chicken Stir-Fry
Vegetable Lo Mein
Steamed Broccoli

*C*hicken was never more at home than in this rich-tasting stir-fry and noodle side dish. Combine the chicken and marinade before you leave for work in the morning and refrigerate it until dinnertime.

GAME PLAN

1. Make the lo mein.
2. Make the stir-fry.
3. Steam broccoli florets; toss with fresh lemon juice.

CHINESE CHICKEN STIR-FRY

SERVES 4

8 *ounces boneless skinless chicken breasts, cut into*
   1" pieces
1 *can (8 ounces) unsweetened pineapple chunks*
   (with juice)
1 *tablespoon reduced-sodium soy sauce*
1 *teaspoon brown sugar*
3 *cloves garlic, minced*
1 *tablespoon cornstarch*
1 *tablespoon hoisin sauce*
1 *sweet red pepper, diced*
1 *green pepper, diced*

Place the chicken, pineapple chunks (with juice), soy sauce, brown sugar, garlic, cornstarch and hoisin sauce in a resealable plastic storage bag. Shake well. Refrigerate for 25 minutes or up to 24 hours, turning occasionally.

Coat a wok with no-stick cooking spray and set it over medium-high heat. When the wok is hot, add the chicken and pineapple chunks; reserve the marinade. Cook and stir for 2 minutes. Add the red and green peppers; cook and stir for 3 minutes. Add the marinade. Bring to a boil; cook and stir for 5 minutes, or until the sauce is thickened and the chicken is no longer pink in the center.

Preparation time: 10 minutes
Cooking time: 10 minutes
Marinating time: 25 minutes

Per serving: 148 calories, 1.7 g. fat (10% of calories), 1.9 g. dietary fiber, 34 mg. cholesterol, 215 mg. sodium.

VEGETABLE LO MEIN

SERVES 4

⅓ *cup defatted chicken broth*
½ *medium onion, sliced*
4 *large stalks bok choy, chopped*
2 *cups cooked Chinese noodles or vermicelli*
1 *cup diagonally sliced snow peas*
1 *tablespoon dark sesame oil*

In a 10″ skillet over medium-high heat, bring the broth to a boil. Add the onions; cook and stir for 3 minutes, or until the onions are soft. Add the bok choy and noodles; cover and cook for 1 minute. Add the snow peas and oil; toss well. Cover and cook for 30 seconds.

Preparation time: 8 minutes
Cooking time: 5 minutes

Chef's note: Bok choy is Chinese cabbage with thick white stalks and dark green leaves. It is available in most supermarkets.

Per serving: 189 calories, 3.6 g. fat (17% of calories), 1.4 g. dietary fiber, no cholesterol, 49 mg. sodium.

Easy Chinese

Asian Chicken Salad
Baked Filled Wontons
Sugar Snap Peas

*T*his whole-meal salad is chock full of nutritious vegetables and tossed with a sweet honey-ginger dressing. The crunchy cheese-filled wontons are a snap to make with prepared wonton skins from the produce section.

Game Plan

1. Make the wontons.
2. Make the salad.
3. Sauté sugar snap peas in apple juice; toss them with a tiny amount of olive oil and salt.

Asian Chicken Salad

SERVES 4

1 tablespoon olive oil
¼ cup honey
1 teaspoon dark sesame oil
1 teaspoon grated fresh ginger
3–4 tablespoons lime juice
1 tablespoon reduced-sodium soy sauce
2 cups shredded cooked chicken
4 cups thinly sliced green cabbage
1 can (8 ounces) mandarin orange slices, drained
1 cup diced sweet red peppers

¼ *cup chopped green onions*

1 *tablespoon grated onions*

1 *teaspoon toasted sesame seeds*

In a large salad bowl, whisk together the olive oil, honey, sesame oil, ginger, lime juice and soy sauce. Add the chicken, cabbage, oranges, peppers, green onions and grated onions; mix well. Sprinkle with the sesame seeds.

Preparation time: 10 minutes

Per serving: 260 calories, 7 g. fat (23% of calories), 2.7 g. dietary fiber, 44 mg. cholesterol, 184 mg. sodium.

BAKED FILLED WONTONS

SERVES 4

1 *cup Asian stir-fry vegetables, finely chopped*

2 *tablespoons finely chopped fresh cilantro*

1 *clove garlic, minced*

1 *green onion, minced*

½ *teaspoon grated fresh ginger*

½ *teaspoon dark sesame oil*

12 *wonton skins*

¼ *cup low-fat cream cheese*

Salt and ground black pepper

Preheat the oven to 350°. In a medium bowl, toss the stir-fry vegetables with the cilantro, garlic, green onions, ginger and oil.

Arrange the wonton skins on a clean counter and place a rounded teaspoon of filling in the center of each skin. Top each with 1 teaspoon of cream cheese. Dampen the edges and fold over to form a triangle. Press the edges with your fingers to seal.

Place the wontons on a no-stick baking sheet and lightly coat with no-stick cooking spray. Sprinkle with salt and pepper. Bake for 10 to 15 minutes, or until lightly browned and crisp.

Preparation time: 15 minutes
Cooking time: 15 minutes

Per serving: 118 calories, 3.4 g. fat (26% of calories), 0.1 g. dietary fiber, 8 mg. cholesterol, 225 mg. sodium.

Savvy Southern Supper

Apricot-Ginger Chicken Thighs
Warm Greens Sauté
Basmati Rice

A great alternative to chicken with cream sauce, this elegant skillet meal is low in fat and ready in minutes. The richness of balsamic vinegar flavors the stir-fry of healthy greens.

Game Plan

1. Make the chicken.
2. Cook the basmati rice according to package directions.
3. Make the greens.

Apricot-Ginger Chicken Thighs

SERVES 4

1	teaspoon canola oil
4	skinless chicken thighs (bone in)
¼	cup white wine or apple juice
2	large green onions, sliced
2	tablespoons low-sugar apricot preserves
8	dried apricots, thinly sliced
1	teaspoon grated fresh ginger
¾	cup defatted chicken broth
2	teaspoons reduced-sodium soy sauce
1	tablespoon cornstarch

Coat a 10″ no-stick skillet with no-stick cooking spray; add the oil and set the pan over medium-high heat. When the oil is hot, add the chicken. Brown for 3 minutes on each side; transfer the chicken to a plate.

Add the wine or apple juice to the pan, scraping to loosen any browned bits. Add the green onions, preserves, apricots, ginger and ½ cup of the broth; bring to a boil. Cook and stir for 1 minute. Add the chicken; reduce the heat to medium. Cover and cook for 15 minutes, or until the chicken is no longer pink.

In a small bowl, combine the remaining ¼ cup of broth, soy sauce and cornstarch. Add to the pan; cook and stir until the sauce has thickened.

Preparation time: 5 minutes
Cooking time: 25 minutes

Per serving: 172 calories, 6.8 g. fat (36% of calories), 0.7 g. dietary fiber, 48 mg. cholesterol, 206 mg. sodium.

WARM GREENS SAUTÉ

SERVES 4

1   *tablespoon olive oil*

4   *cups mixed chopped greens (such as collards, Swiss chard, spinach, kale)*

1   *teaspoon honey*

2   *tablespoons balsamic vinegar*

¼   *teaspoon salt*

Heat the oil in a 10″ no-stick skillet over medium-high heat; when the oil is hot, add the greens. Cover and cook, stirring occasionally, for 3 minutes, or until the greens wilt. Remove the skillet from the heat; stir in the honey, vinegar and salt. Toss well.

Preparation time: 5 minutes
Cooking time: 5 minutes

Per serving: 56 calories, 3.5 g. fat (54% of calories), 1.2 g. dietary fiber, no cholesterol, 167 mg. sodium.

NEW MEXICAN WRAP

*Southwestern Chicken Kabob Wraps
with Yogurt Sauce
Pineapple Salsa
Tossed Green Salad*

Warm pita bread wraps up this spa menu featuring grilled skewers of lime-chili marinated chicken, cooled with a yogurt sauce and pineapple salsa. The salsa is a great topper for any grilled fish or chicken, so make extra.

GAME PLAN

1. Make the salsa.
2. Make the chicken kabobs and yogurt sauce.
3. Make a tossed salad of romaine lettuce, tomatoes and shredded carrots. Add your favorite low-fat vinaigrette dressing.

SOUTHWESTERN CHICKEN KABOB WRAPS WITH YOGURT SAUCE

SERVES 4

1	*pound boneless skinless chicken breasts, cut into 1" pieces*
⅓	*cup honey mustard*
⅓	*cup lime juice*
1	*tablespoon chili powder*
¼	*teaspoon salt*
1	*teaspoon minced garlic*
½	*cup nonfat plain yogurt*

½ cup low-fat sour cream

1 tablespoon chopped fresh cilantro

1 sweet red pepper, cut into 8 pieces

1 green pepper, cut into 8 pieces

4 large pita bread rounds

In a resealable plastic storage bag, combine the chicken, mustard, lime juice, chili powder, salt and garlic. Shake well. Refrigerate for 30 minutes, turning occasionally.

In a small bowl, stir together the yogurt, sour cream and cilantro. Set aside.

Preheat the grill. Drain the chicken, reserving the marinade. Thread the red and green pepper pieces and chicken alternately on skewers. Grill for 10 minutes, turning frequently and basting with the marinade, until the chicken is no longer pink in the center and the vegetables are lightly browned.

Wrap the pita bread in plastic wrap and microwave on high power for 1 minute.

Remove the chicken and peppers from the skewers and divide them among the pita breads; drizzle with yogurt sauce and roll up.

Preparation time: 10 minutes
Cooking time: 10 minutes
Marinating time: 30 minutes

Per serving: 444 calories, 7.8 g. fat (15% of calories), 2.2 g. dietary fiber, 79 mg. cholesterol, 729 mg. sodium.

PINEAPPLE SALSA

SERVES 4

1   can (8 ounces) unsweetened crushed pineapple, drained

2   tablespoons lime juice

1   tablespoon chopped jalapeño peppers (wear plastic gloves when handling)

2   tablespoons chopped dried apricots

1   tablespoon chopped fresh cilantro

In a small bowl, combine the pineapple, lime juice, peppers, apricots and cilantro. Mix well. Let stand at room temperature for 20 minutes, stirring occasionally.

Preparation time: 5 minutes
Marinating time: 20 minutes

Per serving: 47 calories, 0.1 g. fat (2% of calories), 0.7 dietary fiber, no cholesterol, 33 mg. sodium.

15-MINUTE CHICKEN DINNERS

- **Lemon Chicken:** Marinate 4 boneless skinless chicken breast halves in the juice of 1 lemon, 2 teaspoons minced garlic and ¼ teaspoon salt. Grill for 3 to 5 minutes on each side, or until the chicken is no longer pink in the center. Place the marinade in a saucepan and cook over medium-high heat for 5 to 10 minutes, or until reduced by half; serve over the grilled chicken. Serves 4.

- **Chicken with Pesto:** Brush 4 boneless skinless chicken breast halves with 1 teaspoon olive oil. Broil for 3 to 5 minutes on each side, or until the chicken is no longer pink in the center. Place 1 teaspoon prepared pesto on each chicken breast half; cover the pesto with a slice of low-fat mozzarella cheese and broil until the cheese melts. Serves 4.

- **Spicy Barbecued Chicken:** Marinate 4 boneless skinless chicken breast halves in 1 cup reduced-sodium low-fat barbecue sauce, 1 teaspoon hot pepper sauce and 3 cloves garlic, minced. Grill for 3 to 5 minutes on each side, or until the chicken is no longer pink in the center, basting with reserved marinade. Serve on toasted hamburger buns. Serves 4.

- **Mustardy Chicken Wings:** Preheat the oven to 400°. Dip 12 skinned chicken wing drumettes in a mixture of ½ cup Dijon mustard, 1 tablespoon molasses, 1 teaspoon minced garlic and ¼ teaspoon salt. Then dip the coated wings in bread crumbs. Bake for 15 minutes, or until done. Serves 4.

- **Chicken Breasts with Vegetables:** Brown 4 boneless skinless chicken breast halves in 1 tablespoon olive oil for 2 minutes on each side. Add 1 cup sliced yellow squash, 1 cup peeled baby carrots, 1 cup sliced zucchini, 2 tablespoons chopped fresh herbs (such as sage, thyme, rosemary) and ½ cup white wine or apple juice. Cover and cook over medium heat for 8 to 10 minutes, or until the chicken is no longer pink in the center and the vegetables are soft. Serves 4.

Caribbean Barbecue

Jerk Turkey
Minted Peas and Rice
Pineapple Coleslaw

Jamaican jerk seasoning is a delicious low-fat combination of hot and sweet spices. In this menu, it gives a zesty flavor boost to lean turkey.

GAME PLAN

1. Marinate the turkey.
2. Make a coleslaw from shredded cabbage and unsweetened pineapple chunks. Add low-fat coleslaw dressing.
3. Cook the turkey.
4. Make the peas and rice.

JERK TURKEY

SERVES 4

1	tablespoon chopped jalapeño peppers (*wear plastic gloves when handling*)
1	tablespoon grated fresh ginger
1	tablespoon minced garlic
¼	teaspoon ground nutmeg
½	teaspoon ground cinnamon
1	teaspoon ground black pepper
¼	teaspoon ground allspice
½	teaspoon dried thyme
1	tablespoon reduced-sodium soy sauce
2	tablespoons lime juice
1	tablespoon olive oil
4	boneless skinless turkey cutlets

In a blender or food processor, combine the peppers, ginger, garlic, nutmeg, cinnamon, pepper, allspice, thyme, soy sauce, lime juice and oil. Puree.

Spread the spice mixture on one side of the turkey cutlets and place the turkey on a plate; cover with plastic wrap. Refrigerate for 30 minutes or up to 24 hours.

Preheat the grill. Grill the turkey for 5 minutes on each side, or until it is lightly browned and no longer pink in the center, brushing it with any leftover spice mixture.

Preparation time: 5 minutes
Cooking time: 10 minutes
Marinating time: 30 minutes

Chef's note: To make this jerk rub even hotter, substitute Scotch bonnet peppers for the jalapeño peppers.

Per serving: 151 calories, 6 g. fat (36% of calories), 0.3 g. dietary fiber, 44 mg. cholesterol, 204 mg. sodium.

MINTED PEAS AND RICE

SERVES 4

1	teaspoon olive oil
1/4	cup chopped onions
1	cup quick-cooking brown rice
1 1/2	cups defatted chicken broth
3	tablespoons minced fresh mint
1/2	cup frozen peas, thawed

Heat the oil in a large saucepan over medium-high heat. When the oil is hot, add the onions; cook and stir for 1 minute. Add the rice; cook and stir for 1 minute. Add the broth; bring to a boil.

Lower the heat to medium; cover and cook for 5 to 8 minutes, or until the rice is tender and broth is absorbed. Remove the pan from the heat; stir in the mint and peas. Cover and let stand for 5 minutes.

Preparation time: 5 minutes
Cooking time: 12 minutes
Standing time: 5 minutes

Per serving: 211 calories, 2.6 g. fat (11% of calories), 3.6 g. dietary fiber, no cholesterol, 147 mg. sodium.

THANKSGIVING IN A SNAP

Herbed Turkey Tenderloin
Baked Apples and Sweet Potatoes
Butter Beans

Making Thanksgiving dinner doesn't have to take all day. Just cook this savory feast of herbed turkey tenderloin, potatoes, apples and butter beans.

GAME PLAN

1. Make the turkey.
2. Bake the apples and sweet potatoes.
3. Steam frozen butter beans; toss them with snipped fresh chives.

HERBED TURKEY TENDERLOIN

SERVES 4

1   tablespoon olive oil
4   cloves garlic, halved
1   pound turkey tenderloin, quartered
2   tablespoons minced fresh rosemary
1   teaspoon dried thyme
½   cup dry white wine or defatted chicken broth

Preheat the oven to 350°. Heat the oil in a large ovenproof skillet over medium-high heat. When the oil is hot, add the garlic; cook and stir for 2 minutes.

Add the turkey to the skillet and brown it lightly on both sides. Add the rosemary and thyme. Cover the skillet; place it in the oven.

Bake for 30 minutes, or until the turkey is no longer pink in the center. Transfer the turkey to a platter; cover to keep warm.

Add the wine or broth to the skillet. Bring to a boil; cook and stir over medium-high heat for 2 minutes, scraping to loosen the browned bits. Pour the sauce over the turkey.

Preparation time: 5 minutes
Cooking time: 40 minutes

Per serving: 162 calories, 5.9 g. fat (34% of calories), 0.1 g. dietary fiber, 44 mg. cholesterol, 41 mg. sodium.

BAKED APPLES AND SWEET POTATOES

SERVES 4

2 *tart red apples, quartered*
1 *large unpeeled sweet potato, thickly sliced*
½ *cup apple juice*
½ *teaspoon ground cinnamon*

Preheat the oven to 400°. Place the apples, sweet potatoes, apple juice and cinnamon in an 8″ × 8″ baking pan. Cover with foil. Bake for 20 to 25 minutes, or until the apples and sweet potatoes are soft.

Preparation time: 5 minutes
Cooking time: 20 minutes

Per serving: 85 calories, 0.3 g. fat (3% of calories), 2.4 g. dietary fiber, no cholesterol, 4 mg. sodium.

OVEN-BAKED COMFORT

*Turkey Pot Pie
with Buttermilk Biscuit Crust
Chopped Salad
Steamed Green Beans*

*Y*es! You can have old-fashioned turkey pot pie in less than 45 minutes. A low-fat biscuit crust tops a savory mixture of cooked turkey, vegetables and sauce in this shortcut version. Served with steamed green beans and a truly down-home salad, this is a meal you won't want to miss.

GAME PLAN

1. Make the pot pie.
2. Make the salad.
3. Steam green beans; toss them with lemon juice.

TURKEY POT PIE
WITH BUTTERMILK BISCUIT CRUST

SERVES 4

- 1 cup all-purpose flour
- 1 teaspoon baking powder
- ¼ teaspoon baking soda
   Pinch of salt
- 1 tablespoon plus 2 teaspoons chilled butter, cut into small pieces
- ¼ cup low-fat buttermilk
- 3 tablespoons low-fat sour cream
- 1¾ cups defatted chicken broth

⅓	cup chopped onions
2	teaspoons minced garlic
2½	tablespoons cornstarch
¼	teaspoon poultry seasoning
½	teaspoon dried thyme
¼	teaspoon dried sage
2	cups mixed frozen peas, carrots and cauliflower
2	cups diced skinless cooked turkey

In a medium bowl, combine the flour, baking powder, baking soda and salt; cut in the chilled butter with a pastry blender until the mixture resembles fine crumbs. Add the buttermilk and sour cream; mix until smooth. Turn the dough onto a sheet of plastic wrap and flatten it into a large pancake; wrap tightly. Refrigerate while you make the pot pie filling.

Preheat the oven to 425°. In a 10″ no-stick skillet over medium-high heat, bring ¼ cup of the broth to a boil. Add the onions and garlic; cook and stir for 2 minutes.

In a small bowl, combine the cornstarch, poultry seasoning, thyme, sage and remaining 1½ cups of broth; stir into the sauce. Bring to a boil; cook and stir for 1 minute. Remove from the heat; add the mixed vegetables and turkey. Pour into an 8″ × 8″ casserole or baking pan. Cut the biscuit dough into four sections; arrange on top of the filling.

Bake the pot pie for 30 minutes, or until the biscuits are golden brown and the filling is bubbling.

Preparation time: 10 minutes
Cooking time: 35 minutes

Per serving: 331 calories, 6.4 g. fat (18% of calories), 3.2 g. dietary fiber, 64 mg. cholesterol, 536 mg. sodium.

CHOPPED SALAD

1   cup nonfat plain yogurt
2   tablespoons nonfat mayonnaise
2   teaspoons maple syrup
2   cups shredded cabbage
2   cups chopped romaine lettuce
¼   cup shredded carrots
½   cup crushed unsweetened pineapple, drained
¼   cup raisins

In a large salad bowl, whisk together the yogurt, mayonnaise and maple syrup.

Add the cabbage, lettuce, carrots, pineapple and raisins; toss well.

Preparation time: 10 minutes

Per serving: 110 calories, 0.3 g. fat (2% of calories), 2.1 g. dietary fiber, 1 mg. cholesterol, 153 mg. sodium.

TENDER TURKEY NIGHT

> *Turkey Tenderloin with Sun-Dried*
> *Tomato-Mushroom Sauce*
> *Garlic Mashed Potatoes*
> *Snow Peas*

*T*enderloin lives up to its name—despite being low in fat, this cut of lean turkey is very tender. The creamy potatoes get their richness from being cooked in garlic and milk.

GAME PLAN

1. Start the mashed potatoes.
2. While the potatoes cook, make the turkey tenderloin.
3. Finish the mashed potatoes.
4. Steam whole snow peas; toss them with lemon juice.

GARLIC MASHED POTATOES

SERVES 4

1¼ *pounds unpeeled red potatoes, cut into ½" pieces*
¼ *cup skim milk*
8 *large garlic cloves, peeled and crushed*
⅓ *cup low-fat sour cream*
Salt and ground black pepper

In a medium saucepan, combine the potatoes and enough water to cover. Add the milk and garlic. Bring to a boil over medium-high heat; reduce the heat to medium and cook for 20 minutes, or until the potatoes are tender.

Drain the potatoes and garlic, reserving the cooking liquid. Return the potatoes and garlic to the saucepan. Add the sour cream; mash the potatoes until smooth, thinning with reserved cooking liquid if desired. Add salt and pepper to taste.

Preparation time: 5 minutes
Cooking time: 20 minutes

Per serving: 148 calories, 1.4 g. fat (9% of calories), 0.1 g. dietary fiber, 7 mg. cholesterol, 28 mg. sodium.

TURKEY TENDERLOIN WITH SUN-DRIED TOMATO-MUSHROOM SAUCE

SERVES 4

1 *pound turkey tenderloin, cut into 4 pieces*
2 *tablespoons seasoned bread crumbs*
1 *teaspoon olive oil*
¼ *cup defatted chicken broth*
½ *cup chopped onions*
1 *teaspoon minced garlic*
½ *cup diced carrots*
½ *cup diced celery*
1 *cup sliced mushrooms*
2 *ounces dry-pack sun-dried tomatoes, chopped*
1 *cup chopped tomatoes*
¼ *teaspoon dried rosemary, crushed*
   Salt and ground black pepper

Place the turkey and bread crumbs in a resealable plastic storage bag; shake well.

Coat a 10″ no-stick skillet with no-stick cooking spray and set it over medium-high heat; add the oil. When the oil is hot, add the turkey. Cook for 3 minutes on each side. Place the turkey on a plate.

Add the broth, onions, garlic, carrots, celery, mushrooms, sun-dried tomatoes, tomatoes and rosemary to the skillet. Cook and stir for 5 minutes. Add the turkey and cover. Reduce the heat to medium; cook for 20 minutes, or until the turkey is no longer pink in the center.

Preparation time: 10 minutes
Cooking time: 30 minutes

Per serving: 203 calories, 4 g. fat (17% of calories), 2.8 g. dietary fiber, 44 mg. cholesterol, 201 mg. sodium.

POULTRY WITH PIZZAZZ

> *Grilled Raspberry Turkey Breasts*
> *Broccoli Slaw*
> *Steamed Carrots*

*R*aspberry sauce makes turkey taste rich and satisfying. You can pop these turkey breasts in the marinade in the morning before work and grill them before dinner. Add packaged broccoli slaw and steamed baby carrots for color and vitamins.

GAME PLAN

1. Marinate the turkey.
2. Make the slaw.
3. Steam peeled baby carrots; toss them with honey and lemon juice.
4. Grill the turkey.

GRILLED RASPBERRY TURKEY BREASTS

SERVES 4

> 1   *cup raspberry vinegar*
> ½   *cup frozen unsweetened raspberries*
> 2   *cloves garlic, minced*
> 2   *teaspoons grated fresh ginger*
> 1   *tablespoon reduced-sodium soy sauce*
> 1   *large boneless skinless turkey breast half, quartered*

In a resealable plastic storage bag, combine the vinegar, raspberries, garlic, ginger, soy sauce and turkey. Shake well. Refrigerate for 15 minutes or up to 24 hours, turning occasionally.

Preheat the grill. While the grill is heating, strain the marinade into a medium saucepan by pressing through a strainer with rubber spatula; place it over high heat. Cook and stir until the marinade is reduced to ⅓ cup. Remove from the heat; set aside.

Wrap the turkey in foil; place it on the grill. Cook for 20 minutes, then unwrap and place it directly on the grill. Cook for 5 minutes, turning once, or until brown, basting with the reduced marinade. Transfer to a serving platter and top with the remaining reduced marinade.

Preparation time: 5 minutes
Cooking time: 25 minutes
Marinating time: 15 minutes

Per serving: 125 calories, 2.5 g. fat (18% of calories), 0.7 g. dietary fiber, 44 mg. cholesterol, 172 mg. sodium.

BROCCOLI SLAW

SERVES 4

1 *package (1 pound) shredded broccoli slaw*
¼ *cup chopped fresh parsley*
¼ *cup rice vinegar*
2 *tablespoons reduced-sodium soy sauce*
2 *teaspoons dark sesame oil*
¼ *teaspoon crushed red pepper flakes*

In a large bowl, combine the broccoli slaw, parsley, vinegar, soy sauce, oil and red pepper flakes. Toss well.

Preparation time: 5 minutes

Per serving: 58 calories, 2.6 g. fat (34% of calories), 3.4 g. dietary fiber, no cholesterol, 296 mg. sodium.

CHAPTER 7

LIGHT AND
LEAN MEATS

FAST-FIXING BEEF AND PORK DINNERS

Today's beef and pork are leaner, lighter, lower in fat and fit better into healthy weeknight meals. Done right, beef and pork can add iron, B_{12} and high-quality protein to your meals without going overboard on fat. Plus, most thin-sliced steaks or chops cook in under 10 minutes while you prepare a side dish or salad.

Remember to trim away excess fat—even from leaner cuts. To enhance flavor and juiciness, simply marinate the meat in the fridge overnight or during the day while you're at work. Then it's ready to cook when you need it. What could be easier?

EASY ASIAN GRILL

Grilled Marinated Flank Steak
Asian Vegetable Sauté
Quick-Cooking Brown Rice

One of the leanest cuts, flank steak is often over-looked in menus because it can be tough. This recipe keeps it moist and tender by marinating it and cooking it very quickly on the grill. To save time, marinate the steak overnight or during the day while you're at work.

GAME PLAN

1. Marinate the steak.
2. Cook brown rice according to package directions.
3. Make the vegetable sauté.
4. Grill the steak.

GRILLED MARINATED FLANK STEAK

SERVES 4

  1 *pound lean flank steak*
  ¼ *cup lemon juice*
  ¼ *cup reduced-sodium soy sauce*
  1 *teaspoon minced garlic*
  1 *teaspoon grated fresh ginger*
  1 *teaspoon chopped jalapeño peppers (wear plastic gloves when handling)*

In a resealable plastic storage bag, combine the steak, lemon juice, soy sauce, garlic, ginger and peppers. Shake well. Refrigerate for 25 minutes or up to 24 hours, turning occasionally.

Preheat the grill. Grill the steak for 7 minutes on each side, or until done, basting frequently with the marinade. Cut the steak diagonally across the grain into thin slices.

Preparation time: 5 minutes
Cooking time: 14 minutes
Marinating time: 25 minutes

Per serving: 218 calories, 8.2 g. fat (35% of calories), 0.1 g. dietary fiber, 50 mg. cholesterol, 589 mg. sodium.

ASIAN VEGETABLE SAUTÉ

SERVES 4

2 teaspoons olive oil
1 package (16 ounces) Asian stir-fry vegetables
1 cup whole snow peas, trimmed
1 can (15 ounces) whole baby corn, drained
¼ cup defatted chicken broth
1 teaspoon dark sesame oil
2 tablespoons reduced-sodium soy sauce
1 teaspoon grated fresh ginger
1 teaspoon cornstarch

Heat the oil in a wok or 10″ no-stick skillet over medium-high heat. Add the stir-fry vegetables; cook and stir for 2 minutes. Add the snow peas and corn; cook and stir for 2 minutes.

In a small bowl, combine the broth, oil, soy sauce, ginger and cornstarch. Add to the wok. Cook and stir for 1 minute, or until the sauce thickens.

Preparation time: 10 minutes
Cooking time: 5 minutes

Chef's note: Packaged Asian vegetable mixes are found in your supermarket's produce section; you can make your own with sliced bok choy, Chinese cabbage and snow peas.

Per serving: 176 calories, 4.2 g. fat (20% of calories), 6 g. dietary fiber, no cholesterol, 599 mg. sodium.

No-Fuss Pepper Steak

Pepper Steak
Thousand Island Salad
French Bread

$\mathcal{T}$hinly sliced flank steak combines with fast micro-waved red potatoes, green peppers and savory seasonings for a lean one-skillet dish that's a real crowd-pleaser. Our low-fat version of popular Thousand Island salad pairs well with the steak.

Game Plan

1. Marinate the steak.
2. Make the salad.
3. Make the pepper steak.
4. Heat the French bread.

Pepper Steak

Serves 4

1	*pound flank steak, thinly sliced across the grain*
2	*cloves garlic, minced*
1	*tablespoon ground black pepper*
½–1	*teaspoon salt*
4	*red potatoes, cut into ¼" slices*
½	*cup defatted chicken broth*
1	*large onion, thinly sliced*
1	*large green pepper, thinly sliced*
1	*tablespoon olive oil*

In a resealable plastic storage bag, combine the steak, garlic, pepper and salt. Shake well. Refrigerate for 20 minutes, turning occasionally.

Place the potato slices in a paper-towel-lined microwaveable dish and microwave on high power for 10 minutes, or until tender.

Meanwhile, in a 10″ no-stick skillet over medium-high heat, heat ¼ cup of the broth. Add the onions and green peppers. Cook and stir for 10 minutes, or until the onions are soft. Add the potatoes and oil. Cook and stir for 5 to 8 minutes, or until the vegetables begin to brown. Remove the vegetables to a side plate; cover to keep warm.

Add the remaining ¼ cup of broth to the skillet; cook and stir for 1 minute, scraping to loosen any browned bits. Add the beef mixture; cook and stir for 3 to 5 minutes, or until the meat is browned. Add the vegetables; cook and stir for 1 minute.

Preparation time: 5 minutes
Cooking time: 23 minutes
Marinating time: 20 minutes

Per serving: 385 calories, 11.8 g. fat (28% of calories), 4.3 g. dietary fiber, 50 mg. cholesterol, 370 mg. sodium.

THOUSAND ISLAND SALAD

SERVES 4

2½ *tablespoons low-fat mayonnaise*
1 *tablespoon sweet-pickle relish*
1 *tablespoon ketchup*
2 *teaspoons balsamic vinegar*
5 *cups chopped romaine lettuce*
1 *cup shredded carrots*
1 *cup chopped cucumbers*
1 *cup diced sweet red peppers*

In a large salad bowl, whisk together the mayonnaise, relish, ketchup and vinegar. Add the lettuce, carrots, cucumbers and peppers. Toss well.

Preparation time: 15 minutes

Per serving: 83 calories, 2.9 g. fat (29% of calories), 3.2 g. dietary fiber, 3 mg. cholesterol, 107 mg. sodium.

Mom's Meat Loaf in No Time

Easy BBQ Meat Loaf
Smashed Potatoes
Green Peas and Carrots

Who'd ever have thought meat loaf could be this lean, this tasty and ready in less than 45 minutes? We make two loaves (so they cook faster) and use rolled oats to keep the meat moist. Oven baking glazes the loaves; microwaving finishes the cooking. Serve the meat loaf with cheese-spiked potatoes and peas and carrots for a real down-home dinner.

GAME PLAN

1. Make the meat loaf.
2. Make the potatoes.
3. Steam fresh or frozen green peas and carrots; toss them with lemon juice.

EASY BBQ MEAT LOAF

SERVES 4

2	tablespoons Dijon mustard
4½	teaspoons honey
½	teaspoon minced garlic
3	tablespoons tomato puree
¼	cup rolled oats
4½	teaspoons tomato paste
⅛–¼	teaspoon dried thyme
⅛–¼	teaspoon dried oregano
8	ounces extra-lean ground beef

4   ounces ground turkey

2   tablespoons reduced-sodium barbecue sauce

Preheat the oven to 350°. In a large bowl, mix together the mustard, honey, garlic, tomato puree, oats, tomato paste, thyme, oregano, ground beef and turkey. Form into 2 equal loaves and place in an ungreased microwaveable and ovenproof casserole. Brush the tops of the loaves with the barbecue sauce.

Bake for 30 minutes. Transfer to the microwave and cook on high power for 10 minutes, or until the loaves are no longer pink in the center. Slice before serving.

Preparation time: 5 minutes
Cooking time: 40 minutes

Per serving: 233 calories, 11.6 g. fat (45% of calories), 1.1 g. dietary fiber, 52 mg. cholesterol, 278 mg. sodium.

SMASHED POTATOES

SERVES 4

2   *pounds baking potatoes, peeled and cubed*

¼   *cup skim milk*

1   *teaspoon chopped jalapeño peppers (wear plastic gloves when handling)*

¾   *ounce shredded low-fat Monterey Jack cheese*

2   *tablespoons chopped green onions*

Place the potatoes in a medium saucepan; cover with water and bring to a boil. Cover and simmer for 20 minutes, or until the potatoes are very soft.

Drain the potatoes; return them to the saucepan. Mash the potatoes lightly with a fork or potato masher. Add the milk, peppers, Monterey Jack and green onions. Mix well.

Preparation time: 5 minutes
Cooking time: 20 minutes

Per serving: 241 calories, 1.2 g. fat (4% of calories), 0.1 g. dietary fiber, 4 mg. cholesterol, 72 mg. sodium.

JAZZY BURGER DINNER

Spicy Beef Burgers
Low-Fat Waldorf Salad
Tomatoes, Cucumbers, Pickles
and Lettuce

This menu will become a family favorite for summer-time barbecuing because it's fast and easy on the grill. The burgers are spiked with hot peppers and chili powder; adjust the spiciness to your taste. Apples, celery and grapes combine in a light Waldorf salad made with low-fat yogurt dressing to cool off the burgers' heat.

GAME PLAN

1. Make the burgers.
2. Make the salad.
3. Slice tomatoes and cucumbers; arrange them on a platter with lettuce leaves and sweet and dill pickles.

SPICY BEEF BURGERS

SERVES 4

- 1 *pound extra-lean ground round*
- 2 *tablespoons reduced-sodium low-fat barbecue sauce*
- 1 *tablespoon reduced-sodium low-fat steak sauce*
- 1 *tablespoon minced garlic*
- 1 *tablespoon chopped jalapeño peppers (wear plastic gloves when handling)*
- 1 *teaspoon chili powder*
- 4 *whole-wheat hamburger buns*
- 1 *tablespoon nonfat mayonnaise*

Preheat the grill. In a medium bowl, mix the beef, barbecue sauce, steak sauce, garlic, peppers and chili powder. Form into 4 patties. Grill the patties for 6 to 8 minutes, or until done, turning once.

Toast the hamburger buns; spread with the mayonnaise. Arrange the burgers on the buns.

Preparation time: 5 minutes
Cooking time: 8 minutes

Per serving: 261 calories, 6.7 g. fat (23% of calories), 0.3 g. dietary fiber, 55 mg. cholesterol, 400 mg. sodium.

LOW-FAT WALDORF SALAD

SERVES 4

1½	cups chopped red apples
½	cup chopped celery
½	cup halved seedless green grapes
¼	cup raisins
3	cups torn romaine lettuce
¼	cup low-fat mayonnaise
¼	cup nonfat plain yogurt
1	teaspoon honey or sugar
1	tablespoon lemon juice
	Salt and ground black pepper

In a large salad bowl, combine the apples, celery, grapes, raisins and lettuce; toss well.

In a small bowl, whisk together the mayonnaise, yogurt, honey or sugar and lemon juice. Add salt and pepper to taste. Pour over the salad; toss well.

Preparation time: 10 minutes

Per serving: 129 calories, 4.4 g. fat (29% of calories), 2.5 g. dietary fiber, 5 mg. cholesterol, 44 mg. sodium.

TEXAS TACO TIME

Texas Beef Soft Tacos
Sweet Potato Salad
Collard Greens and Black-Eyed Peas

This menu will give you an honorary Texas Ranger badge. By using soft tortillas around the shredded barbecued beef, we eliminate the fat of frying. Sweet and white potatoes combine in a quick salad dressed with a tangy dill sauce.

GAME PLAN

1. Make the salad.
2. Make the tacos.
3. Sauté chopped collard greens and cooked black-eyed peas in defatted chicken broth; season with salt and ground pepper.

TEXAS BEEF SOFT TACOS

SERVES 4

12   *ounces beef tenderloin, trimmed of fat*
1½ *teaspoons ground cumin*
¼   *cup defatted chicken broth*
1   *cup chopped sweet red peppers*
3   *cloves garlic, minced*
2   *canned chipotle chilies in adobo sauce, seeded and minced (wear plastic gloves when handling)*
½   *cup reduced-sodium mild salsa*
8   *(8") low-fat flour tortillas*
3   *ounces shredded low-fat Monterey Jack cheese*
¼   *cup nonfat sour cream*
¼   *cup chopped fresh cilantro*

Cut the beef into very thin strips. In a resealable plastic storage bag, combine the beef and cumin; shake well. Refrigerate.

In a 10″ no-stick skillet over medium-high heat, bring the broth to a boil. Add the red peppers and garlic; cook and stir for 3 minutes. Transfer to a side plate. Add the beef mixture; cook and stir for 5 minutes, or until cooked through. Add the red pepper mixture, chilies and salsa. Cook and stir for 2 minutes.

Wrap the tortillas in plastic wrap and microwave on high power for 1 minute. Divide the beef between the tortillas; top with the Monterey Jack, sour cream and cilantro. Roll up.

Preparation time: 15 minutes
Cooking time: 10 minutes

Per serving: 372 calories, 9.8 g. fat (22% of calories), 12.1 g. dietary fiber, 60 mg. cholesterol, 942 mg. sodium.

SWEET POTATO SALAD

SERVES 4

2	*large sweet potatoes, peeled and cubed*
6	*medium red potatoes, cubed*
½	*cup plain nonfat yogurt*
1	*teaspoon chopped fresh dill*
1	*tablespoon low-fat mayonnaise*
1	*teaspoon honey mustard*
	Salt and ground black pepper
2	*tablespoons chopped fresh parsley*

Place the sweet potatoes and red potatoes on a paper-towel-covered microwaveable plate. Microwave on high power for 15 minutes, or until soft, turning once.

In a large salad bowl, whisk together the yogurt, dill, mayonnaise and mustard. Add the potatoes and toss well. Add salt and pepper to taste. Sprinkle with the parsley.

Preparation time: 5 minutes
Cooking time: 15 minutes

Per serving: 338 calories, 1.4 g. fat (4% of calories), 1.7 g. dietary fiber, 2 mg. cholesterol, 59 mg. sodium.

15 Fast Marinades

Any of these combos is great for marinating lean cuts of beef or pork. Start the meat marinating in the morning and refrigerate it all day; the spices and seasonings will tenderize it as they increase the flavor—plus there will be less prep at dinner time. Then grill, broil or sauté for dinner in a jiffy.

Simply place the marinade in a resealable plastic storage bag, add the beef or pork and shake well. Refrigerate at least 30 minutes or up to 24 hours, turning occasionally.

- **Key West:** Lime juice, chilies and ground cumin

- **Italian:** Tomato sauce, fresh basil and fresh ground pepper

- **Mediterranean:** Onions, garlic, tomatoes and oregano

- **Indian:** Curry powder, nonfat plain yogurt and onions

- **Middle Eastern:** Nonfat plain yogurt, garlic and a small amount of tahini

- **Asian:** Green onions, garlic and a small amount of dark sesame oil

- **Greek:** Thyme, rosemary, garlic and a small amount of olive oil

- **Tuscan:** Balsamic vinegar and fresh basil, tarragon and oregano

- **Thai:** Lemon juice, curry powder and garlic

- **Tex-Mex:** Chipotle chilies in adobo sauce and tomato purée

- **Caribbean:** Chopped papaya, lime juice, lime rind and salt

- **Provençal:** Roasted red peppers, lemon juice and garlic

- **Kansas City:** Tomato juice, lemon juice and thyme

- **Chicago:** Spaghetti sauce and fresh basil

- **Vietnamese:** Fresh cilantro, garlic and lemon juice

GERMAN-STYLE PORK DINNER

Mustardy Broiled Pork Tenderloins
Sweet and Sour Cabbage Sauté
Boiled Parsley Potatoes

Pork tenderloin is quick to prepare when cooked in a skillet or broiled. In this menu it is broiled with a honey mustard glaze that perfectly complements the tangy cabbage side dish.

GAME PLAN

1. Marinate the pork tenderloin.
2. Boil the potatoes; toss them with parsley and a tiny amount of olive oil.
3. Cook the cabbage.
4. Cook the pork medallions.

MUSTARDY BROILED PORK TENDERLOINS

SERVES 4

1 pound pork tenderloin, trimmed of fat and cut into ¾" medallions

2 cloves garlic, minced

¾ cup apple cider

¼ cup honey mustard

1 teaspoon cornstarch

In a resealable plastic storage bag, combine the pork, garlic, cider and mustard; shake well. Refrigerate for 30 minutes or up to 24 hours, turning frequently.

Preheat the broiler. Drain the pork, reserving the marinade. Place the pork on a foil-lined broiler pan. Broil for 3 to 5 minutes on each side, or until the pork is no longer pink in the center.

Pour the marinade into a saucepan and bring it to a boil. Cook rapidly until the marinade is reduced to ½ cup. Pour over the pork medallions and serve.

Preparation time: 5 minutes
Cooking time: 10 minutes
Marinating time: 30 minutes

Per serving: 204 calories, 4.5 g. fat (20% of calories), 0.2 g. dietary fiber, 65 mg. cholesterol, 149 mg. sodium.

SWEET AND SOUR CABBAGE SAUTÉ

SERVES 4

⅓ *cup defatted chicken broth*
⅓ *cup sliced green onions*
2 *cloves garlic, minced*
5 *cups thinly sliced red cabbage*
2–3 *tablespoons brown sugar or maple syrup*
¼ *cup balsamic vinegar*
¼ *cup water*
¼ *cup dried cranberries (craisins) or currants*

In a 10″ no-stick skillet, heat the broth over medium-high heat. When the broth is hot, add the green onions, garlic and red cabbage. Cover and cook for 5 minutes, stirring frequently.

Add the brown sugar or maple syrup, vinegar, water and cranberries or currants. Cover and cook for 15 minutes, or until all the liquid has evaporated and the cabbage is soft. Add more brown sugar or maple syrup to taste, if desired.

Preparation time: 10 minutes
Cooking time: 25 minutes

Per serving: 77 calories, 0.3 g. fat (3% of calories), 2.5 g. dietary fiber, no cholesterol, 43 mg. sodium.

PORK CHOPS IN A FLASH

> *Stuffed Pork Loin Chops*
> *Glazed Honey Carrots*
> *Steamed Green Beans*
> *Cranberry Sauce*

*A*s tasty as a slow-cooked pork roast but done in a fraction of the time, these stuffed pork chops will satisfy the heartiest appetite. Round out our harvest menu with glazed carrots, green beans and cranberry sauce.

GAME PLAN

1. Cook the pork chops.
2. Cook the carrots.
3. Steam green beans; toss them with lemon juice.
4. Make the sauce for the pork chops.

STUFFED PORK LOIN CHOPS

SERVES 4

4	*thick-cut pork loin chops, trimmed of fat*
1½	*cups dry cornbread stuffing*
1	*teaspoon poultry seasoning*
¼	*cup minced onions*
2–2½	*cups defatted chicken broth*
2	*tablespoons balsamic vinegar*
1	*teaspoon cornstarch*
1	*tablespoon water*

Cut a slit in the side of each chop to form a pocket. In a small bowl, mix together the stuffing, poultry seasoning, onions and ½ to 1 cup of the broth, or enough to create a moist stuffing. Pack the stuffing into the pockets; seal the pockets shut with wooden toothpicks, if necessary.

Coat a 10″ no-stick skillet with no-stick cooking spray; set it over medium-high heat. When the pan is hot, add the stuffed pork chops. Brown for 2 to 3 minutes, then carefully turn and brown the other side. Add 1 cup of the broth. Reduce the heat to low; cover and cook for 25 minutes, or until the pork is tender and cooked through.

Place the chops on a serving platter; cover to keep warm. Add the remaining ½ cup of broth and balsamic vinegar. Bring to a boil. In a small bowl, mix the cornstarch and water; add to the pan. Cook and stir until the gravy has thickened; pour over the pork chops.

Preparation time: 10 minutes
Cooking time: 35 minutes

Per serving: 272 calories, 11.2 g. fat (38% of calories), 0.2 g. dietary fiber, 54 mg. cholesterol, 368 mg. sodium.

GLAZED HONEY CARROTS

SERVES 4

1 cup orange juice
1 pound peeled baby carrots
1 tablespoon balsamic vinegar
1 tablespoon honey

Heat the orange juice in a 10″ no-stick skillet over medium-high heat. Add the carrots; cover and cook for 10 minutes, or until the carrots are tender. Push the carrots to the side of the skillet; add the vinegar and honey. Cook and stir for 1 minute; toss with the carrots.

Preparation time: 3 minutes
Cooking time: 15 minutes

Per serving: 72 calories, 0.1 g. fat (1% of calories), 3.2 g. dietary fiber, no cholesterol, 101 mg. sodium.

WHISTLIN' DIXIE DINNER

Cajun Pork Loin Chops
Southern Pineapple Slaw
Sugar Snap Peas

Orange marmalade and Cajun spices flavor these lean and fast-cooking pork chops. Add a tangy pineapple coleslaw and fresh peas, and you'll start whistling *Dixie*. Nonfat yogurt cools down the slaw and cuts the fat.

GAME PLAN

1. Marinate the pork chops.
2. Make the slaw.
3. Cook the pork chops.
4. Steam sugar snap peas; toss them with a tiny amount of olive oil.

CAJUN PORK LOIN CHOPS

SERVES 4

- 4 pork loin chops, trimmed of fat
- ¼ cup low-sugar orange marmalade
- 2 tablespoons lime juice
- 1 tablespoon Cajun spice mix (see note)
- 1 teaspoon chopped jalapeño peppers (wear plastic gloves when handling)

In a resealable plastic storage bag, combine the chops, marmalade, lime juice, Cajun spices and peppers. Shake well. Refrigerate for 30 minutes or up to 24 hours, turning occasionally.

Preheat the grill. Grill the chops for 5 minutes on each side, or until the pork is no longer pink in the center, basting with the marinade.

Preparation time: 5 minutes
Cooking time: 10 minutes
Marinating time: 30 minutes

Chef's note: To make 1 tablespoon of Cajun spice mix, combine 1 teaspoon ground red pepper, 1 teaspoon ground black pepper, ½ teaspoon ground white pepper and ½ teaspoon salt.

Per serving: 255 calories, 10.7 g. fat (38% of calories), 1 g. dietary fiber, 54 mg. cholesterol, 205 mg. sodium.

SOUTHERN PINEAPPLE SLAW

SERVES 4

1 *package (16 ounces) carrot-and-cabbage coleslaw*
1 *can (8 ounces) unsweetened crushed pineapple, drained*
1 *tablespoon currants or raisins*
⅓ *cup nonfat plain yogurt*
1 *tablespoon lime juice*
⅓ *cup low-fat mayonnaise*
1 *teaspoon brown sugar*
   Salt and ground black pepper

In a large salad bowl, combine the coleslaw with the pineapple and currants or raisins. In a small bowl, stir together the yogurt, lime juice, mayonnaise and brown sugar. Pour over the coleslaw; toss well. Add salt and pepper to taste.

Preparation time: 5 minutes

Per serving: 127 calories, 5.4 g. fat (35% of calories), 2.7 g. dietary fiber, 7 mg. cholesterol, 65 mg. sodium.

CALYPSO CHOPS

Caribbean Pork Chops
Island Rice
Sliced Banana, Mango and
Pineapple Platter

*O*range, papaya, garlic and red onions create a piquant yet lean sauce for these skillet-seared pork loin chops.

GAME PLAN

1. Marinate the pork chops.
2. Make the rice.
3. Slice bananas, mangoes and pineapple; arrange them on a plate.
4. Cook the pork chops.

CARIBBEAN PORK CHOPS

SERVES 4

4 *pork loin chops, trimmed of fat*
1 *teaspoon chopped garlic*
¼ *cup orange juice*
¼ *cup papaya nectar*
¼ *cup thinly sliced red onions*
2 *tablespoons water*
2 *tablespoons chopped fresh cilantro*
1 *teaspoon cornstarch*

In a resealable plastic storage bag, combine the pork chops, garlic, orange juice and papaya nectar. Shake well. Refrigerate for 30 minutes, turning occasionally.

Coat a 10″ no-stick skillet with olive oil no-stick cooking spray and set over medium-high heat until hot. Add the onions and water; cook and stir for 2 minutes. Drain the pork chops, reserving the marinade. Add the pork chops; cook for 4 minutes on each side, or until no longer pink in the center.

Stir the cilantro and cornstarch into the marinade; add to the skillet. Cook and stir for 3 minutes, or until the sauce is thick.

Preparation time: 5 minutes
Cooking time: 10 minutes
Marinating time: 30 minutes

Per serving: 225 calories, 10.8 g. fat (44% of calories), 0.3 g. dietary fiber, 54 mg. cholesterol, 57 mg. sodium.

ISLAND RICE

SERVES 4

  2 teaspoons oil
 ½ large ripe plantain, cut into ¼″ slices
 ¼ cup defatted chicken broth
 ¼ cup chopped green onions
  1 cup diced sweet red peppers
  1 teaspoon minced garlic
 ¼ teaspoon crushed red pepper flakes
  4 cups cooked basmati or brown rice
 ¼ cup chopped roasted peanuts

Heat the oil in a 10″ no-stick skillet over medium-high heat. When the oil is hot, add the plantain; cook and stir for 2 to 3 minutes, or until brown and slightly soft. Transfer the plantain to a plate and cover to keep warm.

Add the broth to the pan; bring to a boil, scraping to loosen any browned bits. Add the green onions, peppers, garlic and red pepper flakes. Cook and stir for 1 minute. Add the rice; cook and stir for 5 minutes, or until the rice is lightly browned. Add the plantain and peanuts; heat through.

Preparation time: 5 minutes
Cooking time: 10 minutes

Per serving: 325 calories, 8.4 g. fat (22% of calories), 2.3 g. dietary fiber, no cholesterol, 137 mg. sodium.

Texas Barbecue Dinner

> *Pork BBQ Sandwiches*
> *Oven-Fried Pepper-Dusted*
> *Potato Wedges*
> *Broccoli Slaw*

These hearty sandwiches and steak fries take you back to a Texas barbecue—without the all-day cooking of the barbecue pit. Chipotle chilies (smoked jalapeño peppers) give lean pork tenderloin just the right amount of smoky flavor.

GAME PLAN

1. Marinate the pork.
2. Prepare the potatoes.
3. Make coleslaw from packaged shredded broccoli slaw. Add low-fat coleslaw dressing.
4. Grill the pork and assemble the sandwiches.

PORK BBQ SANDWICHES

SERVES 4

1 pound boneless pork tenderloin, cut into 4 slices
1 tablespoon chopped chipotle chilies in adobo sauce
1 cup plus 1 tablespoon reduced-sodium barbecue sauce
4 hamburger buns or Kaiser rolls, split

In a resealable plastic storage bag, combine the pork, chilies and 1 cup barbecue sauce. Refrigerate for 30 minutes, turning occasionally.

Preheat the grill. Toast the hamburger buns and spread the cut sides with 1 tablespoon barbecue sauce. Set aside.

Grill the pork for 5 minutes on each side, or until slightly charred and no longer pink in the center. Thinly slice and pile onto the hamburger buns.

Preparation time: 5 minutes
Cooking time: 10 minutes
Marinating time: 30 minutes

Per serving: 345 calories, 10.4 g. fat (26% of calories), 0.1 g. dietary fiber, 87 mg. cholesterol, 532 mg. sodium.

OVEN-FRIED PEPPER-DUSTED POTATO WEDGES

SERVES 4

4 *large baking potatoes*
Ground red pepper
Salt and ground black pepper

Pierce each potato several times with a fork; place on a paper-towel-lined microwaveable plate. Microwave on high power for 8 minutes, or until the potatoes are soft. Let cool.

Preheat the oven to 475°. Cut each potato into 8 wedges and place on a no-stick baking sheet. Coat each potato with olive oil no-stick cooking spray; lightly sprinkle with ground red pepper, salt and pepper. Bake for 20 minutes, or until the potatoes are crisp and brown.

Preparation time: 10 minutes
Cooking time: 28 minutes

Per serving: 220 calories, 0.2 g. fat (1% of calories), no dietary fiber, no cholesterol, 16 mg. sodium.

CHAPTER 8

FRESH, SIMPLE
AND FULL
OF FLAVOR

No-FUSS FISH AND SEAFOOD DINNERS

ish and shellfish bring a wealth of flavor and high-value

nutrition to weeknight menus. Yet many cooks avoid fish

because it seems too complicated to cook. So what's the secret to

successful fish dinners? Cook 'em fast. Most fish cooks a little

extra on its way to the table, so chefs in the know slightly under-

cook it to have perfectly done fish when it reaches your plate.

Try these simple recipes to harvest the fruits of the sea.

SPEEDY SWORDFISH

Swordfish with Lime-Soy Marinade
Asian Sesame Coleslaw
Steamed Broccoli
French Bread

Fresh fish couldn't be easier or faster to cook with this three-ingredient marinade. While the swordfish steaks marinate, make the accompanying tangy slaw—it gets its secret richness from a tiny amount of dark sesame oil.

GAME PLAN

1. Marinate the fish.
2. Make the coleslaw.
3. Steam the broccoli; toss it with balsamic vinegar.
4. Warm the French bread.
5. Grill the fish.

SWORDFISH WITH LIME-SOY MARINADE

SERVES 4

  4 *swordfish steaks*
 ¼ *cup reduced-sodium soy sauce*
  1 *tablespoon grated fresh ginger*
 ⅓ *cup lime juice*
     Lime slices

In a resealable plastic storage bag, combine the swordfish, soy sauce, ginger and lime juice. Refrigerate for 25 minutes or up to 24 hours, turning occasionally.

Coat the grill with no-stick cooking spray; preheat the grill. Place the swordfish steaks on the grill and pour the marinade into a 10″ no-stick skillet. Grill the fish for 10 to 14 minutes, or until it flakes when pressed lightly with a fork, turning once.

Meanwhile, boil the marinade over high heat for 2 to 3 minutes, or until it is reduced to ¼ cup. Drizzle it over the swordfish. Garnish with lime slices.

Preparation time: 5 minutes
Cooking time: 14 minutes
Marinating time: 25 minutes

Per serving: 154 calories, 4.6 g. fat (28% of calories), no dietary fiber, 45 mg. cholesterol, 630 mg. sodium.

ASIAN SESAME COLESLAW

SERVES 4

3   cups shredded carrot-and-cabbage coleslaw
1   can (11 ounces) mandarin oranges, drained
¼   cup rice vinegar
1–2   tablespoons honey
2   teaspoons reduced-sodium soy sauce
1   teaspoon dark sesame oil

In a large bowl, combine the coleslaw, oranges, vinegar, 1 tablespoon of the honey, soy sauce and oil. Toss well. Let the salad marinate for 10 minutes at room temperature. Add more honey to taste, if desired.

Preparation time: 5 minutes
Marinating time: 10 minutes

Per serving: 66 calories, 1.2 g. fat (14% of calories), 1 g. dietary fiber, no cholesterol, 102 mg. sodium.

SOLE FOOD

*L*emon and Mediterranean herbs like thyme and bay permeate this simple yet elegant menu. The thin fillets of sole cook in less than 10 minutes on sizzle plates or in a skillet.

GAME PLAN

1. Cook the orzo. Toss it with a tiny amount of olive oil and chopped fresh herbs.
2. Start the fish.
3. Make the asparagus.

POACHED SOLE WITH HERBS

SERVES 4

4	*fillets of sole*
½	*cup dry white wine or fish stock*
	Juice of 1 lemon
2	*shallots, thinly sliced*
4	*bay leaves*
2	*teaspoons dried thyme*
1	*tablespoon olive oil*

Preheat the oven to 450°. Wash the fish and pat dry with paper towels. Place on two sizzle plates. Sprinkle with the wine or stock and lemon juice; arrange the shallots, bay leaves and thyme on top. Drizzle with the oil.

Cover the sizzle plates with foil, crimping the edges tightly. With a knife, puncture a steam vent in each piece of foil. Place the sizzle plates over high heat on the stovetop until you can see steam coming out of the top. Transfer them to the oven. Bake for 5 minutes, or until the fish flakes easily when lightly pressed with a fork. Remove the bay leaves.

Preparation time: 5 minutes
Cooking time: 8 minutes

Chef's note: The sizzle plate, described on page 27, is a time-saving tool that's gaining popularity in home kitchens. If you don't have sizzle plates on hand, cook this recipe in a skillet. Place all ingredients in a 10″ no-stick skillet; cover and cook over medium-high heat for 5 minutes, or until the fish flakes easily when lightly pressed with a fork.

Per serving: 162 calories, 4.8 g. fat (27% of calories), no dietary fiber, 60 mg. cholesterol, 95 mg. sodium.

CITRUS-STEAMED ASPARAGUS

SERVES 4

1   *pound fresh asparagus*
1   *teaspoon olive oil*
3   *tablespoons finely minced red onions*
6   *tablespoons defatted chicken broth*
1   *teaspoon lemon juice*
1   *tablespoon orange juice*
½   *teaspoon grated lemon rind*
    Salt and ground black pepper

Trim any tough ends from the asparagus. In a 10″ no-stick skillet, combine the asparagus, oil, onions, broth, lemon juice, orange juice and lemon rind; cover. Bring to a boil over medium-high heat; cook for 3 minutes, or until the asparagus is tender. Add salt and pepper to taste.

Preparation time: 5 minutes
Cooking time: 5 minutes

Per serving: 42 calories, 1.5 g. fat (27% of calories), 0.2 g. dietary fiber, no cholesterol, 44 mg. sodium.

FRENCH DINNER

Baked Stuffed Sole
Oven-Roasted Red Potatoes
Steamed Baby Carrots

A French dinner like this used to take hours, but with the food processor this elegant baked sole is ready in less than 30 minutes. The slender fillets are stuffed with an easy shrimp filling, then baked. Bake the red potatoes alongside. Voilà!

GAME PLAN

1. Make the sole.
2. Make the potatoes.
3. Steam baby carrots; toss them with lemon juice and parsley.

BAKED STUFFED SOLE

SERVES 4

6	ounces cooked baby shrimp
¼	cup evaporated skim milk
1	egg white
½–1	teaspoon minced garlic
½	teaspoon lemon juice
4	fillets of sole
¼	teaspoon salt
½	teaspoon ground black pepper
	Pinch of ground nutmeg
	Pinch of ground red pepper

½   cup minced green onions

1   teaspoon prepared pesto

2   cups sliced mushrooms

¼   cup white wine or apple juice

¼   cup fish stock or water

3   tablespoons shredded low-fat cheese (such as mozzarella)

Preheat the oven to 350°. Wash the fish and pat it dry with paper towels.

In a blender or food processor, combine the shrimp, skim milk, egg white, garlic, lemon juice, salt, pepper, red pepper and nutmeg. Puree to a thick paste. Stir in ¼ cup of the green onions and the pesto. Set aside.

In an ovenproof skillet, combine the mushrooms, wine or apple juice and remaining ¼ cup of green onions; bring to a boil over medium-high heat. Cook and stir for 1 minute; remove from the heat.

Spread each fillet of sole with a fourth of the shrimp paste. Fold the fillet in half to enclose the filling. Place the stuffed fillets on top of the mushrooms in the ovenproof skillet. Add the fish stock or water and the cheese. Cover and bring to a boil over medium-high heat. Transfer to the oven; bake for 10 to 12 minutes, or until the fish flakes easily when lightly pressed with a fork. Serve the sauce over the fish.

Preparation time: 10 minutes
Cooking time: 15 minutes

Per serving: 219 calories, 3.8 g. fat (16% of calories), 0.8 g. dietary fiber, 130 mg. cholesterol, 412 mg. sodium.

OVEN-ROASTED RED POTATOES

SERVES 4

 8 small red potatoes
 1 tablespoon olive oil
    Salt and ground black pepper
 ¼ cup chopped fresh chives or parsley

Pierce the potatoes with a knife tip; place them on a paper-towel-lined microwaveable plate. Microwave on high power for 15 minutes, or until tender.

Preheat the oven to 350°. Quarter the potatoes; place them on a baking sheet covered with foil. Drizzle with the oil and sprinkle with salt and pepper. Bake for 15 minutes, or until lightly browned. Toss with the chives or parsley.

Preparation time: 5 minutes
Cooking time: 30 minutes

Per serving: 362 calories, 3.7 g. fat (9% of calories), no dietary fiber, no cholesterol, 24 mg. sodium.

CATCH OF THE DAY: HOW TO SELECT THE BEST FISH

First step to creating successful fish dishes? Make sure your fish is fresh or fresh frozen. Fresh fish lasts about 3 days, fresh frozen about 3 months. To see how long your fish has been off the boat, follow these important tips:

Fresh whole fish:
   Bright red color under the gills
   Smooth, shiny scales or skin
   Clear, slightly protruding eyes

Fresh fillets and steaks:
   Firm texture
   Clear, shiny flesh that looks moist and fresh

Fresh frozen fillets and steaks:
   Vacuum-packed or sealed to prevent moisture loss
   Rich color on darker fish; milky white on lighter fish

Easy Island Feast

Sautéed Swordfish with Pepper Relish
Roasted Green Beans
Coleslaw

The delicate flavor of swordfish is enhanced by a mildly spicy sauce—and it all cooks in one pan in less than 10 minutes.

Game Plan

1. Make the green beans.
2. Mix bagged cabbage-and-carrot slaw with low-fat coleslaw dressing.
3. Make the fish.

Sautéed Swordfish with Pepper Relish

serves 4

4   swordfish steaks
   Juice of 2 medium limes
4   cloves garlic, thinly sliced
1   tablespoon Asian fish sauce
1   teaspoon chopped jalapeño peppers (wear plastic gloves when handling)
¾   cup diced papaya
¼   cup diced red onions
¼   cup diced green peppers
2   tablespoons chopped fresh cilantro
   Salt and ground black pepper

Wash the fish and pat it dry with paper towels. Measure 2 tablespoons of the lime juice into a small bowl. Set aside.

In a 10″ no-stick skillet over medium-high heat, combine the swordfish, remaining lime juice, garlic, fish sauce and jalapeño peppers. Cover and cook for 10 minutes, or until the fish flakes easily when lightly pressed with a fork.

In a small bowl, combine the papaya, onions, green peppers, cilantro and reserved 2 tablespoons lime juice. Add salt and pepper to taste. Spoon the relish over the hot fish.

Preparation time: 10 minutes
Cooking time: 10 minutes

Per serving: 167 calories, 4.7 g. fat (26% of calories), 0.7 g. dietary fiber, 45 mg. cholesterol, 339 mg. sodium.

ROASTED GREEN BEANS

SERVES 4

1   *pound fresh green beans*
½   *teaspoon olive oil*
1   *teaspoon balsamic vinegar*
2   *teaspoons minced fresh basil*
     Salt and ground black pepper

Preheat the oven to 500°. In a large bowl, toss together the green beans, oil, vinegar and basil. Place on a no-stick baking sheet in one layer; roast for 10 minutes, or until wilted, stirring once. Add salt and pepper to taste.

Preparation time: 5 minutes
Cooking time: 10 minutes

Per serving: 33 calories, 0.7 g. fat (17% of calories), no dietary fiber, no cholesterol, 13 mg. sodium.

ORIENT EXPRESS

Teriyaki Salmon
Tropical Fruit Salad on Bitter and Sweet
Lettuce
Quick-Cooking Brown Rice

Flavors of the Orient inspire this easy menu. If you can marinate the salmon longer (over the workday is best), it will taste even better.

GAME PLAN

1. Marinate the salmon.
2. Cook the brown rice according to package directions; toss it with chopped fresh parsley.
3. Make the fruit salad.
4. Cook the salmon.

TERIYAKI SALMON

SERVES 4

⅓ cup reduced-sodium soy sauce
2 tablespoons mirin (rice wine) or apple juice
2 tablespoons chopped green onions
2 teaspoons grated fresh ginger
2 tablespoons honey
3 tablespoons lemon juice
4 salmon steaks

In a resealable plastic storage bag, combine the soy sauce, mirin or apple juice, green onions, ginger, honey, lemon juice and salmon. Shake well. Refrigerate for 30 minutes or up to 24 hours, turning occasionally.

Preheat the broiler. Transfer the salmon to a no-stick broiler pan. Place the marinade in a medium saucepan; bring to a boil over medium-high heat. Cook, stirring occasionally, for 8 minutes, or until reduced by half.

Meanwhile, broil the salmon about 4 inches from the heat for 10 to 12 minutes, turning once, or until the fish flakes easily when lightly pressed with a fork. Spoon the reduced marinade over the fish before serving.

Preparation time: 5 minutes
Cooking time: 12 minutes
Marinating time: 30 minutes

Per serving: 183 calories, 3.8 g. fat (19% of calories), 0.1 g. dietary fiber, 58 mg. cholesterol, 779 mg. sodium.

TROPICAL FRUIT SALAD ON BITTER AND SWEET LETTUCE

SERVES 4

¼   *fresh pineapple, cut into chunks*
1   *mango, diced*
½   *large papaya, diced*
½   *cantaloupe, diced*
1   *large seedless orange, chopped*
2   *tablespoons maple syrup*
⅓   *cup fresh orange juice*
¼   *cup chopped fresh mint*
2   *cups mixed leaf lettuce and endive*

In a large bowl, combine the pineapple, mango, papaya, cantaloupe, orange, maple syrup, orange juice and mint; toss well. Cover the bowl with plastic wrap; refrigerate for 20 minutes.

Arrange the lettuce on a platter; spoon the fruit on top.

Preparation time: 15 minutes
Marinating time: 20 minutes

Per serving: 207 calories, 0.9 g. fat (4% of calories), 6.4 g. dietary fiber, no cholesterol, 42 mg. sodium.

Mediterranean Medley

Baked Seafood Packets
Roasted Vegetables
Orzo

ast and foolproof, cooking fish in parchment or foil is the way to go on rushed weeknights. You assemble the packets, pop them in the oven and steam heat does the rest—for tasty, moist fillets. Add oven-roasted vegetables and orzo, a tiny Italian pasta that cooks in minutes, and you've got a Mediterranean feast.

Game Plan

1. Make the roasted vegetables.
2. Make the seafood packets and bake them alongside the vegetables.
3. Cook the orzo according to package directions.

BAKED SEAFOOD PACKETS

SERVES 4

1   pound salmon, orange roughy or other fish fillets
2   tablespoons prepared pesto
2   tablespoons plain nonfat yogurt
1   small tomato, thinly sliced
¼   cup shredded carrots
¼   cup chopped green onions
1   tablespoon lemon juice

Preheat the oven to 400°. Tear off 4 large pieces of cooking parchment or foil. Divide the fish into 4 equal portions; place one portion on each sheet of parchment or foil.

In a small bowl, combine the pesto and yogurt. Layer the tomato slices, carrots, green onions, pesto mixture and lemon juice on each piece of fish; fold the parchment or foil to create 4 sealed packets. Transfer the packets to a baking sheet.

Bake the packets for 20 to 25 minutes, or until the fish flakes easily when lightly pressed with a fork. Remove the fish from the packets and serve with the vegetables and cooking juices.

Preparation time: 5 minutes
Cooking time: 25 minutes

Per serving: 183 calories, 7.7 g. fat (39% of calories), 0.7 g. dietary fiber, 59 mg. cholesterol, 140 mg. sodium.

ROASTED VEGETABLES

SERVES 4

1   cup cooked diced red or baking potatoes
1   cup whole baby carrots
1   cup broccoli florets
1   sweet red pepper, quartered
1   green pepper, quartered
1   tablespoon garlic-and-red-pepper-flavored olive oil
½   teaspoon salt
     Ground black pepper

Preheat the oven to 400°. In a large bowl, combine the potatoes, carrots, broccoli and red and green peppers. Drizzle with the oil; toss well. Arrange the vegetables on a no-stick baking sheet. Sprinkle with the salt and with pepper to taste. Bake for 25 minutes, or until the vegetables are tender.

Preparation time: 10 minutes
Cooking time: 25 minutes

Chef's note: Look for garlic-and-red-pepper-flavored olive oil in the specialty section of your supermarket.

Per serving: 119 calories, 3.7 g. fat (26% of calories), 3.9 g. dietary fiber, no cholesterol, 313 mg. sodium.

EASY ELEGANT EVENING

> *Broiled Orange Roughy*
> *with Sun-Dried Tomatoes*
> *Orange-Sweet Potato Puree*
> *Tossed Salad*

In this menu, orange roughy is sauced with a rich-tasting Italian blend of sun-dried and fresh tomatoes, garlic and a tiny amount of pesto. The sweet potato puree complements the fish in both flavor and bright color. Steam or microwave the sweet potatoes ahead of time so they're ready to puree.

GAME PLAN

1. Make the sweet potatoes.
2. Make a salad with romaine lettuce, cucumbers and cherry tomatoes. Add your favorite low-fat creamy dressing.
3. Make the fish.

BROILED ORANGE ROUGHY
WITH SUN-DRIED TOMATOES

SERVES 4

- 1 cup diced tomatoes
- ¼ cup defatted chicken broth
- 4 dry-pack sun-dried tomatoes, chopped
- 2 teaspoons minced garlic
- ¼ cup chopped fresh parsley
- 1 teaspoon prepared pesto
- 4 orange roughy fillets
- 1 teaspoon olive oil
  Salt and ground black pepper

Preheat the broiler. In a 10″ skillet combine the tomatoes, broth, sun-dried tomatoes and garlic; bring to a boil over medium-high heat. Cook and stir for 3 minutes. Add the parsley and pesto; stir well and remove from the heat.

Place the orange roughy fillets on a no-stick broiler pan. Sprinkle with the oil, salt and pepper. Broil for 3 to 5 minutes, or until the fish is lightly browned and flakes easily when lightly pressed with a fork. Spoon the sauce over each portion before serving.

Preparation time: 10 minutes
Cooking time: 8 minutes

Per serving: 129 calories, 2.9 g. fat (20% of calories), 0.7 g. dietary fiber, 22 mg. cholesterol, 249 mg. sodium.

ORANGE-SWEET POTATO PUREE

SERVES 4

4 *large sweet potatoes or garnet yams, cooked and cooled*

  Juice of 1 medium orange

½ *teaspoon grated orange rind*

1 *teaspoon grated lemon rind*

1 *teaspoon grated fresh ginger*

  Pinch of ground nutmeg

2–3 *tablespoons maple syrup*

Preheat the oven to 350°. Peel the sweet potatoes or yams; place them in a blender or food processor with the orange juice, orange rind, lemon rind, ginger, nutmeg and 2 tablespoons of the maple syrup. Puree. Add more maple syrup to taste, if desired. Spoon into a lightly oiled 8″ × 8″ casserole dish; bake for 15 minutes, or until hot.

Preparation time: 10 minutes
Cooking time: 15 minutes

Chef's note: The puree can be spooned into halved, hollowed-out orange shells after baking for an elegant presentation.

Per serving: 149 calories, 0.2 g. fat (1% of calories), 3.6 g. dietary fiber, no cholesterol, 13 mg. sodium.

Viva L'Italia!

Shrimp Marinara
Garlicky Angel-Hair Pasta
Sautéed Carrots and Zucchini

*S*campi is a fast Italian shrimp dish that traditionally drips with butter. Our skinny version is equally rich-tasting but makes a healthy and satisfying one-skillet meal for rushed weeknights. Serve it with garlic-laden angel-hair pasta.

GAME PLAN

1. Make the pasta.
2. Cook baby carrots and zucchini in defatted chicken broth until crisp-tender.
3. Make the shrimp marinara.

SHRIMP MARINARA

SERVES 4

1	teaspoon olive oil
¼	cup white wine or defatted chicken broth
3–4	tablespoons minced garlic
¼	cup minced red onions
3	cups coarsely chopped tomatoes
1–2	teaspoons lemon juice
1¼	pounds large uncooked shrimp, peeled and deveined
¼	cup minced fresh parsley
	Pinch of crushed red pepper flakes
¼	cup grated Parmesan cheese
	Salt and ground black pepper

In a 10″ no-stick skillet over medium-high heat, bring the oil and wine or broth to a boil. Add the garlic and red onions; cook and stir for 3 minutes. Add the tomatoes and 1 teaspoon of the lemon juice; cook and stir for 8 minutes, or until the sauce is thick. Add the shrimp; cook and stir for 5 minutes. Add the parsley, red pepper flakes and Parmesan; add salt and pepper to taste and additional lemon juice, if desired.

Preparation time: 5 minutes
Cooking time: 16 minutes

Per serving: 213 calories, 4.8 g. fat (20% of calories), 2.3 g. dietary fiber, 224 mg. cholesterol, 385 mg. sodium.

GARLICKY ANGEL-HAIR PASTA

SERVES 4

1   *tablespoon olive oil*
5   *cloves garlic, minced*
¼   *cup chopped green onions*
1   *cup minced green peppers*
¼   *cup minced sweet red peppers*
4   *cups cooked angel-hair pasta*
    Salt and ground black pepper

Heat the oil in a 10″ no-stick skillet over medium-high heat; when the oil is hot, add the garlic, green onions, and green and red peppers. Cook and stir for 5 minutes, or until the vegetables are crisp-tender. Add the pasta. Cook and stir for 2 minutes, or until the pasta is hot. Add salt and pepper to taste.

Preparation time: 10 minutes
Cooking time: 7 minutes

Per serving: 249 calories, 6 g. fat (21% of calories), 3 g. dietary fiber, 72 mg. cholesterol, 26 mg. sodium.

Sautéed Swordfish with Pepper Relish (page 191)

Teriyaki Salmon (page 193)

Bouillabaisse (page 212) and Herbed Crouton Toast (page 213)

Chinese Vegetables in Parchment (page 215)

Vegetarian Souvlaki with Pita Wraps (page 217)
and Tsiziki Dip (page 218)

Vegetarian Spring Rolls (page 221)

East Indian Curried Couscous Platter (page 274)

Shallot and Corn Risotto (page 278)

5 FRESH SAUCES FOR GRILLED FISH

- **Caribbean Fruit Sauce:** In a food processor, coarsely chop ½ medium red onion. In a large bowl, combine the chopped onions with 1 cubed papaya, 1 cubed mango, 2 tablespoons minced fresh cilantro and the juice of 1 lime. Let the sauce sit for 15 minutes before spooning it over grilled tuna, halibut, swordfish or shark.

- **Mama's Traditional Italian Sauce:** In a no-stick skillet, bring to a boil 1 can (8 ounces) Italian-style stewed tomatoes and 2 tablespoons tomato paste. Add salt, ground black pepper, chopped fresh parsley and minced garlic to taste. Serve hot over grilled cod or halibut.

- **Uptown Herb Sauce:** Make a low-fat pesto from 1 cup chopped spinach, 1 cup chopped parsley, 1 tablespoon dried basil and ¼ cup grated Parmesan cheese. Spread it over grilled sole, orange roughy or trout.

- **Greek Get-Away Sauce:** Sauté ½ medium onion, chopped, and 1 tablespoon minced garlic in 1 teaspoon olive oil. Add 2 cups diced tomatoes and ⅓ cup crumbled feta cheese. Add dried oregano, salt and ground black pepper to taste. Toss with grilled shrimp or spoon over grilled cod or orange roughy.

- **Vietnamese Sauce:** In a small bowl, stir together the juice of 1 lime, ½ teaspoon grated lime rind, 1 teaspoon honey and ½ teaspoon chopped fresh cilantro. Drizzle it over grilled salmon.

EAST MEETS WEST

Spicy Shrimp Kabobs
Vegetable Rice Pilaf
Steamed Baby Artichokes

While the shrimp is marinating in its own spicy sauce, steam halved baby artichokes until tender (they take much less time than their bigger cousins). Use the marinade as a dipping sauce.

GAME PLAN

1. Marinate the shrimp.
2. Steam baby artichokes.
3. Cook the rice pilaf.
4. Grill the shrimp kabobs.

SPICY SHRIMP KABOBS

SERVES 4

¼ cup lime juice
2 cloves garlic, minced
2 teaspoons reduced-sodium soy sauce
1 teaspoon olive oil
¼ teaspoon crushed red pepper flakes
1 teaspoon honey
24 uncooked medium shrimp, peeled and deveined
2 sweet red peppers, cut into 8 pieces each
2 green peppers, cut into 8 pieces each

In a resealable plastic storage bag, combine the lime juice, garlic, soy sauce, oil, red pepper flakes, honey and shrimp. Shake well. Refrigerate for 30 minutes, turning frequently.

Preheat the grill. Remove the shrimp from the marinade; transfer the marinade to a medium saucepan. Thread the shrimp on 4 skewers, alternating with the red and green peppers.

Bring the marinade to a boil over medium-high heat. Cook for 3 to 5 minutes, or until it is reduced by half.

Coat the grill with no-stick cooking spray. Preheat the grill. Grill the kabobs for 8 minutes, or until the shrimp is pink and the vegetables lightly browned, turning once and basting with the reduced marinade. Serve the reduced marinade as a dipping sauce.

Preparation time: 5 minutes
Cooking time: 13 minutes
Marinating time: 30 minutes

Per serving: 117 calories, 2.3 g. fat (17% of calories), 2.8 g. dietary fiber, 65 mg. cholesterol, 152 mg. sodium.

VEGETABLE RICE PILAF

SERVES 4

¾ cup uncooked basmati rice
1 cup sliced green onions
1 cup diced sweet red peppers
1 tablespoon minced garlic
¼ cup white wine or apple juice
2 cups defatted chicken broth
   Salt and ground black pepper

Rinse the rice under cold water until the water runs clear; drain well.

In a 10″ no-stick skillet over medium-high heat, combine the green onions, red peppers, garlic and wine or apple juice. Cook and stir for 5 minutes, or until the peppers are soft. Add the rice; cook and stir for 1 minute. Add the broth; bring to a boil. Lower the heat to medium; cover and cook for 10 to 15 minutes, or until the rice is tender and all the liquid has been absorbed. Add salt and pepper to taste.

Preparation time: 5 minutes
Cooking time: 15 minutes

Per serving: 165 calories, 1 g. fat (5% of calories), 1.6 g. dietary fiber, no cholesterol, 193 mg. sodium.

SIMPLY PROVENCE

Bouillabaisse
Herbed Crouton Toast
Tossed Green Salad

This well-seasoned French stew used to take all day to make, but we've streamlined and slimmed it down with fewer ingredients. It still has that rich flavor that makes it an ideal meal for wintry evenings. Serve it in big crockery bowls with crunchy toast and a green salad.

GAME PLAN

1. Make the bouillabaisse.
2. Make the croutons.
3. Make a salad with baby lettuces. Add your favorite low-fat vinaigrette dressing.

BOUILLABAISSE

SERVES 4

1	*tablespoon olive oil*
2	*bottles (8 ounces each) clam juice*
1	*cup chopped onions*
2	*leeks, thinly sliced*
5	*cloves garlic, minced*
12	*ounces small red potatoes, quartered*
1	*can (28 ounces) reduced-sodium chopped Italian plum tomatoes (with juice)*
1	*pound halibut, cut into 2" cubes*
8	*ounces bay scallops*

8 ounces large shrimp, peeled and deveined

2–3 tablespoons chopped fresh herbs (such as tarragon, basil, thyme, parsley)

Salt and ground black pepper

In a Dutch oven over medium-high heat, bring the oil and ¼ cup of the clam juice to a boil; add the onions, leeks, garlic and potatoes. Cook and stir for 3 to 5 minutes, or until the onions are lightly browned. Add the tomatoes (with juice); bring to a boil. Cook and stir for 10 minutes.

Add the halibut, scallops and shrimp; cook and stir for 5 minutes or until the fish is opaque and flakes easily when lightly pressed with a fork. Stir in the fresh herbs and salt and pepper to taste.

Preparation time: 10 minutes
Cooking time: 20 minutes

Per serving: 420 calories, 7.9 g. fat (17% of calories), 3.4 g. dietary fiber, 148 mg. cholesterol, 474 mg. sodium.

HERBED CROUTON TOAST

SERVES 4

8 slices French or Italian bread (1″ thick)

1 tablespoon dried herbs (such as thyme, marjoram, basil, oregano)

Salt and ground black pepper

Preheat the oven to 400°. Arrange the bread on a large no-stick baking sheet. Coat each slice with no-stick spray; sprinkle with herbs, salt and pepper. Bake for 15 minutes, or until crisp and golden brown.

Preparation time: 5 minutes
Cooking time: 15 minutes

Per serving: 139 calories, 1.6 g. fat (11% of calories), no dietary fiber, no cholesterol, 304 mg. sodium.

CHAPTER 9

TASTEBUD-
TANTALIZING
MAIN DISHES

EASY MEATLESS MEALS

eatless main dishes are showing up on the best tables as diners discover filling, fast and satisfying recipes like the ones in this chapter. You won't miss a beat (or the meat!) with these weeknight menus because you'll get plenty of great-tasting protein from light cheeses, tofu, whole grains and legumes. And because vegetarian means vegetables, your five-a-day goals will be easily met.

CHINESE RUSH HOUR

Chinese Vegetables in Parchment
Noodles with Low-Fat Peanut Sauce
Pineapple and Mandarin Oranges

The flavors of ginger and garlic in these parchment-cooked vegetables pair nicely with cooked noodles tossed with savory peanut sauce. The pineapple and mandarin oranges add a bright sweetness to the meal.

GAME PLAN

1. Make the parchment packets.
2. Make the noodles and peanut sauce.
3. Toss together mandarin oranges and pineapple chunks; arrange in salad bowls.

CHINESE VEGETABLES IN PARCHMENT

SERVES 4

1	*cup sliced onions*
1	*cup peeled cubed eggplant*
2	*cups thickly sliced bok choy or Chinese cabbage*
1	*sweet red pepper, cut into 8 pieces*
2	*tomatoes, quartered*
1	*teaspoon minced fresh ginger*
1	*teaspoon minced garlic*
1	*cup diagonally sliced snow peas*
1	*cup thickly sliced yellow squash*
1	*tablespoon rice wine or vegetable broth*
½	*teaspoon dark sesame oil*
1	*tablespoon minced fresh cilantro*
	Reduced-sodium soy sauce

Preheat the oven to 400°. Tear off 2 large sheets of parchment paper.

In a large bowl, combine the onions, eggplant, bok choy or cabbage, peppers, tomatoes, ginger, garlic, snow peas, squash, wine or broth, oil and cilantro. Divide evenly between the 2 sheets of parchment and fold to seal the vegetables inside. Place on two baking sheets. Bake for 15 minutes.

Open the packets and divide the vegetables between 4 plates. Add soy sauce to taste.

Preparation time: 10 minutes
Cooking time: 15 minutes

Per serving: 87 calories, 1.3 g. fat (12% of calories), 4 g. dietary fiber, no cholesterol, 16 mg. sodium.

Noodles with Low-Fat Peanut Sauce

SERVES 4

1   package (9 ounces) Japanese udon noodles
2   teaspoons peanut butter
1   tablespoon low-sodium soy sauce
2   teaspoons honey
½   teaspoon minced garlic
1   teaspoon minced green onions
1   teaspoon water

Cook the noodles according to package directions; drain well.

Meanwhile, in a large bowl, stir together the peanut butter, soy sauce, honey, garlic, green onions and water. Toss with the noodles.

Preparation time: 5 minutes
Cooking time: 12 minutes

Per serving: 156 calories, 1.5 g. fat (8% of calories), 3 g. dietary fiber, no cholesterol, 214 mg. sodium.

GREEK FAST FOOD

> *Vegetarian Souvlaki with Pita Wraps*
> *Tsiziki Dip*
> *Tomato and Basil Salad*

*G*reeks love their garlic, and both the vegetables in this vegetarian shish kebab and the cooling yogurt dip are rich in the healthy herb. This fast and colorful trio of recipes will send your taste buds on a Mediterranean cruise.

GAME PLAN

1. Marinate the souvlaki.
2. Make the dip.
3. Make a salad of sliced tomatoes and basil.
4. Make the souvlaki.

VEGETARIAN SOUVLAKI WITH PITA WRAPS

SERVES 4

½ large eggplant, cubed

12 large button mushrooms

1 green pepper, cubed

6 pineapple rings, cut into 24 chunks

2 tablespoons balsamic vinegar

1 tablespoon chopped fresh oregano or 1 teaspoon dried

2 teaspoons olive oil

1 teaspoon minced garlic

8 large pita bread rounds

In a large bowl, combine the eggplant, mushrooms, peppers, pineapple, vinegar, oregano, oil and garlic. Let marinate for 20 minutes at room temperature, stirring frequently.

Preheat the grill. Thread the vegetables and pineapple on metal shish kebab skewers, alternating colors. Grill for 10 minutes, turning once, or until lightly browned, basting with any leftover marinade.

Warm the pita rounds on the grill, turning once. Wrap 1 pita around each shish kebab.

Preparation time: 10 minutes
Cooking time: 10 minutes
Marinating time: 20 minutes

Per serving: 421 calories, 6.2 g. fat (12% of calories), 1.5 g. dietary fiber, no cholesterol, 685 mg. sodium.

TSIZIKI DIP

SERVES 4

1   large cucumber, peeled, seeded, grated and squeezed dry
1   cup plain nonfat yogurt
1   teaspoon apple cider vinegar
    Pinch of salt
1   teaspoon dried dill
4   large cloves garlic, minced

In a medium bowl, combine the cucumber, yogurt, vinegar, salt, dill and garlic. Let stand for 20 minutes at room temperature, stirring occasionally.

Preparation time: 5 minutes
Marinating time: 20 minutes

Per serving: 46 calories, 0.2 g. fat (4% of calories), 0.1 g. dietary fiber, 1 mg. cholesterol, 46 mg. sodium.

FEAST FROM TAJ MAHAL

Indian Vegetables with Baked Tempeh
Raita
Mango Chutney
Basmati Rice

*F*oil packets of curried vegetables and strips of meaty soy tempeh are baked in the oven. Their intricate Eastern flavors blend with the traditional side dishes of chutney and raita, a cucumber-yogurt sauce, in this fast Indian feast.

GAME PLAN

1. Assemble the vegetable packets.
2. Make the raita.
3. Cook the basmati rice according to package directions.
4. Bake the vegetable packets.

INDIAN VEGETABLES WITH BAKED TEMPEH

SERVES 4

2 *sweet potatoes, cut into medium-size chunks*
1 *package (8 ounces) tempeh, cut into 1" squares*
3 *cups nonfat plain yogurt*
4 *cloves garlic, minced*
2 *tablespoons grated fresh ginger*
1 *teaspoon curry powder*
½ *teaspoon whole cumin seeds, toasted*
2 *green peppers, cut into 8 pieces*
2 *sweet red peppers, cut into 8 pieces*
2 *cups whole small mushrooms*
1 *large zucchini, cut into chunks*

Place the sweet potatoes and tempeh in a steamer basket; set it over boiling water in a 3-quart pot. Cover and steam for 10 minutes; drain well.

In a shallow pan, combine the yogurt, garlic, ginger, curry powder and cumin. Gently stir in the warm sweet potatoes and tempeh. Cover with plastic wrap; refrigerate for 20 minutes, stirring occasionally.

Preheat the oven to 400°. Tear off 4 large sheets of foil. Drain the sweet potatoes and tempeh; divide evenly between the sheets of foil. Top with the green and red peppers, mushrooms and zucchini. Seal the packets and place on two baking sheets; bake for 15 minutes, or until piping hot.

Preparation time: 10 minutes
Cooking time: 25 minutes
Marinating time: 20 minutes

Per serving: 341 calories, 5.7 g. fat (14% of calories), 10.2 g. dietary fiber, 3 mg. cholesterol, 142 mg. sodium.

RAITA

SERVES 4

3 *teaspoons whole cumin seeds*
½–1 *teaspoon salt*
3 *cups nonfat plain yogurt*
2 *large cucumbers, peeled, seeded and coarsely shredded*
Pinch of ground red pepper

In a small no-stick skillet over low heat, combine the cumin and salt. Cook and stir for 5 minutes, or until fragrant. Grind in a spice grinder or crush with a mortar and pestle.

In a medium bowl, combine the cumin mixture, yogurt, cucumbers and red pepper. Stir well. Let marinate for 15 minutes at room temperature.

Preparation time: 10 minutes
Cooking time: 5 minutes
Marinating time: 15 minutes

Per serving: 120 calories, 0.9 g. fat (6% of calories), no dietary fiber, 3 mg. cholesterol, 403 mg. sodium.

BANGKOK HOLIDAY

Vegetarian Spring Rolls
Thai Noodles
Sliced Tropical Fruit

*S*pring rolls are lighter, more delicate uncooked versions of Chinese egg rolls—and the lack of cooking time makes them quicker to prepare. This menu pairs them with a speedy stir-fry of ginger-flavored vegetables and noodles.

GAME PLAN

1. Make the spring rolls and sauce.
2. Make the noodles.
3. Slice an assortment of fresh tropical fruit; arrange it on a platter.

VEGETARIAN SPRING ROLLS

SERVES 4

 2 *large carrots, julienned*
 2 *tablespoons slivered green onions*
 ⅓ *cup thinly sliced napa cabbage*
 1 *tablespoon olive oil*
 1 *tablespoon minced fresh cilantro*
 ¼ *teaspoon ground black pepper*
 1 *package (3 ounces) dried bean thread noodles*
 16 *(8″) rice-paper rounds, softened (see note)*
 2 *teaspoons slivered fresh basil or mint*
 1 *tablespoon reduced-sodium soy sauce*
 1 *teaspoon dark sesame oil*

In a large bowl, combine the carrots, green onions, cabbage, olive oil, cilantro and pepper; toss well. Let marinate at room temperature for 10 minutes, stirring frequently.

Meanwhile, place the noodles in a medium bowl. Cover with boiling water and soak for 10 minutes, or until the noodles are softened. Drain well and snip into 2″ pieces. Set aside.

Place about 2 tablespoons of the noodles and about 2 tablespoons of the vegetable mixture about 1″ from the lower edge of each rice-paper round. Sprinkle with the basil or mint leaves. Fold the bottom edge over the filling, fold in both sides and roll up tightly. Press to seal. Place on a plate; cover with plastic wrap. Refrigerate for 10 minutes.

Meanwhile, in a small bowl, combine the soy sauce and sesame oil. Serve as a dipping sauce with the spring rolls.

Preparation time: 25 minutes
Chilling time: 10 minutes
Marinating time: 10 minutes

Chef's note: To soften the rice-paper rounds before rolling them, fill a large bowl with warm water. Dip each rice-paper round into the water for 10 seconds, or until softened and translucent. Remove and let drain on a clean dish towel. (Do not stack the rice papers or they will stick together.)

Per serving: 181 calories, 4.6 g. fat (23% of calories), 1 g. dietary fiber, no cholesterol, 186 mg. sodium.

THAI NOODLES

SERVES 4

¼ cup dry sherry or water

¼ cup plus 2 tablespoons vegetable broth

1 tablespoon chopped fresh ginger

1 tablespoon minced garlic

1 tablespoon reduced-sodium soy sauce

1 teaspoon cornstarch

¼ teaspoon chili powder

1–2 teaspoons chopped fresh cilantro

3 tablespoons white wine or apple juice

1 cup peeled, seeded and sliced cucumbers

1 cup julienned sweet red peppers

1 cup fresh mung bean sprouts

½ cup sliced water chestnuts

8 ounces spaghettini, cooked and drained

In a saucepan, whisk together the sherry or water, ¼ cup of the broth, ginger, garlic, soy sauce, cornstarch, chili powder and cilantro; set the pan over medium-high heat and bring to a boil. Reduce the heat to medium; cook and stir for 2 minutes, or until the sauce thickens slightly. Set aside.

In a wok set over high heat, bring the remaining 2 tablespoons of broth to a boil; add the wine or apple juice, cucumbers and peppers. Cook and stir for 2 minutes. Add the bean sprouts and water chestnuts; cook and stir for 2 minutes. Add the noodles and sauce; cook and stir for 1 minute, or until hot.

Preparation time: 10 minutes
Cooking time: 5 minutes

Per serving: 332 calories, 1.5 g. fat (4% of calories), 1.6 g. dietary fiber, no cholesterol, 148 mg. sodium.

MEXICAN VEGETARIAN DINNER

Low-Fat Vegetable Enchiladas with Salsa
Brown Rice and Black Beans
Tossed Salad

The enchilada filling is a quick sauté of frozen vegetables, which reduces baking time because the ingredients are already softened and the flavors are already developed. Faster and leaner than frying, the tortillas are dipped in salsa to soften them before filling.

GAME PLAN

1. Make the enchiladas.
2. Make the rice and beans.
3. Make a salad of cucumbers, tomatoes and leaf lettuce. Add your favorite low-fat vinaigrette.

LOW-FAT VEGETABLE ENCHILADAS WITH SALSA

SERVES 4

⅓	cup vegetable broth or white wine
3	cups frozen mixed vegetables (such as pearl onions, sweet red peppers, corn)
¾	cup canned diced mild green chilies
1½	teaspoons ground coriander
¾	teaspoon ground cumin
1½	cups reduced-sodium Mexican-style stewed tomatoes
1½	cups shredded low-fat farmer cheese
¾	cup shredded fat-free Cheddar cheese
¾	teaspoon ground black pepper
¼–½	teaspoon salt

8 (6″) corn tortillas

2 cups reduced-sodium salsa

1 cup low-fat sour cream

⅓ cup chopped fresh cilantro

Coat a microwaveable 9″ × 13″ baking dish with no-stick cooking spray. In a 10″ no-stick skillet over medium-high heat, bring the broth or wine to a boil. Add the mixed vegetables, chilies, coriander and cumin. Cook and stir for 2 minutes, or until the vegetables are soft. Remove from the heat. Add the tomatoes, farmer cheese, Cheddar and pepper. Add salt to taste.

Wrap the tortillas in plastic wrap; microwave on high power for 1 minute to soften and prevent cracking. Place 1 cup of the salsa in the baking dish. Dip each tortilla in the remaining 1 cup of salsa to coat both sides; lay the tortillas in the baking dish with edges overlapping. Divide the filling between the tortillas and roll each up tightly. Pack into the baking dish. Cover with the remaining salsa.

Preheat the broiler. Cover the baking dish with plastic wrap. Microwave on high power for 5 minutes. Remove the wrap and transfer to the broiler; broil for 2 to 3 minutes, or until the enchiladas are brown and bubbly. Top with sour cream and cilantro.

Preparation time: 15 minutes
Cooking time: 15 minutes

Per serving: 423 calories, 9.9 g. fat (21% of calories), 4.4 g. dietary fiber, 26 mg. cholesterol, 971 mg. sodium.

Brown Rice and Black Beans

1½ cups canned black beans, rinsed and drained

2 cups cooked brown rice

1 cup chopped tomatoes

½ teaspoon ground cumin

2 teaspoons chopped garlic

2 tablespoons chopped fresh cilantro

Salt and ground black pepper

In a 10″ no-stick skillet over medium-high heat, combine the beans, rice, tomatoes, cumin and garlic. Cover and cook for 5 minutes, stirring occasionally, or until the beans are hot. Add the cilantro and salt and pepper to taste.

Preparation time: 5 minutes
Cooking time: 5 minutes

Per serving: 177 calories, 1.7 g. fat (8% of calories), 6.1 g. dietary fiber, no cholesterol, 210 mg. sodium.

MEATLESS MARVELS: CUTTING BACK ON MEAT

*I*t makes sense to include vegetarian meals in a healthy diet. Meatless menus give you variety, use the best seasonal produce and can be as fast and easy as grilling a steak.

• **Caesar Pasta Salad Bar:** In a large salad bowl, combine 4 cups chopped fresh vegetables (from the supermarket salad bar), 1 cup cooked leftover pasta, ¼ cup low-fat Italian dressing and 1 tablespoon grated Parmesan cheese; toss well. Serves 4.

• **Skillet Tex-Mex Grain and Bean Casserole:** In a 10″ no-stick skillet over medium-high heat, combine ½ cup chopped frozen onions, 1 teaspoon olive oil, 1 teaspoon minced fresh garlic and ½ teaspoon ground cumin; cook and stir for 3 minutes. Add 2 cups cooked brown rice, 2 cups cooked pinto or kidney beans, 1 cup chopped tomatoes, 1 cup frozen mixed peas and corn and ½ cup medium salsa; cover and cook for 5 minutes. Add ½ cup grated low-fat Monterey Jack cheese; cover and cook for 1 minute, or until the cheese melts. Serves 4.

New Mexican Night

> *Eggplant Cheese Quesadillas*
> *Warm Artichoke Dip with Vegetables*
> *Quick-Cooking Brown Rice*

A fast evening meal that's a hit with cheese lovers, this New Mexican combination plate boasts a low-fat vegetable-and-melted-cheese tortilla sandwich alongside creamy warm artichoke dip, vegetables and brown rice.

GAME PLAN

1. Make the dip and vegetables.
2. Cook the brown rice according to package directions.
3. Make the quesadillas.

EGGPLANT CHEESE QUESADILLAS

SERVES 4

   1 *cup finely cubed peeled eggplant*
  ½ *cup diced tomatoes*
  ⅓ *cup chopped green onions*
  ¼ *cup apple juice*
   1 *cup shredded low-fat Monterey Jack cheese*
  ½ *cup nonfat sour cream*
  ¼ *cup grated Parmesan cheese*
   8 *(10″) low-fat flour tortillas*

In a 10″ no-stick skillet over medium-high heat, combine the eggplant, tomatoes, green onions and apple juice. Cover and cook for 3 minutes, or until the vegetables are soft. Uncover; cook and stir for 5 minutes, or until the liquid has evaporated. Transfer to a plate.

In a small bowl, combine the Monterey Jack, sour cream and Parmesan; spread on 4 tortillas. Top with the vegetables. Cover each with another tortilla.

In a clean 10″ no-stick skillet, brown each quesadilla for 1 minute on each side, or until the cheese melts. Cut into wedges.

Preparation time: 10 minutes
Cooking time: 20 minutes

Per serving: 285 calories, 7.1 g. fat (20% of calories), 11.3 g. dietary fiber, 25 mg. cholesterol, 930 mg. sodium.

WARM ARTICHOKE DIP WITH VEGETABLES

SERVES 4

1   *can (14 ounces) artichoke hearts, drained*
2   *cloves garlic, minced*
1   *tablespoon lemon juice*
⅓   *cup low-fat sour cream*
⅓   *cup nonfat mayonnaise*
1   *teaspoon cornstarch*
3   *tablespoons grated Parmesan cheese*
2   *tablespoons bread crumbs*
4   *cups precut vegetables (such as celery, carrots, jicama, cucumbers)*

Preheat the oven to 375°. In a blender or food processor, chop the artichoke hearts; add the garlic, lemon juice, sour cream, mayonnaise, cornstarch and Parmesan. Pulse until mixed.

Coat a 1-quart casserole dish with no-stick cooking spray. Transfer the artichoke dip to the casserole; top with the bread crumbs. Bake for 20 minutes, or until golden brown and bubbly. Serve with the vegetables.

Preparation time: 10 minutes
Cooking time: 20 minutes

Per serving: 153 calories, 2.8 g. fat (15% of calories), 5.9 g. dietary fiber, 7 mg. cholesterol, 482 mg. sodium.

TIMELY TOFU DINNER

Tofu Piccata
Herbed Basmati Rice Pilaf
Green Beans

ofu lovers will flip over this vegetarian piccata. The tofu absorbs the flavors of the lemon-and-caper sauce even better than veal.

GAME PLAN

1. Marinate the tofu.
2. Make the rice.
3. Steam green beans.
4. Make the tofu.

TOFU PICCATA

SERVES 4

2½ *cups cubed extra-firm reduced-fat tofu*
2 *tablespoons plus ⅓ cup lemon juice*
¾ *cup all-purpose flour*
½ *teaspoon salt*
1 *teaspoon ground black pepper*
1½ *teaspoons minced garlic*
⅓ *cup chopped fresh parsley*
1 *tablespoon capers*
2 *tablespoons minced fresh dill*
½ *lemon, thinly sliced*

Place the tofu in a resealable plastic storage bag. Add 2 tablespoons of the lemon juice. Shake gently. Refrigerate for 20 minutes, turning frequently.

In a second bag, combine the flour, salt and pepper. Transfer the tofu to the flour mixture (discard the lemon juice). Shake gently.

Coat a 10″ no-stick skillet with olive oil no-stick cooking spray. Place the skillet over medium-high heat. When the skillet is hot, add the garlic and tofu. Cook for 5 to 8 minutes, stirring occasionally, or until browned. Transfer the tofu to a plate; set aside.

Add the parsley, capers and remaining ⅓ cup of lemon juice to the skillet. Cook and stir for 1 minute, scraping to loosen any browned bits. Add the dill and tofu. Heat through. Garnish with lemon slices.

Preparation time: 10 minutes
Cooking time: 10 minutes
Marinating time: 20 minutes

Per serving: 146 calories, 1.6 g. fat (9% of calories), 0.8 g. dietary fiber, no cholesterol, 449 mg. sodium.

HERBED BASMATI RICE PILAF

SERVES 4

- 1 tablespoon olive oil
- ¼ cup white wine or apple juice
- ½ cup chopped onions
- ½ cup chopped celery
- ½ cup chopped apples
- 2 teaspoons minced garlic
- 3 cups cooked basmati rice
- ¼ cup chopped fresh parsley
- 2 tablespoons chopped fresh herbs (such as tarragon, basil, marjoram, chervil)

  Salt and ground black pepper

In a 10″ no-stick skillet over medium-high heat, combine the oil and the wine or apple juice. Bring to a boil; add the onions, celery and apples. Cook and stir for 5 minutes, or until the onions are soft. Add the garlic and rice. Cook and stir for 5 to 8 minutes, or until the rice is slightly browned. Stir in the parsley and fresh herbs; add salt and pepper to taste.

Preparation time: 10 minutes
Cooking time: 15 minutes

Per serving: 214 calories, 4.5 g. fat (19% of calories), 0.9 g. dietary fiber, no cholesterol, 47 mg. sodium.

Meet a Nutritional Superstar

What makes tofu such a headliner in nutrition news today? Soyfoods like tofu contain phytochemicals, important substances in our battle with cancer and heart disease, says Mark Messina, Ph.D., a researcher who worked with the National Cancer Institute's Division of Cancer Prevention and Control. "As little as one serving of soyfoods a day may be enough to reduce cancer risk," says Dr. Messina. Soyfoods like tofu, miso and tempeh are unique because they contain isoflavones, which inhibit an enzyme that controls cell growth in our bodies.

Substituting soy protein for animal products can reduce LDL (bad) cholesterol levels by an average of 15 percent in people with high cholesterol, Dr. Messina says. This is above and beyond the effects of a low-fat diet. LDL cholesterol goes down in these people, but HDL (good) cholesterol does not.

Tasty Ways with Tofu

• **Stuffed Pasta:** Substitute crumbled firm tofu for half the amount of ricotta or other cheeses in lasagna or manicotti.

• **Soup Power:** Add finely diced firm tofu to minestrone and other thick grain or bean soups just before serving them.

• **Salad Toss:** Marinate cubed firm tofu in low-fat vinaigrettes, then toss it with your favorite vegetable salad.

• **Egg Salad:** Add finely diced extra firm tofu to egg salad sandwich filling.

• **Creamy Topping:** Puree 4 ounces soft tofu with 1 teaspoon chives and 1 teaspoon lemon juice. Spoon over 2 hot, split baked potatoes or use in place of sour cream.

• **Stir-Fry:** Include cubed firm tofu in a vegetable stir-fry. It will absorb the flavors of any sauce you use.

• **Chocolate Mousse:** In a food processor, puree 1 (10.5-ounce) box lite silken tofu with ¾ cup low-fat chocolate chips (melted) and ½ teaspoon vanilla. Chill for 30 minutes and enjoy!

PASSING THROUGH PROVENCE

> *Easy Ratatouille*
> *Garlic Rotelle*
> *Tossed Salad*

*R*atatouille is a simple vegetable stew beloved by southern French cooks; it is versatile enough to serve over polenta, pasta or bread, or to enjoy alone. Make extra for a weekend lunch—this dish gets even tastier as the flavors mellow.

GAME PLAN

1. Make the ratatouille.
2. Make the rotelle.
3. Make a salad of baby lettuces; add your favorite creamy low-fat dressing.

EASY RATATOUILLE

SERVES 4

½ cup orange juice
1 cup sliced onions
1 sweet red pepper, diced
1 zucchini, sliced
3 cups cubed eggplant
3 cups chopped tomatoes
3 cloves garlic, minced
1 teaspoon dried Italian herb seasoning

In a 10″ no-stick skillet over medium-high heat, bring the orange juice to a boil. Add the onions, peppers, zucchini and eggplant. Cook and stir for 5 minutes, or until the vegetables soften. Add the tomatoes, garlic and Italian seasoning. Cook and stir for 3 minutes.

Cover and reduce the heat to medium. Cook for 10 minutes, or until the stew thickens.

Preparation time: 10 minutes
Cooking time: 18 minutes

Per serving: 108 calories, 1 g. fat (7% of calories), 4.3 g. dietary fiber, no cholesterol, 20 mg. sodium.

GARLIC ROTELLE

SERVES 4

4 *cups cooked rotelle*
1 *tablespoon olive oil*
1 *tablespoon minced garlic*
¼ *cup chopped fresh parsley*
¼ *cup freshly grated Romano cheese*
Salt and ground black pepper

In a 10″ no-stick skillet over medium-high heat, combine the pasta, oil and garlic. Cook and stir for 5 minutes, or until the garlic softens. Add the parsley and Romano; stir well. Remove from the heat; add salt and pepper to taste.

Preparation time: 5 minutes
Cooking time: 5 minutes

Per serving: 213 calories, 6 g. fat (26% of calories), 1.8 g. dietary fiber, 7 mg. cholesterol, 88 mg. sodium.

ITALIAN COMFORT FOOD DINNER

Green Vegetable Risotto
Marinated Tomato Salad
Steamed Asparagus

*A*romatic vegetables like garlic and onions make this low-fat risotto taste as good as classical buttery versions. Use arborio rice, a creamy white grain from Italy, for the richest flavor. A light marinated tomato salad looks beautiful alongside the green vegetable rice.

GAME PLAN

1. Make the risotto.
2. Make the salad.
3. Steam asparagus; toss it with lemon juice.

GREEN VEGETABLE RISOTTO

SERVES 4

1	medium onion, finely chopped
3–5	cups vegetable broth, warmed
1	cup sliced mushrooms
1	green bell pepper, diced
3	tablespoons minced garlic
2	cups chopped spinach
2	cups arborio rice
1	tablespoon grated Parmesan cheese
	Salt and ground black pepper

Coat a 2-quart saucepan with no-stick cooking spray; set it over medium-high heat until hot. Add the onions and ¼ cup of the broth; cook and stir for 5 minutes, or until the onions are soft. Add the mushrooms, peppers and garlic. Cook and stir for 5 minutes.

Add the spinach and rice; cook and stir for 1 minute. Add ½ cup of the broth. Stirring continuously, cook until the liquid has completely evaporated. Add another ½ cup of the broth; cook and stir until the liquid has completely evaporated. Cook and stir for 25 minutes, continuing to add broth by ½ cupfuls after previous additions have been absorbed, or until the rice is creamy and just tender.

Remove from the heat; add the Parmesan and salt and pepper to taste.

Preparation time: 10 minutes
Cooking time: 30 minutes

Per serving: 500 calories, 0.8 g. fat (1% of calories), 4.1 g. dietary fiber, 1 mg. cholesterol, 117 mg. sodium.

MARINATED TOMATO SALAD

SERVES 4

4   *medium tomatoes, thickly sliced*
1   *teaspoon olive oil*
2   *tablespoons balsamic vinegar*
2   *tablespoons chopped fresh basil*
    Salt and ground black pepper

Place the tomatoes on a large platter, overlapping as needed. In a small bowl, whisk together the oil and vinegar. Drizzle over the tomatoes. Top with the basil. Add salt and pepper to taste. Let marinate for 20 minutes.

Preparation time: 10 minutes
Marinating time: 20 minutes

Per serving: 43 calories, 1.5 g. fat (29% of calories), 1.6 g. dietary fiber, no cholesterol, 12 mg. sodium.

LIGHTHEARTED ALFREDO DINNER

Lean Fettuccine Alfredo
Sautéed Tomatoes and Onions
Sugar Snap Peas

This one-dish version of fettuccine Alfredo is rich-tasting but low in fat due to lean cheeses. It looks elegant on a plate with homemade stewed tomatoes and sugar snap peas.

GAME PLAN

1. Make the noodles.
2. Make the tomatoes and onions.
3. Steam sugar snap peas.

LEAN FETTUCCINE ALFREDO

SERVES 4

½ *cup nonfat cottage cheese*
¼ *cup evaporated skim milk*
¼ *cup low-fat ricotta cheese*
¼ *cup shredded low-fat Monterey Jack cheese*
¼ *cup grated Parmesan cheese*
1 *teaspoon minced garlic*
5 *cups hot cooked egg noodles*
2 *tablespoons minced fresh parsley*

In a blender or food processor, combine the cottage cheese, milk and ricotta; puree. Transfer to a 10″ no-stick skillet; add the Monterey Jack, Parmesan and garlic. Cook and stir over medium heat for 3 to 5 minutes, or until the cheeses are melted and the sauce is smooth.

Add the noodles and parsley; stir well.

Preparation time: 10 minutes
Cooking time: 7 minutes

Per serving: 360 calories, 6.5 g. fat (16% of calories), 3.8 g. dietary fiber, 79 mg. cholesterol, 292 mg. sodium.

SAUTÉED TOMATOES AND ONIONS

SERVES 4

1   *red onion, thinly sliced*
2   *teaspoons minced garlic*
¼   *cup apple juice*
2   *teaspoons olive oil*
1   *pint cherry tomatoes, quartered*
½   *teaspoon sugar*
1   *tablespoon slivered fresh basil*
     Salt and ground black pepper

In a 10″ no-stick skillet over medium-high heat, combine the onions, garlic, apple juice and oil. Cook and stir for 5 minutes, or until the onions are soft but not browned. Add the tomatoes and sugar. Cook and stir for 5 minutes, or until the tomatoes are soft. Add the basil; stir well. Add salt and pepper to taste.

Preparation time: 8 minutes
Cooking time: 10 minutes

Per serving: 72 calories, 2.7 g. fat (31% of calories), 2.1 g. dietary fiber, no cholesterol, 12 mg. sodium.

SICILIAN SPECIALTIES

*P*roper Italian comfort food, polenta is an almost-instant dinner made from a thick cornmeal. It's served here with vegetables and wedges of garlic bread.

GAME PLAN

1. Make the vegetables.
2. Make the polenta.
3. Coat sliced Italian bread with olive oil no-stick cooking spray; sprinkle with minced garlic. Wrap in foil and warm in a 350° oven for 10 minutes.

POLENTA

SERVES 4

1   cup yellow cornmeal
1   cup vegetable broth
3   cups boiling water
½   teaspoon salt
½   cup shredded part-skim mozzarella cheese
2   tablespoons grated Parmesan cheese

In a 2-quart saucepan, combine the cornmeal and broth. Set over medium-high heat; whisk in the boiling water and salt. Cook and stir for 5 minutes, or until the polenta thickens and boils. Cover; reduce the heat to low. Cook for 10 minutes, stirring frequently. Remove from the heat; stir in the mozzarella and Parmesan.

Preparation time: 5 minutes
Cooking time: 15 minutes

Per serving: 169 calories, 4.3 g. fat (22% of calories), 4.7 g. dietary fiber, 10 mg. cholesterol, 422 mg. sodium.

ITALIAN VEGETABLE SAUTÉ

SERVES 4

¼	*cup white wine or water*
1	*tablespoon olive oil*
1	*cup sliced onions*
2	*cups diced sweet red peppers*
1	*cup cubed unpeeled eggplant*
1	*cup sliced zucchini*
1	*can (16 ounces) Italian-style stewed tomatoes*
½	*teaspoon honey*
	Salt and ground black pepper

In a 10″ no-stick skillet over medium-high heat, combine the wine or water, oil and onions. Cook and stir for 5 minutes. Add the peppers, eggplant and zucchini; cook and stir for 3 minutes. Add the tomatoes and honey; bring to a boil. Cook and stir for 5 minutes. Add salt and pepper to taste.

Preparation time: 12 minutes
Cooking time: 15 minutes

Per serving: 140 calories, 3.9 g. fat (24% of calories), 3.9 g. dietary fiber, no cholesterol, 219 mg. sodium.

PANCAKES FOR DINNER

*Hearty Dutch Oven Pancake
with Cheddar Cheese
Sautéed Spiced Fruit
Melon Wedges*

*I*f you're too rushed for the one-at-a-time cooking style of pancakes, try this simple oven-baked version. It serves four in large wedges and looks impressive right out of the oven, especially topped with sautéed fruit. This menu is great for brunch, too.

GAME PLAN

1. Make the pancake.
2. Make the fruit.
3. Slice the melon into wedges; arrange them on a platter.

HEARTY DUTCH OVEN PANCAKE
WITH CHEDDAR CHEESE

SERVES 4

1   *cup all-purpose flour*
1   *tablespoon brown sugar or honey*
1   *cup skim milk*
2   *teaspoons melted butter or oil*
3   *eggs*
½   *cup shredded low-fat Cheddar cheese*
½   *teaspoon salt*

Preheat the oven to 425°. Coat an ovenproof no-stick skillet with no-stick cooking spray.

In a medium bowl, combine the flour, brown sugar or honey, milk, butter or oil, eggs, Cheddar and salt. Beat well. Pour into the skillet; transfer to the oven. Bake for 20 to 25 minutes, or until the pancake is puffed and golden brown. Cut into 4 wedges.

Preparation time: 5 minutes
Cooking time: 25 minutes

Per serving: 257 calories, 8.1 g. fat (29% of calories), 0.8 g. dietary fiber, 174 mg. cholesterol, 559 mg. sodium.

SAUTÉED SPICED FRUIT

SERVES 4

3 *large sweet apples (such as Golden Delicious), sliced*
1 *large pear, sliced*
1 *teaspoon butter or oil*
½ *teaspoon ground cinnamon*
  Pinch of ground nutmeg
¼ *cup maple syrup*

In a 10″ no-stick skillet over medium-high heat, combine the apples, pears, butter or oil, cinnamon and nutmeg. Cover and cook, stirring occasionally, for 3 to 5 minutes, or until the fruit softens slightly. Add the maple syrup; cook and stir for 5 minutes, or until the syrup is thick.

Preparation time: 5 minutes
Cooking time: 10 minutes

Per serving: 143 calories, 1.5 g. fat (9% of calories), 3.4 g. dietary fiber, 3 mg. cholesterol, 12 mg. sodium.

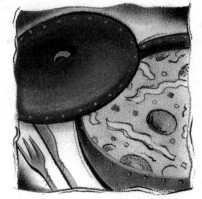

CHAPTER 10

FROM SKILLET
TO TABLE
IN MINUTES

QUICK CASSEROLES AND ONE-DISH MEALS

One pot, one dish—what could be easier? These classic recipes have been updated to meet our under-an-hour requirements, making good use of quick-cooking tools like no-stick skillets, microwaves and woks. Prepare extra portions of these hearty comfort foods to augment menus later in the week. You can even assemble some recipes ahead of time and pop them into the oven when you get home from work.

AUTUMN SUPPER ON THE VERANDAH

Braised Chicken with Root Vegetables
Cooked Noodles
French Bread

*L*ooking for an aromatic cool-weather dinner? This chicken skillet dish gets its richness from lots of autumn vegetables, garlic, onions and herbs—instead of fat.

GAME PLAN

1. Make the chicken.
2. Cook the noodles.
3. Warm the French bread.

BRAISED CHICKEN WITH ROOT VEGETABLES

SERVES 4

4	*skinless chicken breast halves (bone-in)*
2	*teaspoons olive oil*
¼	*cup defatted chicken broth*
1	*medium onion, sliced*
12	*baby carrots*
1	*teaspoon minced garlic*
1	*parsnip, thickly sliced*
2	*red potatoes, cubed*
½	*teaspoon dried thyme*
2	*bay leaves*
½	*teaspoon ground nutmeg*
1	*cup apple cider*
1	*teaspoon cornstarch*
2	*tablespoons cold water*

In a Dutch oven over medium-high heat, brown the chicken in the oil for 4 to 8 minutes, turning once. Transfer to a plate and cover to keep warm. Add the broth; cook and stir for 1 minute, scraping to loosen any browned bits. Add the onions, carrots and garlic; cook and stir for 1 minute. Add the parsnips, potatoes, thyme, bay leaves, nutmeg, cider and chicken. Bring to a boil; reduce the heat to medium. Cover and cook for 20 to 25 minutes, or until the chicken is no longer pink in the center.

In a small bowl, combine the cornstarch and water; add to the sauce. Cook and stir for 1 minute, or until the sauce thickens slightly. Remove the bay leaves.

Preparation time: 10 minutes
Cooking time: 35 minutes

Per serving: 294 calories, 5.7 g. fat (17% of calories), 2.5 g. dietary fiber, 69 mg. cholesterol, 99 mg. sodium.

GREAT GREEK DINNER

Greek Chicken and Orzo
Carrot Raisin Salad

Feta cheese, pasta and cooked chicken mingle with tomatoes and Mediterranean flavors in this skillet supper. Since the flavors are even better the next day, make the casserole on a weekend and heat it up for Monday night football suppers.

GAME PLAN

1. Make the chicken and orzo.
2. Make a salad of shredded carrots and raisins; add low-fat coleslaw dressing.

Greek Chicken and Orzo

1   *cup chopped onions*

2   *cups defatted chicken broth*

1   *teaspoon olive oil*

2   *teaspoons dried oregano*

4   *boneless skinless chicken breast halves*

1   *can (15 ounces) whole peeled tomatoes (with juice), chopped*

½   *cup crumbled feta cheese*

2   *cups cooked orzo*

In a 10″ no-stick skillet over medium-high heat, combine the onions, ¼ cup of the broth and the oil; cook and stir for 5 minutes. Add the oregano and chicken; brown for 3 minutes, turning once. Add the tomatoes (with juice) and remaining 1¾ cups of broth; cover and bring to a boil. Cook for 10 minutes, or until the chicken is no longer pink in the center.

Transfer the chicken to a plate and cover to keep warm. Bring the sauce to a boil; cook and stir for 5 minutes, or until thick. Add the feta and orzo; cook and stir for 1 minute, or until the cheese melts. Add the chicken.

Preparation time: 10 minutes
Cooking time: 15 minutes

Per serving: 331 calories, 7.9 g. fat (22% of calories), 2.5 g. dietary fiber, 81 mg. cholesterol, 560 mg. sodium.

SUNSET DINNER FROM NICE

Chicken Pasta Niçoise
Steamed Greens

A bouquet of herbs and a small amount of black olives give extraordinary flavor to this one-pot meal from southern France.

GAME PLAN

1. Make the chicken.
2. Steam chopped greens (such as collards, spinach, kale); toss them with lemon juice.

CHICKEN PASTA NIÇOISE

SERVES 4

1¼   cups white wine or defatted chicken broth
  2   skinless chicken breast halves (bone-in)
  2   skinless chicken thighs
  1   tablespoon minced garlic
 ½   cup sliced onions
  1   can (15 ounces) whole peeled tomatoes (with juice), chopped
  1   cup sliced sweet red peppers
  1   cup sliced green peppers
  1   tablespoon dried Italian herb seasoning
  5   niçoise olives, pitted and chopped
  3   cups cooked hot noodles, such as fettuccine

In a 10″ no-stick skillet over medium-high heat, bring the wine or broth to a boil. Add the chicken breasts and thighs; brown on both sides. Add the garlic, onions, tomatoes (with juice), red and green peppers, Italian seasoning and olives. Reduce the heat to medium. Cook for 30 minutes, or until the chicken is no longer pink in the center. Serve over the noodles.

Preparation time: 10 minutes
Cooking time: 35 minutes

Per serving: 403 calories, 7.9 g. fat (17% of calories), 4.5 g. dietary fiber, 112 mg. cholesterol, 278 mg. sodium.

SUMMER BAYOU BASH

Vegetable and Chicken Jambalaya
Basmati Rice
French Bread

The rich and spicy flavors of this Creole dish can be on your table in less than 45 minutes with quick-cooking rice, precut vegetables and canned tomatoes.

GAME PLAN

1. Make the jambalaya.
2. Cook basmati rice according to package directions.
3. Slice the French bread.

VEGETABLE AND CHICKEN JAMBALAYA

SERVES 4

1 cup chopped onions

1 tablespoon minced garlic

¾ cup defatted chicken broth

1 teaspoon olive oil

¾ cup diced celery

½ cup diced green peppers

4 cups cooked rice

1 cup diced cooked chicken

1 cup frozen peas

½ cup frozen whole-kernel corn

1 can (15 ounces) whole peeled tomatoes (with juice), chopped

1 teaspoon hot-pepper sauce

⅓ cup chopped fresh parsley

Salt and ground black pepper

In a Dutch oven over medium-high heat, combine the onions, garlic, broth and oil; cook and stir for 5 minutes, or until the onions are soft but not browned. Add the celery and peppers; cook and stir for 3 minutes.

Add the rice, chicken, peas, corn, tomatoes (with juice) and hot-pepper sauce. Bring to a boil; reduce the heat to medium. Cover and cook, stirring occasionally, for 20 minutes, or until the vegetables are tender and sauce is thick. Add the parsley and salt and pepper to taste.

Preparation time: 10 minutes
Cooking time: 30 minutes

Per serving: 367 calories, 3 g. fat (7% of calories), 4.3 g. dietary fiber, 22 mg. cholesterol, 321 mg. sodium.

LIGHT AND LIVELY MEXICAN MEAL

Layered Taco Salad
Fresh Pineapple and Papaya with Lime

*B*oth kids and adults love this layered Mexican salad, made leaner and faster with low-fat cheese, low-fat sour cream and precut salad bar vegetables.

GAME PLAN

1. Make the salad.
2. Slice pineapple and papaya; arrange on a platter with lime wedges.

LAYERED TACO SALAD

SERVES 4

½ cup diced red onions
2 cloves garlic, minced
1 teaspoon olive oil
1 can (15 ounces) kidney or pinto beans, drained and rinsed
2 dashes of hot-pepper sauce
¼ cup orange juice
8 corn tortillas
3 cups chilled chopped leaf lettuce
2 cups shredded cooked skinless chicken breasts
2 cups diced tomatoes
1 cup shredded low-fat Monterey Jack cheese
⅓ cup low-fat sour cream
2 tablespoons chopped fresh cilantro

Preheat the oven to 400°. In a 10″ no-stick skillet over medium-high heat, combine the onions, garlic and oil; cook and stir for 3 minutes. Add the beans, hot-pepper sauce and orange juice. Cook and stir for 2 minutes. Set aside.

Cut the tortillas into thin strips. Place them on an ungreased baking sheet; bake for 10 minutes, or until they are crisp. Set aside.

Place half the lettuce in the bottom of a large salad bowl. Top with the bean mixture, chicken, half the tomatoes, half the Monterey Jack and half the tortilla strips. Repeat with the remaining lettuce, tomatoes, Monterey Jack and tortilla strips. Top with the sour cream and cilantro.

Preparation time: 15 minutes
Cooking time: 5 minutes
Baking time: 10 minutes

Per serving: 445 calories, 11.3 g. fat (23% of calories), 7.9 g. dietary fiber, 70 mg. cholesterol, 735 mg. sodium.

FIFTIES' FAMILY FAVORITE

Turkey Noodle Casserole
Steamed Broccoli
Baked Potatoes

This old-fashioned casserole has been updated and streamlined with cooked turkey and a low-fat cheese sauce. Steamed broccoli and baked potatoes round out a classic dinner.

GAME PLAN

1. Make the casserole.
2. Microwave red potatoes.
3. Steam broccoli florets and toss them with lemon juice.

Turkey Noodle Casserole

SERVES 4

4	cups sliced mushrooms
1	tablespoon water
2	teaspoons olive oil
1/3	cup minced onions
2	tablespoons white wine or apple juice
1/4	cup all-purpose flour
1¾	cups skim milk
2	cups defatted reduced-sodium chicken broth
1/2	teaspoon dried thyme
1/4	cup low-fat cream cheese
10	ounces uncooked yolk-free noodles
1	cup frozen peas
1	jar (2 ounces) diced pimentos
1/3	cup grated Parmesan cheese
2	cups chopped cooked turkey breasts
1/3	cup seasoned bread crumbs
1/2	teaspoon ground black pepper

In a 2-quart saucepan over medium-high heat, combine the mushrooms, water and oil; cook and stir for 7 minutes, or until the mushrooms brown and the pan is dry. Add the onions and wine or apple juice; cook and stir for 2 minutes. Add the flour; cook and stir for 3 minutes. Gradually add the milk, broth, thyme and cream cheese; cook and stir for 5 minutes, or until the sauce has slightly thickened.

Cook the noodles according to package directions; drain well.

Preheat the oven to 375°. Coat a 3-quart casserole with no-stick cooking spray. Set aside.

In a large bowl, combine the mushroom sauce, noodles, peas, pimentos, Parmesan and turkey. Mix well. Spoon into the casserole. Top with the bread crumbs and pepper. Bake for 20 to 30 minutes, or until bubbling.

Preparation time: 5 minutes
Cooking time: 40 minutes

Per serving: 617 calories, 12.6 g. fat (18% of calories), 3.3 g. dietary fiber, 129 mg. cholesterol, 642 mg. sodium.

ITALIAN SUPPER STEW

Italian Sausage Stew
Crusty Rolls
Green Salad

Italian sausage plays a minor role in the total fat content of this hearty stew, but it contributes major flavor. Serve the stew with crusty rolls to soak up the sauce.

GAME PLAN

1. Make the stew.
2. Heat crusty Italian rolls.
3. Make a salad of baby lettuces; add low-fat Italian dressing.

ITALIAN SAUSAGE STEW

SERVES 4

6 ounces sweet Italian-style turkey sausage, crumbled
¼ cup red wine or water
1 teaspoon olive oil
1 large onion, sliced
2 cloves garlic, minced
½ teaspoon dried basil
　Pinch of crushed red pepper flakes
1 can (16 ounces) whole peeled tomatoes (with juice), chopped
1 can (16 ounces) Italian-style stewed tomatoes
2 cups cubed new potatoes
⅓ cup chopped fresh parsley
　Salt and ground black pepper

In a 10″ no-stick skillet over medium-high heat, brown the sausage for 5 minutes. Drain the fat.

Add the wine or water; scrape the pan to loosen any browned bits. Add the oil, onions and garlic; cook and stir for 5 minutes. Add the basil, red pepper flakes, tomatoes (with juice), stewed tomatoes and potatoes; bring to a boil. Reduce the heat to medium; cover and cook for 25 minutes, or until the potatoes are tender. Stir in the parsley. Add salt and pepper to taste.

Preparation time: 5 minutes
Cooking time: 35 minutes

Per serving: 304 calories, 9.1 g. fat (27% of calories), 4 g. dietary fiber, 34 mg. cholesterol, 711 mg. sodium.

FAMILY-STYLE SKILLET SUPPER

*Skillet Pork Tenderloins
with Dried Cranberry-Mushroom Gravy
French Bread
Baby Lettuce and Tomato Salad*

Tender medallions of lean pork cook in a savory mushroom gravy spiced with dried cranberries in this easy skillet dinner.

GAME PLAN

1. Make the pork.
2. Make a salad of baby lettuces and tomato wedges; add balsamic vinegar.
3. Warm the French bread.

Skillet Pork Tenderloins
with Dried Cranberry-Mushroom Gravy

SERVES 4

1   *cup dried cranberries (Craisins)*

1   *cup port wine or apple cider*

1   *tablespoon oil*

1   *small onion, chopped*

3   *cups sliced mushrooms*

1   *pound pork tenderloin, trimmed of fat and cut into 1" slices*

Salt and ground black pepper

In a small saucepan over medium heat, combine the cranberries and wine or cider; bring to a boil. Turn off the heat and let it sit for 10 minutes.

Meanwhile, heat the oil in a 10″ no-stick skillet over medium-high heat; add the onions and mushrooms. Cook and stir for 5 to 8 minutes, or until the mushrooms begin to brown. Transfer them to a plate.

Strain out ⅓ cup of the soaking wine or cider; add it to the skillet. Bring to a boil. Add the pork; brown for 8 to 10 minutes, turning once. Add the mushrooms, cranberries and remaining soaking wine or cider. Bring to a boil. Cook and stir for 2 to 3 minutes, or until the pork is no longer pink in the center. Add salt and pepper to taste.

Preparation time: 15 minutes
Cooking time: 20 minutes
Soaking time: 10 minutes

Per serving: 603 calories, 8.9 g. fat (13% of calories), 1 g. dietary fiber, 65 mg. cholesterol, 57 mg. sodium.

An Evening in Crete

Greek Eggplant Feta Casserole
Sliced Cucumbers with Dill

Fresh flavors from the Greek isles permeate this easy casserole: feta cheese, oregano, eggplant and tomatoes. We've made it simple and fast with precut vegetables. Salting and rinsing the eggplant is an old Mediterranean method to soften it without cooking it in oil.

GAME PLAN

1. Make the casserole.
2. Slice cucumbers; toss them with nonfat plain yogurt and chopped fresh dill.

GREEK EGGPLANT FETA CASSEROLE

SERVES 4

1   *large eggplant, peeled and cubed*
1   *teaspoon olive oil*
8   *ounces lean ground lamb*
2   *onions, chopped*
1   *tablespoon minced garlic*
1   *sweet red pepper, diced*
2   *teaspoons dried oregano*
1   *can (15 ounces) peeled whole tomatoes (with juice), chopped*
1   *cup uncooked orzo*
1½ *cups defatted chicken broth*
½   *cup crumbled feta cheese*
⅓   *cup minced fresh parsley*

Place the eggplant in a medium bowl; sprinkle it generously with salt. Let it sit at room temperature for 20 minutes, stirring occasionally.

Meanwhile, coat a large Dutch oven or a large ovenproof saucepan with no-stick cooking spray; set it over medium-high heat. Add the oil; when the oil is hot, add the lamb and onions. Cook and stir for 3 to 5 minutes. Add the garlic, peppers and oregano; cook and stir for 3 minutes.

Preheat the oven to 375°. Rinse the eggplant well; squeeze it dry. Add the eggplant, tomatoes (with juice), orzo, broth and ¼ cup of the feta to the pot; bring to a boil.

Cover the pot and transfer it to the oven; bake for 20 minutes, or until the orzo is tender and all the liquid has been absorbed. Sprinkle the parsley and the remaining ¼ cup feta over the top. Cover and cook for 5 minutes, or until the cheese melts.

Preparation time: 10 minutes
Cooking time: 30 minutes

Per serving: 311 calories, 9.4 g. fat (26% of calories), 3.8 g. dietary fiber, 51 mg. cholesterol, 499 mg. sodium.

Mediterranean Bean, Potato and Vegetable Salad Platter (page 280)

Vegetable Pizza with Goat Cheese (page 281)

Parchment-Baked Winter Fruit (page 287)

Sautéed Oranges with Italian Amaretti Cookies (page 294)

Quick Chocolate Cake (page 295)

Melon Mango Sorbet (page 297)

- **Chicken in Black Bean Sauce:** Stir-fry ½ sliced onion, 2 cups broccoli florets, 2 tablespoons minced garlic, 1 tablespoon grated fresh ginger and 2 sliced boneless skinless chicken breast halves in ½ cup defatted chicken broth. Add 1 tablespoon rinsed and drained black bean paste, 1 tablespoon hoisin sauce and ¼ cup pineapple juice mixed with 1 teaspoon cornstarch. Spoon over hot cooked rice. Serves 4.

- **Sweet-and-Sour Tofu and Vegetables:** Stir-fry 1 tablespoon minced garlic and 2 cups chopped mixed Asian vegetables in ½ cup defatted chicken broth. Add 8 ounces cubed firm tofu, 2 teaspoons reduced-sodium soy sauce, 1 tablespoon mirin (rice wine) or rice vinegar, and 2 tablespoons cornstarch mixed with ½ cup pineapple juice. Serve over hot cooked Asian pasta. Serves 4.

- **Oriental Rice and Vegetables:** Stir-fry 2 cups chopped mixed Asian vegetables, ½ sliced onion and 1 tablespoon each grated fresh ginger and minced garlic in ½ cup apple juice. Add 2½ cups cooked rice and 1 beaten egg. Stir in 2 tablespoons low-sodium soy sauce before serving. Serves 4.

- **Spicy Shrimp:** Stir-fry 2 tablespoons minced garlic, 1 tablespoon grated fresh ginger, 2 chopped green onions, 1 cup mixed vegetables and ½ pound shelled large uncooked shrimp in ½ cup defatted chicken broth. Add 1 tablespoon each hoisin sauce, chili sauce and mirin (rice wine) or apple juice. Serve over hot cooked rice. Serves 4.

- **Garlicky Pasta and Greens:** Stir-fry ½ sliced onion, 3 tablespoons minced garlic, 1 cup sliced mushrooms and 4 cups chopped greens (such as bok choy, spinach, collards, Chinese cabbage) in ½ cup defatted chicken broth. Add 2 cups cooked spaghetti, 1 tablespoon low-sodium soy sauce and 1 tablespoon honey. Serves 4.

A Taste of Thai

Thai Fish Stew with Asian Noodles
Sliced Cucumbers

*S*picy yet sweet, this stew transforms plain white fish into a quick exotic meal. The side dish of vinegary cucumbers is a crunchy contrast.

GAME PLAN

1. Make the stew.
2. Slice hothouse (unwaxed) cucumbers; sprinkle them with balsamic vinegar.

THAI FISH STEW WITH ASIAN NOODLES

SERVES 4

1	cup sliced onions
1	tablespoon minced garlic
1	tablespoon olive oil
3	cups Asian stir-fry vegetables, finely chopped
½	cup defatted chicken broth
8	ounces halibut or other white fish fillets, cubed
1	tablespoon chopped jalapeño peppers (wear plastic gloves when handling)
8	ounces medium shrimp, peeled and deveined
4	ounces bay scallops
1	tablespoon fish sauce
1	tablespoon reduced-sodium soy sauce
1	tablespoon packed brown sugar
1	package (3 ounces) Asian ramen noodles (without seasoning packet)

In a 10″ no-stick skillet over medium-high heat, cook and stir the onions and garlic in the oil for 5 minutes, or until the onions are soft but not browned. Add the vegetables and broth; cook and stir for 5 minutes.

Add the fish, peppers, shrimp, scallops, fish sauce, brown sugar and ramen. Cook and stir for 5 minutes, or until the ramen is tender.

Preparation time: 5 minutes
Cooking time: 15 minutes

Chef's note: Look for packaged stir-fry vegetables in your supermarket's produce section, or make your own from bok choy, Chinese (napa) cabbage and snow peas.

Per serving: 319 calories, 9 g. fat (25% of calories), 1.8 g. dietary fiber, 131 mg. cholesterol, 954 mg. sodium.

CURRY IN A HURRY

Thai Shrimp Curry with Basmati Rice
Sliced Kiwifruit

If you love Thai food, you'll love this easy curry. It depends on small amounts of two essential Thai ingredients for its rich flavor: fish sauce and shrimp paste, both available in Asian markets.

GAME PLAN

1. Make the curry.
2. Peel and slice kiwifruit; arrange it on a plate.

Thai Shrimp Curry with Basmati Rice

SERVES 4

1½ teaspoons ground red pepper
1 teaspoon ground ginger
½ teaspoon ground black pepper
4 cloves garlic, minced
5 shallots, minced
½ cup fresh cilantro
½ teaspoon grated lime rind
1 teaspoon lemon juice
½ teaspoon shrimp paste
½ cup low-fat coconut milk
1¾ cups evaporated skim milk
1–2 tablespoons fish sauce
1 tablespoon brown sugar
1 pound uncooked medium shrimp, peeled and deveined
4 cups hot cooked basmati rice

In a blender or food processor, combine the red pepper, ginger, black pepper, garlic, shallots, cilantro, lime rind, lemon juice and shrimp paste; puree. Transfer to a 3-quart saucepan; add the coconut milk and skim milk. Cook and stir for 5 minutes over medium-high heat. Add the fish sauce, brown sugar and shrimp. Cook and stir for 3 to 5 minutes, or until the shrimp are pink. Serve over the hot rice.

Preparation time: 15 minutes
Cooking time: 10 minutes

Per serving: 432 calories, 4.3 g. fat (9% of calories), 0.1 g. dietary fiber, 179 mg. cholesterol, 604 mg. sodium.

FUSION CUISINE

Shrimp, Orzo and Broccoli Stir-Fry
Sliced Tomatoes

Orzo, also called rosamarina, is a fast-cooking, rice-shaped pasta that extends this stir-fry into a one-dish feast. Sliced tomatoes alongside are an easy addition.

GAME PLAN

1. Slice tomatoes; sprinkle them with chopped fresh basil.
2. Make the stir-fry.

SHRIMP, ORZO AND BROCCOLI STIR-FRY

SERVES 4

2 teaspoons oil
1 tablespoon minced garlic
1 tablespoon grated fresh ginger
1 teaspoon curry powder
¼ cup water
2 cups sliced onions
2 cups broccoli florets
8 ounces uncooked medium shrimp, peeled and deveined
3 cups cooked orzo
½ cup defatted chicken broth
1 teaspoon cornstarch
1 teaspoon dark sesame oil
3 tablespoons reduced-sodium soy sauce

Heat the oil in a wok over medium-high heat. Add the garlic and ginger; cook and stir for 1 minute. Add the curry powder, water and onions; cook and stir for 3 minutes. Add the broccoli, shrimp and orzo; cover and cook for 3 minutes, or until the shrimp is bright pink.

In a small bowl, whisk together the broth, cornstarch, sesame oil and soy sauce. Add to the wok; cook and stir for 3 to 4 minutes, or until the sauce has thickened.

Preparation time: 10 minutes
Cooking time: 15 minutes

Per serving: 276 calories, 4.9 g. fat (16% of calories), 4.6 g. dietary fiber, 87 mg. cholesterol, 554 mg. sodium.

SOUTHERN FRENCH PICNIC

Provençal Tuna Loaf (Pan Bagna)
Coleslaw

A large loaf of French bread, hollowed out and stuffed with vegetables, is a common sight on picnics in southern France. This meal assembles in minutes, and it can be made ahead and refrigerated overnight, wrapped tightly in plastic wrap.

GAME PLAN

1. Make the tuna loaf.
2. Make a coleslaw from shredded cabbage and carrots; add low-fat coleslaw dressing.

PROVENÇAL TUNA LOAF

SERVES 4

1 *small round loaf crusty Italian bread*

1 *tablespoon olive oil*

2 *tablespoons balsamic vinegar*

1 *garlic clove, halved*

⅛ *teaspoon crushed red pepper flakes*

1 *teaspoon dried thyme*

1 *jar (7 ounces) roasted sweet red peppers, drained*

1 *can (7 ounces) reduced-sodium water-packed tuna, drained*

1 *large tomato, thinly sliced*

½ *cup thinly sliced red onions*

1 *teaspoon capers, drained*

1 *cup watercress or baby lettuces*

   Salt and ground black pepper

Halve the bread horizontally; remove the soft crumbs from inside the top half. Brush the cut sides of both halves with the oil and vinegar, then rub with the cut garlic. Sprinkle with red pepper flakes and thyme.

On the bottom half of the loaf, layer the red peppers, tuna, tomatoes, onions, capers and watercress or lettuce. Sprinkle with salt and pepper. Press the top half of the loaf over the filling; wrap tightly in plastic wrap. Let it sit at room temperature for 15 minutes; slice into 4 wedges.

Preparation time: 20 minutes
Marinating time: 15 minutes

Per serving: 356 calories, 7.7 g. fat (19% of calories), 1.8 g. dietary fiber, 17 mg. cholesterol, 552 mg. sodium.

WHITE NIGHTS

*Mushroom Vegetable Stroganoff
with Noodles
Green Beans*

*R*ussian vegetable stroganoff tastes rich yet uses lean dairy products to fit into a low-fat diet. Adding cornstarch to the low-fat sour cream keeps it from separating when it's heated.

GAME PLAN

1. Make the stroganoff.
2. Steam green beans; toss them with lemon juice.

MUSHROOM VEGETABLE STROGANOFF

SERVES 4

1	teaspoon olive oil
½	cup sliced onions
3	cups halved mushrooms
2	cloves garlic, minced
1	cup sliced green beans
2	carrots, chopped
2	tablespoons tomato paste
1	cup white wine or defatted chicken broth
2	teaspoons cornstarch
¼	cup plain nonfat yogurt
¼	cup nonfat sour cream
4	cups hot cooked egg noodles

In a 10″ no-stick skillet over medium-high heat, heat the oil; add the onions. Cook and stir for 2 to 3 minutes, or until the onions are soft. Add the mushrooms and garlic; cook and stir for 5 minutes. Add the beans, carrots, tomato paste and wine or broth; bring to a boil. Lower the heat to medium; cover and cook, stirring frequently, for 15 minutes, or until the vegetables are tender.

In a small bowl, stir together the cornstarch, yogurt and sour cream. Remove the skillet from the heat; stir in the sour cream mixture. Serve over cooked noodles.

Preparation time: 10 minutes
Cooking time: 25 minutes

Per serving: 128 calories, 1.6 g. fat (11% of calories), 2.9 g. dietary fiber, no cholesterol, 105 mg. sodium.

MARRAKESH EXPRESS

East Indian Curried Couscous Platter
Yogurt
Mango Chutney

This elegant platter blends Middle Eastern and Indian cooking with sweet couscous and curried vegetables. To make this meal even quicker, use precut vegetables from the supermarket salad bar.

GAME PLAN
1. Make the couscous platter.
2. Spoon yogurt and chutney into two bowls.

EAST INDIAN CURRIED COUSCOUS PLATTER

SERVES 4

1	teaspoon olive oil
½	cup sliced green onions
½	cup shredded carrots
1	cup broccoli florets
¼	cup currants
¼	cup chopped dried apricots
2	cups uncooked couscous
1½	cups defatted chicken broth
1	cup apple juice
1–2	teaspoons curry powder
1	cup chopped yellow summer squash
½	cup diced tomatoes
	Salt and ground black pepper
¼	cup chopped fresh cilantro or mint

Heat the oil in a 10″ no-stick skillet over medium-high heat; add the onions, carrots and broccoli. Cook and stir for 5 minutes, or until the vegetables are soft but not browned. Add the currants, apricots and couscous. Cook and stir for 1 minute.

Add the broth, apple juice and curry powder; bring to a boil. Add the squash and tomatoes; cover and remove from the heat. Let stand for 5 to 8 minutes, or until all the liquid has been absorbed. Fluff the couscous with a fork and add salt and pepper to taste. Transfer to a platter; top with the cilantro or mint.

Preparation time: 5 minutes
Cooking time: 6 minutes
Standing time: 8 minutes

Per serving: 444 calories, 2.2 g. fat (4% of calories), 17.5 g. dietary fiber, no cholesterol, 153 mg. sodium.

QUICK BRUNCH OR SUPPER MENU

Baked Eggs Florentine
Fresh Berries with Maple Syrup

So much easier than last-minute omelets, a baked egg dish can be a fast brunch entrée or light supper. This version is lower in fat because we've replaced the traditional heavy cream with evaporated skim milk.

GAME PLAN

1. Make the eggs.
2. Combine raspberries, blueberries and blackberries with maple syrup.

BAKED EGGS FLORENTINE

SERVES 4

1	cup chopped onions
¼	cup defatted chicken broth
4	cups torn spinach
5	large mushrooms, sliced
½	cup shredded low-fat Colby or mild Cheddar cheese
4	large eggs
	Salt and ground black pepper
1	cup evaporated skim milk
1	cup nonfat cottage cheese
1–2	drops hot-pepper sauce
¼	cup toasted bread crumbs

Preheat the oven to 325°. Lightly oil a shallow 8-cup baking dish.

In a small skillet over medium-high heat, combine the onions and broth; cook and stir for 5 minutes, or until the onions are soft but not browned. Transfer to the baking dish; add the spinach, mushrooms and Colby or Cheddar. Make 4 depressions in the spinach for the eggs; carefully break 1 egg into each hole. Sprinkle with salt and pepper.

In a blender or food processor, puree the milk and cottage cheese. Pour over the eggs. Top with the hot pepper sauce and bread crumbs. Bake for 30 minutes, or until the eggs are set.

Preparation time: 10 minutes
Cooking time: 35 minutes

Per serving: 260 calories, 8.4 g. fat (29% of calories), 2.5 g. dietary fiber, 225 mg. cholesterol, 523 mg. sodium.

FRENCH FANTASY

Crustless Vegetable Quiche
Sliced Tomatoes
Steamed Carrots and Peas

Quiche off your diet? Put it back on the menu with this easy low-fat version. It assembles in 5 minutes with precut vegetables from the salad bar, and the fat content is low because we've omitted the rich crust.

GAME PLAN

1. Make the quiche.
2. Slice tomatoes; arrange them on a platter.
3. Steam baby carrots and peas.

CRUSTLESS VEGETABLE QUICHE

SERVES 4

1 cup chopped onions

1 cup finely chopped carrots

1 cup diced sweet red peppers

2 cups sliced mushrooms

¼ cup reduced-sodium defatted chicken broth

1 teaspoon olive oil

1 egg

3 egg whites

½ cup part-skim ricotta cheese

1½ cups nonfat cottage cheese

1 teaspoon cornstarch

2 tablespoons grated Parmesan cheese

¼ teaspoon hot-pepper sauce

1 cup shredded low-fat extra-sharp Cheddar cheese

¾ teaspoon dry mustard

⅓ cup chopped fresh parsley

Preheat the oven to 350°. Coat a 10″ pie plate with no-stick cooking spray. Set aside.

In a 10″ no-stick skillet over medium-high heat, combine the onions, carrots, peppers, mushrooms, broth and oil; cook and stir for 5 minutes, or until the vegetables are soft and all the liquid has evaporated.

In a food processor or blender, combine the egg, egg whites, ricotta, cottage cheese, cornstarch and Parmesan; puree until very smooth. Stir in the hot-pepper sauce, Cheddar, dry mustard, parsley and vegetables. Pour into the pie plate.

Bake for 35 minutes, or until the quiche is set and lightly browned. Let it sit for 5 minutes before serving.

Preparation time: 5 minutes
Cooking time: 40 minutes

Per serving: 265 calories, 8.8 g. fat (29% of calories), 3.3 g. dietary fiber, 75 mg. cholesterol, 785 mg. sodium.

FRENCH WINTER SUPPER

Shallot and Corn Risotto
French Bread
Romaine and Radish Salad

The ultimate comfort food—creamy risotto—is made rich yet low-fat with corn, chicken broth and sweet red peppers. The crunchy radish and romaine salad provides a nice texture contrast.

GAME PLAN

1. Make the risotto.
2. Warm a loaf of French bread.
3. Make a salad from romaine lettuce, sliced radishes and tomatoes. Add your favorite low-fat dressing.

SHALLOT AND CORN RISOTTO

SERVES 4

1	teaspoon olive oil
¼	cup dry sherry or water
3	tablespoons minced shallots
3½	cups defatted chicken broth, warmed
2	tablespoons minced sweet red peppers
1	cup arborio rice
2	cups whole-kernel corn
1	tablespoon minced fresh parsley
	Salt and ground black pepper

In a 2-quart saucepan, heat the oil and sherry or water to bubbling over medium-high heat. Add the shallots and ¼ cup of the broth; cook and stir for 3 minutes, or until the shallots are soft but not browned. Add the red peppers; cook and stir for 3 minutes.

Add the rice; cook and stir for 1 minute. Add ½ cup of the broth. Stirring continuously, cook until the liquid has completely evaporated. Add another ½ cup of the broth; cook and stir until the liquid has completely evaporated. Cook and stir for 25 minutes, adding more broth only after previous additions have been absorbed, or until the rice is creamy and just tender.

Remove from the heat; add the corn and parsley. Add salt and pepper to taste.

Preparation time: 10 minutes
Cooking time: 35 minutes

Chef's note: For a creamier risotto, puree 1 cup of the corn.

Per serving: 301 calories, 1.5 g. fat (4% of calories), 2.1 g. dietary fiber, no cholesterol, 300 mg. sodium.

SUMMERY ANTIPASTO PLATTER

*Mediterranean Bean, Potato and
Vegetable Salad Platter
Breadsticks*

This summery menu will remind you of the best antipasto at your favorite Italian restaurant. Our version is low in fat because we've substituted the rich flavor of balsamic vinegar for most of the oil in the dressing.

GAME PLAN

1. Make the salad platter.
2. Warm the breadsticks.

Mediterranean Bean, Potato and Vegetable Salad Platter

SERVES 4

2 *cups canned kidney beans, drained and rinsed*

2 *cups sliced cooked red potatoes*

½ *cup balsamic vinegar*

2 *tablespoons minced garlic*

2 *tablespoons lemon juice*

3 *tablespoons honey*

1 *tablespoon olive oil*

¼ *cup minced red onions*

¼ *teaspoon salt*

3 *cups torn leaf lettuces*

½ *cup sliced sweet red peppers*

½ *cup sliced green peppers*

½ *cup whole-kernel corn*

1 *large tomato, cut into wedges*

Ground black pepper

In a large bowl, combine the beans, potatoes, vinegar, garlic, lemon juice, honey, oil, onions and salt. Stir gently. Let marinate at room temperature for 20 minutes.

Line a platter with the lettuce; arrange the red and green peppers, corn and tomatoes around the edge. Strain the beans and potatoes from the marinade; pile in the center of the platter. Drizzle the marinade over the vegetables. Add pepper to taste.

Preparation time: 10 minutes
Marinating time: 20 minutes

Per serving: 390 calories, 4.3 g. fat (10% of calories), 11.1 g. dietary fiber, no cholesterol, 598 mg. sodium.

PERFECT PIZZA

Vegetable Pizza with Goat Cheese
Tossed Salad

Faster than pizza delivery, this homemade pie is in the oven in 10 minutes if you use precut vegetables, prepared pizza dough and prepared sauce.

GAME PLAN

1. Make the pizza.
2. Make a salad of sweet and bitter lettuces. Add your favorite low-fat vinaigrette dressing.

VEGETABLE PIZZA WITH GOAT CHEESE

SERVES 4

- 1 teaspoon cornmeal
- 1 pound reduced-sodium fresh pizza dough
- 2 tablespoons prepared pesto
- 1 red onion, thinly sliced
- 1 large tomato, sliced
- 1 jar (7 ounces) roasted sweet red peppers, drained
- 1 cup chopped broccoli florets
- ⅓ cup crumbled goat cheese
- 2 tablespoons grated Parmesan cheese

Preheat the oven to 500°. Set the oven rack at its lowest position.

Sprinkle the cornmeal on a large ungreased baking sheet. Roll out the pizza dough and place it on the baking sheet, pressing to fit.

Spread the pesto on the crust; top with the onions and tomatoes. Sprinkle the peppers, broccoli, goat cheese and Parmesan on top. Bake for 10 to 15 minutes, or until the underside is browned and the cheese has melted. Cut into wedges.

Preparation time: 10 minutes
Cooking time: 15 minutes

Per serving: 375 calories, 10.1 g. fat (24% of calories), 2.9 g. dietary fiber, 11 mg. cholesterol, 668 mg. sodium.

BISTRO BRUNCH OR SUPPER

> *Garlic and Tomato Frittata*
> *Whole-Wheat Toast with Apple Butter*
> *Sliced Fruit*

A fast entrée for a weekend brunch or light supper, this frittata takes only about 20 minutes of total cooking time.

GAME PLAN

1. Make the frittata.
2. Slice melon, oranges and bananas; arrange them on a platter.
3. Toast whole-wheat bread; serve it with apple butter.

GARLIC AND TOMATO FRITTATA

SERVES 4

1 cup chopped red onions
1 tablespoon minced garlic
2 teaspoons olive oil
¼ cup defatted chicken broth
2 cups chopped tomatoes
⅓ cup shredded raw potatoes
⅓ cup shredded carrots
1 cup broccoli florets

½ teaspoon dried thyme
½ teaspoon salt
¼ teaspoon ground black pepper
4 eggs
4 egg whites
¼ cup shredded low-fat sharp Cheddar cheese
4 sprigs fresh thyme

Preheat the broiler. In a 10″ no-stick ovenproof skillet, combine the onions, garlic, oil and broth; cook and stir for 5 minutes over medium-high heat, or until the onions are soft but not browned. Add the tomatoes, potatoes, carrots, broccoli and thyme; cook and stir for 3 minutes. Add the salt and pepper.

In a blender or food processor, combine the eggs, egg whites and Cheddar; puree. Stir into the vegetable mixture. Reduce the heat to low; cook for 5 to 8 minutes, or until the underside is golden brown. Transfer to the broiler.

Broil the frittata for 1 to 2 minutes, or until the top is puffed and golden brown. Cut into wedges and garnish with fresh thyme.

Preparation time: 10 minutes
Cooking time: 20 minutes

Per serving: 202 calories, 8.9 g. fat (39% of calories), 3.1 g. dietary fiber, 217 mg. cholesterol, 521 mg. sodium.

CHAPTER 11

NATURALLY
QUICK FINALES

SIMPLY DELICIOUS DESSERTS

o ahead. Indulge in that dessert. The delectable treats in this chapter will tempt your taste buds without the guilt. Full of flavor yet quick to prepare, they're optimal for everyday occasions. Most revolve around fruit, converting their natural good taste into light, refreshing finales for weeknight menus. After all, what's life without dessert?

INDIVIDUAL PEACH-RASPBERRY GRATINS

SERVES 4

*F*resh raspberries and peaches create a succulent oven-baked dessert for the lazy days of mid and late summer. Use frozen or dried fruit when fresh is hard to find.

> 2 *cups chopped fresh peaches*
> 1 *cup fresh raspberries*
> ½ *cup apple juice*
> ⅓ *cup packed brown sugar*
> 2 *teaspoons lemon juice*
> 1 *teaspoon ground ginger*
> 4 *gingersnap cookies, chopped*

Preheat the oven to 425°. In a medium bowl, combine the peaches, raspberries, apple juice, brown sugar, lemon juice and ginger. Divide the fruit mixture among 4 shallow gratin dishes. Sprinkle with the gingersnaps. Bake for 15 to 20 minutes, or until the fruit is tender and the syrup thickens.

Preparation time: 5 minutes
Cooking time: 20 minutes

Per serving: 166 calories, 1 g. fat (5% of calories), 2.8 g. dietary fiber, no cholesterol, 54 mg. sodium.

MAPLE BANANA BAKE

SERVES 4

*T*his warm winter treat takes only 10 minutes to assemble. Pop it into the oven to bake while you enjoy dinner.

4   *bananas, diagonally sliced*
¼   *cup maple syrup*
1   *teaspoon lime juice*
1   *teaspoon butter or oil*
¼   *cup all-purpose flour*
½   *cup rolled oats*
½   *teaspoon vanilla*
   Pinch of ground nutmeg
   Pinch of ground cinnamon
2   *tablespoons apple juice*
2   *tablespoons packed brown sugar*
¼   *cup low-fat sour cream*

Preheat the oven to 400°. Lightly oil a shallow casserole dish. Arrange the bananas in the casserole dish; drizzle them with the maple syrup and lime juice.

In a small bowl, mix the butter or oil, flour, oats, vanilla, nutmeg, cinnamon and apple juice. Sprinkle over the bananas. Bake for 25 minutes, or until the fruit is soft and the topping is crisp.

In a small bowl, stir together the brown sugar and sour cream. Serve over the crisp.

Preparation time: 10 minutes
Cooking time: 25 minutes

Per serving: 277 calories, 3.2 g. fat (10% of calories), 3.1 g. dietary fiber, 7 mg. cholesterol, 25 mg. sodium.

PARCHMENT-BAKED WINTER FRUIT

SERVES 4

*B*aking fruit in parchment concentrates its natural sweetness and creates a moist, tender dessert. For a finishing touch, top the fruit with pureed frozen strawberries and nonfat vanilla frozen yogurt.

2	*tart apples, cored, peeled and sliced into 4 rings each*
2	*Bosc pears, quartered*
16	*dried apricot halves*
1	*tablespoon dried currants*
1	*tablespoon red wine or apple juice*
1	*teaspoon maple syrup*
½	*teaspoon ground cinnamon*

Preheat the oven to 400°. Tear off 4 large sheets of parchment paper. Divide the apples, pears, apricots and currants evenly between the pieces of parchment. Drizzle each pile of fruit with wine or apple juice and maple syrup, then sprinkle with cinnamon. Seal the packets tightly. Place on two baking sheets. Bake for 20 minutes, or until the fruit is tender.

Preparation time: 10 minutes
Cooking time: 20 minutes

Per serving: 171 calories, 0.7 g. fat (3% of calories), 6 g. dietary fiber, no cholesterol, 6 mg. sodium.

QUICK APPLE CRISP

SERVES 4

his fall dessert bakes in 30 minutes if you slice the apples very thinly. To shortcut the crust, use low-fat granola in place of the flour, baking powder, butter, oil and plain yogurt.

3 *tart apples, peeled and thinly sliced*
½ *cup raisins*
2 *tablespoons grated orange rind*
1 *cup packed brown sugar or honey*
½ *teaspoon ground cinnamon*
Pinch of ground nutmeg
1 *cup all-purpose flour*
1 *teaspoon baking powder*
2 *teaspoons butter*
1 *tablespoon oil*
⅔ *cup nonfat plain yogurt*
1 *teaspoon sugar*
2 *cups nonfat vanilla yogurt*

Preheat the oven to 400°. In a shallow 1-quart baking dish, combine the apples, raisins, orange rind, brown sugar or honey, cinnamon and nutmeg.

In a medium bowl, stir together the flour and baking powder. Add the butter and oil, stirring until the mixture resembles coarse cornmeal. Add the plain yogurt; stir well. Drop spoonfuls of the dough on top of the apples. Sprinkle with the sugar.

Cover and bake for 30 minutes, then uncover and bake for 5 minutes to brown the top. Serve with the vanilla yogurt.

Preparation time: 10 minutes
Cooking time: 35 minutes

Per serving: 618 calories, 8.5 g. fat (12% of calories), 3.1 g. dietary fiber, 3 mg. cholesterol, 215 mg. sodium.

8 EASY DESSERTS

- **Tropical Treat:** Slice bananas, mango, papaya and pineapple; arrange on dessert plates. Stir 1 tablespoon lime juice and 2 tablespoons honey into 1 cup low-fat vanilla yogurt. Drizzle over the fruit.

- **Italian Custard:** Puree 2 cups low-fat ricotta cheese with 1 teaspoon each vanilla extract and grated lemon rind. Add sugar or honey to taste. Spoon into custard cups, chill and serve with black or green seedless grapes.

- **Foil-Wrapped Summer Fruit:** Brush the cut sides of 4 peach and 4 apricot halves with maple syrup, then wrap the fruit in foil. Grill the fruit for 10 minutes, or until it is soft and warm. Serve with low-fat vanilla frozen yogurt.

- **Poached Peaches:** Simmer 4 halved, pitted peaches in 1 cup red grape juice or red wine, 3 cups orange juice, 1 cinnamon stick and ¼ cup honey for 15 minutes. Remove the cinnamon stick. Serve warm with a curl of orange rind.

- **Creamy Pineapple Topping:** Combine ½ cup each chopped dates and dried apricots with 1 cup low-fat cream cheese and 2 tablespoons orange juice. Spoon over pineapple rings and garnish with mint leaves.

- **Super Bowl Sundae:** Fill 4 dessert bowls with scoops of low-fat chocolate frozen yogurt; top each sundae with sliced bananas and crushed chocolate amaretti or other low-fat cookies.

- **Orange Ecstasy:** Drizzle sliced navel oranges with warmed honey and sprinkle with ground cinnamon. Serve the oranges with low-fat biscotti.

- **Quartet of Ices:** Spoon small scoops of 4 different Italian ices onto chilled plates. Garnish with grated lemon rind.

GRILLED SUMMER FRUIT WITH BERRY SAUCE

SERVES 4

*G*rilling brings out the sweetest flavors in fresh summer fruit. And the bright raspberry sauce gives it a crowning touch of color and flavor.

1	*cup fresh or frozen raspberries*
1½–2	*teaspoons lemon juice*
1–2	*tablespoons packed brown sugar*
2	*medium fresh apricots, halved and pitted*
2	*medium fresh plums, halved and pitted*
1	*medium fresh peach, halved and pitted*
1	*teaspoon olive oil*
2	*teaspoons honey*

In a blender or food processor, combine the raspberries, 1½ teaspoons of the lemon juice and 1 tablespoon of the brown sugar; puree. With a spatula, push the sauce through a sieve into a bowl to strain out the seeds. Add more lemon juice or brown sugar to taste, if desired.

Preheat the grill. Brush the cut sides of the apricot, plum and peach halves with the oil. Grill the fruit, oiled side down, for 2 to 3 minutes, or until lightly browned. Remove from the grill. While the fruit is still hot, drizzle it with the honey. Arrange the fruit on 4 dessert plates and top with the raspberry sauce.

Preparation time: 5 minutes
Cooking time: 3 minutes

Per serving: 85 calories, 1.6 g. fat (15% of calories), 2.8 g. dietary fiber, no cholesterol, 2 mg. sodium.

Strawberry Crêpes

SERVES 4

A lot lower in fat than traditional strawberry shortcake, these crêpes have all the same elegance and flavor. Look for prepared crêpes in the produce section of your supermarket and whip together this almost-instant dessert during strawberry season.

8 *crêpes*
4 *ounces nonfat cream cheese*
1 *cup nonfat sour cream*
½ *teaspoon vanilla*
1 *teaspoon grated orange rind*
¼ *cup packed brown sugar*
3 *cups sliced fresh strawberries*
1 *tablespoon honey*

Wrap the crêpes in plastic wrap and microwave them on high power for 1 minute.

In a food processor or blender, combine the cream cheese, sour cream, vanilla, orange rind and brown sugar; puree. Spread a small amount of the cream cheese mixture inside each crêpe; divide 2 cups of the strawberries among the crêpes. Roll up the crêpes and place them seam side down in a serving dish.

In a blender or food processor, combine the remaining 1 cup of strawberries and honey. Puree. Drizzle the sauce over the crêpes.

Preparation time: 10 minutes

Per serving: 249 calories, 4.1 g. fat (15% of calories), 2 g. dietary fiber, 23 mg. cholesterol, 381 mg. sodium.

GOLDEN POACHED PEARS

SERVES 4

Poaching is a quick cooking method to infuse fruit with extra flavor. This dessert tastes especially refreshing after a stir-fry menu.

- 2 medium pears, quartered
- ⅓ cup dried apricots
- ¼ cup currants or raisins
- 2 cups white grape juice or dry white wine
- ¼ cup maple syrup or packed brown sugar
- ⅓ cup nonfat plain yogurt
- ¼ teaspoon ground nutmeg

In a 2-quart saucepan, combine the pears, apricots, currants or raisins, grape juice or wine, and maple syrup or brown sugar; bring to a boil over medium-high heat. Lower the heat to medium and cook for 15 minutes, or until the pears are soft. Remove from the heat; place 2 pear quarters in each of 4 dessert bowls. Top each with a dollop of yogurt; sprinkle with nutmeg.

Preparation time: 5 minutes
Cooking time: 15 minutes

Chef's note: If desired, reduce any leftover cooking liquid to a thick syrup by boiling it rapidly for 3 to 5 minutes.

Per serving: 202 calories, 0.5 g. fat (2% of calories), 3.5 g. dietary fiber, no cholesterol, 18 mg. sodium.

BROILED PINEAPPLE WITH PAPAYA PUREE

SERVES 4

*A*ny tropical fruit broils beautifully and can be substituted for the pineapple in this fast dessert. Mango can replace the papaya in the puree.

> 1   *can (8 ounces) unsweetened pineapple rings, drained*
> 3   *tablespoons lime juice*
> 2   *cups peeled, seeded and chopped papaya*
> 2   *tablespoons maple syrup*
>   *Pinch of ground nutmeg*
> ½   *cup nonfat plain yogurt*
> 8   *fresh mint leaves*

Preheat the broiler. Place the pineapple on a broiler pan; drizzle with 2 tablespoons of the lime juice. Broil 4″ from the heat for 2 to 5 minutes, or until the pineapple is light brown. Turn and broil the other side for 2 to 5 minutes.

In a blender or food processor, puree the remaining 1 tablespoon of lime juice, papaya, maple syrup and nutmeg. Divide the pineapple between 4 dessert plates and top with the puree. Garnish each plate with a dollop of yogurt and 2 mint leaves.

Preparation time: 10 minutes
Cooking time: 10 minutes

Per serving: 105 calories, 0.2 g. fat (2% of calories), 1 g. dietary fiber, 1 mg. cholesterol, 26 mg. sodium.

SAUTÉED ORANGES
WITH ITALIAN AMARETTI COOKIES

SERVES 4

*L*ook for very sweet oranges for this easy dessert. The amaretti cookies crush best with a rolling pin between two sheets of wax paper.

> 4 *large seedless oranges, peeled and sliced into rounds*
> 1 *teaspoon butter*
> 2 *tablespoons packed brown sugar*
> 1–2 *teaspoons frozen orange juice concentrate, thawed, or orange liqueur*
> ⅔ *cup crushed amaretti cookies*

In a 10″ no-stick skillet over medium-high heat, combine the oranges, butter, brown sugar and 1 teaspoon of the orange juice or liqueur. Cook and stir for 3 minutes, or until the butter and sugar melt and the oranges soften slightly. Add more orange juice or liqueur to taste, if desired.

Spoon the oranges onto 4 dessert plates and top with the crushed cookies.

Preparation time: 10 minutes
Cooking time: 3 minutes

Per serving: 199 calories, 4.4 g. fat (21% of calories), 4.3 g. dietary fiber, 3 mg. cholesterol, 38 mg. sodium.

QUICK CHOCOLATE CAKE

SERVES 12

*T*his rich-tasting snacking cake is fast yet has a great old-fashioned chocolatey flavor and extra lightness from the buttermilk. Extra pieces make great lunchbox treats.

> 2 *tablespoons canola or safflower oil*
> ½ *cup unsweetened applesauce or prune puree*
> 1 *tablespoon vanilla*
> 1 *cup date sugar or packed brown sugar*
> 1 *egg*
> 1 *cup all-purpose flour*
> ½ *cup unsweetened cocoa powder*
> 1 *teaspoon ground cinnamon*
> ½ *teaspoon ground nutmeg*
> ½ *teaspoon baking powder*
> ½ *teaspoon baking soda*
> ½ *cup low-fat buttermilk*
> 2 *egg whites, stiffly beaten*
> *Confectioner's sugar (optional)*

Preheat the oven to 350°. Lightly oil an 8″×8″ cake pan.

In a small bowl, combine the oil, applesauce or prune puree, vanilla, date sugar or brown sugar and whole egg. In another bowl, sift together the flour, cocoa, cinnamon, nutmeg, baking powder and baking soda.

Fold the dry ingredients into the wet ingredients, alternating with the buttermilk. Fold in the egg whites. Spoon the mixture into the baking pan. Bake for 25 to 30 minutes, or until a toothpick inserted in the center of the cake comes out clean. Let cool. Sprinkle with confectioner's sugar (if using) before slicing.

Preparation time: 15 minutes
Cooking time: 30 minutes

Per serving: 235 calories, 4.9 g. fat (18% of calories), 0.7 g. dietary fiber, 27 mg. cholesterol, 152 mg. sodium.

SPICED OATMEAL COOKIES

MAKES 36

These soft and chewy gems are a hit with kids. Extra cookies can be frozen.

3   cups rolled oats

1   cup unbleached white flour

4   teaspoons ground cinnamon

2   teaspoons baking powder

2   teaspoons baking soda

¼   teaspoon ground nutmeg

½   teaspoon ground allspice

½   cup packed brown sugar or date sugar

⅓   cup plus 2 tablespoons frozen apple juice concentrate, thawed, or honey

2   tablespoons butter or oil

2   teaspoons vanilla

1   cup shredded peeled apple

¾   cup raisins

4   egg whites, stiffly beaten

Preheat the oven to 375°. In a food processor or blender, combine 1 cup of the oats with the flour, cinnamon, baking powder, baking soda, nutmeg, allspice and brown sugar or date sugar. Process until the oats are coarsely ground and ingredients well mixed. Stir in the remaining oats.

In another bowl, combine the juice concentrate or honey, butter or oil, vanilla, apples and raisins. Mix well. Combine the contents of the two bowls, stirring just until incorporated, then fold in the egg whites.

Drop the batter by heaping tablespoonfuls onto 2 no-stick 9″ × 13″ baking sheets. Bake for 12 to 15 minutes, checking frequently during the last 5 minutes to avoid overbaking. Allow the cookies to cool on the baking sheets for 2 minutes before transferring them to a cooling rack.

Preparation time: 10 minutes
Cooking time: 15 minutes

Per cookie: 77 calories, 1.2 g. fat (13% of calories), 1 g. dietary fiber, 2 mg. cholesterol, 104 mg. sodium.

MELON MANGO SORBET

SERVES 4

*S*orbet is one of the easiest—and most elegant—summer desserts. This one is made in chilled margarita glasses or individual custard cups. Use fruits from the salad bar for the fastest prep time.

    1   mango, peeled and cubed
    2   cups frozen unsweetened melon balls
    ½   cup superfine sugar or maple syrup
    ¼   cup lime juice

In a blender or food processor, combine the mango cubes, melon balls, sugar or maple syrup and lime juice; puree. Spoon into 4 margarita glasses or glass custard cups. Cover with plastic wrap and freeze for 30 to 40 minutes, or until firm, stirring once to break up any ice crystals.

Preparation time: 5 minutes
Freezing time: 40 minutes

Per serving: 163 calories, 0.4 g. fat (2% of calories), 2.5 g. dietary fiber, no cholesterol, 28 mg. sodium.

CHAPTER 12

EFFORTLESS
ENTERTAINING
AND 15-MINUTE
MEALS

$\mathscr{S}$PECIAL NIGHTS

ome nights you need a meal that's a little different. You might have unexpected company. Or you might have only 15 minutes to get dinner on the table. Whatever the occasion—fast or fancy—the menus that follow will put the perfect meal on your table without a minute's thought.

SPRING DINNER

Paella Primavera (page 76)   *Strawberry Crêpes (page 291)*
Roasted Asparagus (page 127)

FRENCH DINNER

Butternut Squash Bisque (page 42)
Red Pepper–Ricotta Bruschetta
  (page 43)
Onion, Caper and Orange Salad
  (page 97)

Sautéed Chicken in Rosemary-
  Mushroom Sauce (page 134)
Grilled Summer Fruit with Berry
  Sauce (page 290)

HOLIDAY FEAST

Cheesy Whole-Wheat Breadsticks
  (page 51)
Minted Sugar Snap Peas
  (page 112)
Escarole Salad with Parmesan
  (page 122)

Herbed Turkey Tenderloin
  (page 152)
Baked Apples and Sweet Potatoes
  (page 153)
Individual Peach-Raspberry
  Gratins (page 285)

AUTUMN HARVEST DINNER

Cheddar Corn Muffins (page 53)
Warm Artichoke Dip with Vegetables (page 228)

Stuffed Pork Loin Chops (page 175)
Glazed Honey Carrots (page 176)
Quick Apple Crisp (page 288)

GREEK ISLAND GRILL

Lemon Vegetable Pasta and
  Grilled Shrimp (page 105)

Greek Salad (page 104)
Melon Mango Sorbet (page 297)

CHINESE NEW YEAR DINNER

Chinese Chicken Stir-Fry
  (page 140)
Vegetable Lo Mein (page 141)
Vegetarian Spring Rolls (page 221)

Baked Filled Wontons (page 143)
Broiled Pineapple with Papaya
  Puree (page 293)

SUNDAY COMPANY SUPPER

Apple-Romaine Salad (page 108)
Garlic Mashed Potatoes (page 157)
Grilled Raspberry Turkey Breasts
  (page 159)

Saffron Rice (page 70)
Parchment-Baked Winter Fruit
  (page 287)

CARIBBEAN DINNER

Black Bean and Corn Salad
  (page 79)
Caribbean Pork Chops (page 179)

Island Rice (page 180)
Maple Banana Bake (page 286)

SUMMER BRUNCH BUFFET

Herbed Egg-White Popovers
  (page 66)
Sautéed Spiced Fruit (page 241)
Crustless Vegetable Quiche
  (page 277)

Marinated Vegetable Salad
  (page 48)
Quick Chocolate Cake (page 295)

SEA-FARING FEAST

Chive Biscuits (page 36)
Asian Sesame Coleslaw (page 185)
Bouillabaisse (page 212)

Swordfish with Lime-Soy
  Marinade (page 184)
Grilled Summer Fruit with Berry
  Sauce (page 290)

15-MINUTE MENUS

Poached Sole with Herbs (page 186)
Citrus-Steamed Asparagus (page 187)

Bean-and-Grain Burgers (page 85)
Salad of Bitter Greens and Mint (page 71)

Mediterranean Pasta with Feta and Olives (page 103)
Greek Salad (page 104)

Spicy Beef Burgers (page 168)
Low-Fat Waldorf Salad (page 169)

Sautéed Swordfish with Pepper Relish (page 191)
Roasted Green Beans (page 192)

15-MINUTE DINNER IDEAS

Great Cooks' 15-Minute Dinners (page 6)
15-Minute Chicken Dinners (page 149)

Index

Note: Underscored page references indicate sidebars. **Boldface** references indicate photographs.
Italic references indicate tables.